D1056091

CAUSE *of* DEATH

CAUSE of DEATH

A Perfect Little Guide to What Kills Us

*Edited by Jack Mingo, Erin Barrett,
and Lucy Autrey Wilson*

POCKET BOOKS

NEW YORK • LONDON • TORONTO • SYDNEY

POCKET BOOKS
A Division of Simon & Schuster, Inc.
1230 Avenue of the Americas
New York, NY 10020

First Pocket Books trade paperback edition April 2008

POCKET and colophon are registered trademarks of Simon & Schuster, Inc.

For information about special discounts for bulk purchases, please contact
Simon & Schuster Special Sales at 1-800-456-6798 or business@simonandschuster.com

Designed by Timothy Shaner@nightanddaydesign.biz

Manufactured in the United States of America

10 9 8 7 6 5 4 3 2 1

Library of Congress Cataloging-in-Publication Data is available.

ISBN-13: 978-1-4165-5479-0   ISBN-10: 1-4165-5479-3

Contents

Introduction

by George Lucas

As it must to all men, death came to Charles Foster Kane in one of the most famous movies of all time. The eloquence of that notion—that death will come to every single one of us—has always been a bit of a morbid fascination for me. But is it really so morbid to be curious about the only thing in this world that is truly certain? (Remember, you don't have to pay taxes in some states and countries.) Thousands of books have been written about birth, a subject we love; it's the other end of life that's so strangely troubling.

We're more fearful of dying than perhaps at any other time in human history. Our ancestors worshipped death, prepared their dead for an extraordinary journey of the soul, and were eager to learn what happened once our human form had expired. Death is all around us, wherever we turn—the media love to report about it, artists love to depict it, though in ways that are decidedly less eloquent and inquisitive than in centuries past.

But death is truth—and it's undeniably fascinating. So, I hope that *Cause of Death* will intrigue, inform, illuminate, and perhaps even inspire you to action—because when we learn a little about how we die, we also learn a lot about how we live.

Foreword

by Robert Young Pelton

In my chosen profession as an Adventurer, someone who focuses on studying the odds to overcome danger, I have learned to differentiate fear from danger. More importantly, I have learned to never let fear of death stop me from enjoying that fine line between excitement and terror, or fortune and misfortune, I call life.

What do we fear? In rough order of magnitude, humans have inordinate fears or phobias of spiders, flying, heights, confined spaces, dentists, needles, and blood. People fear a lot of things but not necessarily the things that will kill them. Deer will kill a lot more people than spiders, flying is a lot safer than walking, and dentists, needles, and blood are more likely to help you than kill you.

We are all going to die. Those of us who die from "natural causes" do not have absolute control over how we die, but we can shave the odds, game the system, and even guarantee that we will not die of many of the afflictions that kill millions of the less fortunate by doing simple things like wearing a seatbelt, skipping dessert, and never smoking.

On a recent visit to my doctor, he happily informed me that my high-mileage fifty-two-year-old body was not only in perfect shape, but that

I should be thankful to be part of the last generation that would outlive the previous one. Life expectancy a century ago was around forty-seven, now it's seventy-seven! But even with safety advances and medical breakthroughs, we may have maxed out our natural life span. Now "good living" killers like heart disease, cancer, and obesity-related problems are estimated to knock years off the next generation's lifespan unless aggressive efforts are made to slow rising death rates from these causes.

There are few people on battlefields or in jungle villages who are keeping track of exactly what kills people, so death statistics in many regions of the world are best guesses. Roughly, in a world of over 6 billion people, about 60 million will die in a given year, over half of those from preventable deaths. Disease will kill over 33 million, accidents and suicide around 5 million and half a million will be murdered.

Death . . . it's something we will all come in touch with but it's probably the least popular thing to think about. There is something about the finality and inevitability that keeps death as both an unspoken fear and the topic of most popular entertainment. Shouldn't it be our love of life that guides us? Rather than fear death, it's better to stare it straight in the face and examine it closely. A good reason for this book, and a great way to focus your energies, is to determine the things that will help you live longer . . . and better.

You will discover in these pages that life is a gift in much of the world, yet taken for granted in some areas and severely abused in others. Many people in low-income regions of the world die before they ever get a chance to learn how to read, let alone grow up to know what a book is. That you are reading this book means you are likely to live longer. Why? You are probably English-speaking, have the disposable income to afford books, have the leisure time to read, and are interested in the topic. More than likely some of the information in this book will rub off on you and you will make lifestyle adjustments. Why? Because affluent, educated people live longer. North Americans, Europeans, and Southeast Asians live longer. Statistically you lose twenty years of life if you live in Africa. Your life expectancy increases if you live in Japan, but drops if you live next door in China.

Even a brief look through this wonderfully informative book will show you very quickly that much of what you think will kill you . . . will not. And much of what you fear will kill you . . . won't. I am more likely to die in a car accident on the way to a war zone than die from a bullet, more likely to lose years of my life from a debilitating disease I pick up on an expedition than be attacked by a wild animal. I am often doing more harm to myself at home by eating too well, drinking, relaxing, and just doing nothing. It is an active body and an inquisitive mind that keeps us young. So get out there and enjoy life!

Robert Young Pelton is the author of The World's Most Dangerous Places *and hosts the website www.comebackalive.com.*

DANGER OF DEATH

Note to the Reader
by The Authors

There are many numbers in this book. But our purpose is not simply to give you a list of raw data: No matter how recent, they would become history with every passing day. What we tried to do instead was to compare numbers, to show you how the frequency of an occurrence can vary by region, age, lifestyle, and myriad other factors.

So we needed benchmark years for which the data have completely been recorded and counted, early enough for us to sift through the reports and produce this book. Therefore, unless we indicate otherwise:

- Worldwide data are taken from the year 2002
- U.S. data are taken from the year 2001

We will remind you of this from time to time, and we will make exceptions that we'll duly note. But you can trust that, as much as humanly possible, we will compare apples to apples.

Acknowledgments

Cause of Death took many years to develop. To satisfy George Lucas's curiosity meant creating a massive framework of statistical data that would allow one provocative mortality number to be viewed in context against the entire spectrum of facts about death. And the information needed to be factual. Finally, the book had to be written in a way to appeal even to those suffering from *arithmophobia* and *numerophobia* (also known as fear of numbers). The results presented here couldn't have happened without the help of the following people and resources:

PEOPLE THANK-YOUS

To TOM DUPREE for his masterful editorial touch and his help making sense out of nonsense and consistency in presentation

To JACK MINGO and ERIN BARRETT for their ability to turn facts into fun

To JANE ELLEN STEVENS for her help with early research and for opening the door to the many global organizations that track statistical data

To TOM GRACE for his initial research identifying the World Health Organization (WHO) Global Burden of Disease (GBD) mortality reports and the International Classification of Disease (ICD10) codes used by both the Centers for Disease Control (CDC) and the WHO to track deaths in the United States and throughout the world

PRIMARY RESOURCES

1. World Health Organization "GBD Mortality Reports" and other reports available at www.who.int/
2. The Centers for Disease Control "National Vital Statistics Reports" and other reports available at www.cdc.gov/
3. The National Safety Council "Injury Facts" book and other reports available at www.nsc.org/
4. The National Highway Traffic Safety Administration "Traffic Safety Facts" book and other reports available at www.nhtsa.dot.gov/
5. The U.S. Census Bureau "Statistical Abstract of the United States" and other material available at www.census.gov/

6. The U.S. Department of Health and Human Services book "Health, United States" and other reports available at www.hhs.gov/
7. The Bureau of Labor Statistics "Census of Fatal Occupational Injuries" available at www.bls.gov/
8. The Central Intelligence Agency "World Factbook" and other information available at www.cia.gov/
9. The Federal Bureau of Investigation "Crime in the United States" and other reports and information available at www.fbi.gov/
10. The Bureau of Justice statistics "Capital Punishment" and other bulletins available at www.usdoj.gov/
11. The United Nations Office on Drugs and Crime and their "Survey on Crime Trends and the Operation of Criminal Justice Systems" reports available at www.unodc.org/
12. The U.S. Department of Defense (DoD) "Casualty" and other reports and information available at www.defenselink.mil/
13. The U.S. National Library of Medicine/National Institutes of Health "Medical Encyclopedia," "Dictionary," and other information available at www.nlm.nih.gov/medlineplus/
14. *Warfare and Armed Conflicts: A Statistical Reference to Casualty and Other Figures, 1500–2000* by Micheal Clodfelter
   Additional sources can be found beginning on page 440.

OTHER INSPIRATIONAL REFERENCE BOOKS ON RELATED SUBJECTS

Freakonomics by Steven D. Levitt and Stephen J. Dubner
Last Breath: Cautionary Tales from the Limits of Human Endurance by Peter Stark
Stiff: The Curious Lives of Human Cadavers by Mary Roach
The Visual Display of Quantitative Information by Edward R. Tufte

And finally, thanks to Google and the Internet, without which the research required for this book would have taken many more years.

Lucy Autrey Wilson
Director of Publishing, George Lucas Books

Canc

#3 Cause of premature death in the world
2002 (under age 70)

#1 Cause of premature death in the USA
2001 (under age 75)

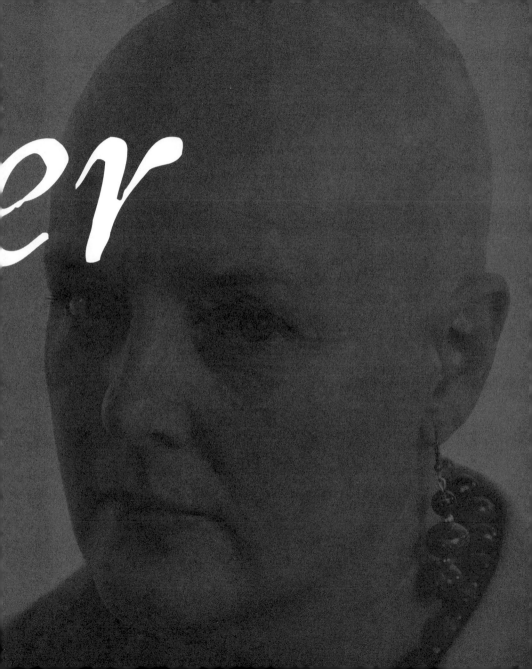

Q UESTION: What percentage of world cancer deaths are caused by viruses? **Answer: 18%**

Of the approximately 9 million worldwide cancer deaths in 1995, 1,100,000 were caused by viruses, 490,000 by bacteria, and 10,000 by parasites.

Q How many lung cancer deaths are there for every $500,000 spent on cigarettes? **A: 1**

Americans spent $77.8 billion on cigarettes in 2001, and about 156,000 of them died of lung cancer.

Q Are you more likely to die of skin cancer in California or Maine? **A: Maine**

The rate of death in 2002 was 5.0 per 100,000 in Maine versus 3.0 in California.

Q Are you more likely to die of breast cancer in California or New Jersey? **A: New Jersey**

The rate of death in 2002 was 17.4 in New Jersey versus 11.9 in California.

Q Between sun lovers in the U.S. and Germany, who is more likely to die from melanoma? **A: It's a tie**

In 2000, the rate of death was 2.6 per 100,000 people in both the U.S. and Germany. In contrast, the rate in Japan was only 0.3.

Q If you're an American male, how much more likely are you to die from homicide at work than breast cancer? **A: 30%**

In 2003, 511 American men were murdered at work, while 390 died from breast cancer.

Q Which cancer has better survival rates: breast or prostate?

A: Prostate

96% of prostate cancer patients are alive after 5 years versus 86% of breast cancer patients.

Q Are you more likely to die from bacterial-caused syphilis or lymphoma cancer—thought to be caused by viruses? **A: Lymphoma**

In the world in 2002, 333,855 people died from lymphoma cancers (affecting the lymphatic system) versus 156,927 who died from syphilis.

Q Which diet is more likely to result in colon cancer: Asian or American? **A: American**

In the U.S. in 2000, white Americans died of colon cancer at an age-adjusted rate of 20.3 per 100,000 versus 12.7 for Asian Americans.

Q How much more likely are you to die of prostate cancer if you're black versus Hispanic?

A: 3 times

Hispanics died of prostate cancer at an age-adjusted rate of 21.6 per 100,000 in 2000 versus 68.1 for African Americans

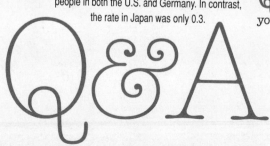

Cancer World Death Rates
by WHO Region (per 100,000 population)

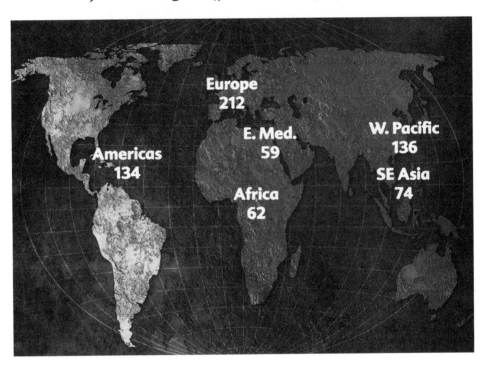

CANCER DEATHS, 2002—ALL AGES

Americas (incl USA): **1,145,104**

USA: **567,444***

Europe: **1,860,084**

E. Mediterranean: **296,614**

Africa: **418,268**

W. Pacific: **2,343,772**

Southeast Asia: **1,178,595**

* USA totals are for 2001.

Cancer Deaths and Death Rates Worldwide, 2002

Location of Cancer	Deaths	Death Rates per 100,000
Lung, trachea, & bronchus	1,238,867	19.9
Stomach	849,477	13.6
Colon & rectum	620,071	9.9
Liver	618,791	9.9
Breast	476,746	7.6
Esophagus	445,895	7.1
Lymph & marrow	333,854	5.3
Mouth & oropharynx	317,428	5.1
Prostate	268,293	4.3
Blood	263,613	4.2
Cervix	238,805	3.8
Pancreas	229,399	3.7
Bladder	178,123	2.8
Ovary	133,663	2.1
Uterus	71,256	1.1
Skin	65,896	1.1
All other	904,615	14.52
TOTAL	**7,254,792**	**116.02**

CANCER is difficult for many people to think about rationally. It inspires a level of fear that may not be commensurate with its actual danger.

True, the cumulative fatalities from all kinds of cancer make it the #1 premature killer in the U.S., and the #3 premature killer worldwide. And cancer seems a frightening thing to contemplate: something malignant growing inside us that can end our lives. But in truth, cancer is a part of us, both literally and in its relation to our own choices of the foods we eat, the chemicals we ingest, the drugs we take, the smoke we

THE TOPIC OF CANCER

inhale, and the medical tests we forgo. It is we who are in collusion with cancer, and it is we who need to face it rationally. A recent survey found that women are ten times more afraid of breast cancer than lung cancer—even though many more women actually die from lung cancer. Let's take a sober look at the facts.

Note: All deaths cited are for 2001 in the U.S. and for 2002 in the world, unless otherwise noted

Quick & Dead Summary for the U.S.

567,444 Number of U.S. cancer deaths

44 Percentage of those over age 75

4 Percentage of those under 45

3 Number of men who die of lung cancer for every two women

3 Number of women who die from breast cancer for every

TOP 5 MOST LETHAL CANCERS IN THE U.S.

RANK	TYPE OF DISEASE	NUMBER OF DEATHS
1	Respiratory	162,958
2	Digestive	131,745
3	Genital (male & female)	58,139
4	Leukemia/Lymphoma	45,210
5	Breast	41,809

Malignancies

10 million
Number of annual new cancer diagnoses worldwide

22 million
Number of people who are living with cancer at any given time

90 Percentage of cancer deaths in people over 45

212 Cancer death rate per 100,000 in Europe, 2002

194.4 The same rate in the USA, 2001

62 The same rate in Africa

What's Money Got to Do with It?

More affluent people tend to live longer and reach the age when they're more likely to die from cancer.

U.S. WHITE AND BLACK ECONOMICS VS. CANCER DEATH RATES, 2003
(per 100,000 population by race)

RACE	MEDIAN INCOME	CANCER DEATH RATE
White	$54,633	208.9
Black	$33,525	167.2

Cancers Killing American Women and Men

(by type and % distribution, 2001)

273,634 Female deaths   **293,812** Male deaths

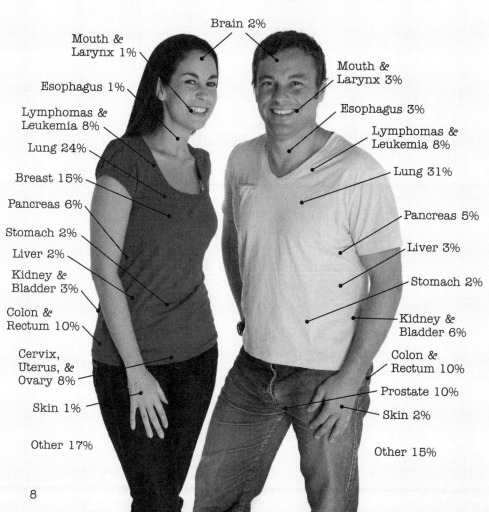

Brain 2%

Mouth &
Larynx 1%

Mouth &
Larynx 3%

Esophagus 1%

Esophagus 3%

Lymphomas &
Leukemia 8%

Lymphomas &
Leukemia 8%

Lung 24%

Lung 31%

Breast 15%

Pancreas 6%

Pancreas 5%

Stomach 2%

Liver 3%

Liver 2%

Kidney &
Bladder 3%

Stomach 2%

Colon &
Rectum 10%

Kidney &
Bladder 6%

Cervix,
Uterus, &
Ovary 8%

Colon &
Rectum 10%

Prostate 10%

Skin 1%

Skin 2%

Other 17%

Other 15%

Fear vs. Reality

22 Percentage of American women who say that breast cancer is the disease they fear most

41,394 Number of breast cancer deaths among U.S. women

2.4 Percentage of American women who say that lung cancer is the disease they fear most

65,632 Number of lung cancer deaths among U.S. women

1 Ranking of Washington State in diagnosed breast cancer rates (a diagnosis rate doesn't necessarily correlate with a death rate from cancer—it can be a sign of good cancer detection in early stages)

1 Number of states in the breast cancer high-detection top 10 that are also in the top 10 of breast cancer death rates: Massachusetts

TOP 10 WORST STATES FOR BREAST CANCER
(per 100,000)

RANK	STATE	DEATH RATES
1	Pennsylvania	18.9
2	New Jersey	17.4
3	Ohio	16.8
4	Montana	16.7
5	Massachusetts	16.5
6	Iowa	16.5
7	North Dakota	16.4
8	Maryland	16.3
9	Louisiana	16.2
10	Kentucky	16.1

TOP 10 BEST STATES FOR BREAST CANCER
(per 100,000)

RANK	STATE	DEATH RATES
1	Alaska	7.3
2	Hawaii	9.2
3	Utah	9.6
4	Wyoming	10.8
5	Colorado	11.0
6	Texas	11.6
7	New Mexico	11.8
8	California	11.9
9	Arizona	12.3
10	Georgia	12.3

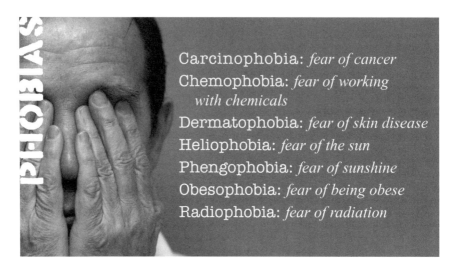

PHOBIAS

Carcinophobia: *fear of cancer*
Chemophobia: *fear of working with chemicals*
Dermatophobia: *fear of skin disease*
Heliophobia: *fear of the sun*
Phengophobia: *fear of sunshine*
Obesophobia: *fear of being obese*
Radiophobia: *fear of radiation*

Ounce of Prevention

1 in 3 Proportion of cancer deaths that are preventable, according to a 2005 Harvard report

9 Number of modifiable risk factors that the Harvard researchers identified: smoking, weight, lack of exercise, diet, alcohol use, unsafe sex, solid-fuel use in the household (coal, wood, etc.), contaminated injections, and air pollution

30 Percentage of cancers attributed to each of tobacco use and diet

18 Percentage attributed to chronic infections

4 Percentage attributed to each of environmental causes and genetics

Cancer Sticks to Lungs

1 Rank of lung cancer in cause of death from all cancers

156,058 Number of American trachea, bronchus, and lung cancer deaths

58 Percentage of lung cancer fatalities who are male

U.S. MALE LUNG CANCER DEATH RATES, 2001
(per 100,000 population by race)

White	78.4
Black	59.2
Hispanic	13.1

---

90 Percentage of lung cancer diagnoses who are smokers

2 Percentage of lung cancer diagnoses who live or work with smokers

24 Percentage increase in chance of contracting lung cancer if regularly exposed to secondhand smoke

1–5 Percentage of lung cancer cases believed to come from air pollution. Before a huge rise in smoking during the 1930s, lung cancer was uncommon, even among people who worked in factories and mines built when pollution standards were unknown

30 Percentage of all tumors in developed nations that are attributable to tobacco use

6–8 Number of years that a regular smoker typically loses in life expectancy

50 Percentage by which a smoker who quits at age 50 reduces the risk of lung cancer. A quitter at age 30 eliminates nearly all of the smoking-related risk

11

Although some lung, throat, esophageal, or oral cancer victims have never touched a cigarette, so many more die from these cancers because of smoking. Among the many celebrities who have died too soon from smoking-related cancer: Desi Arnaz (age 69), Wilhelmina Behmenburg (40), Humphrey Bogart (57), Yul Brynner (65), Nat "King" Cole (45), Sammy Davis Jr. (64), Walt Disney (65), Sigmund Freud (83), Peter Jennings (67), Michael Landon (54), Lee Remick (55), Babe Ruth (53), Lana Turner (74), Mary Wells (49), and Carl Wilson (51).

Boys Against Girls

7 to 2 Ratio of deaths from esophagus cancer among men and women

12 to 7 The same ratio for deaths from liver cancer

7 to 5 For lung cancer

7 to 4 For skin cancer

2 to 5 For cancer of the anus

Demon Alcohol

5–10 times Magnitude of risk of head and neck cancers among heavy drinkers compared to teetotalers

2 times Increased risk of breast cancer among women who are heavy drinkers

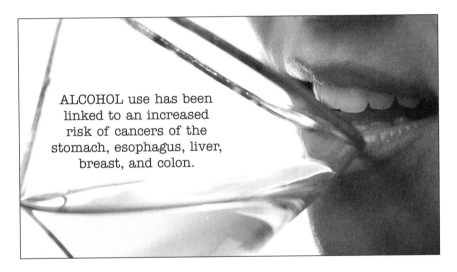

ALCOHOL use has been linked to an increased risk of cancers of the stomach, esophagus, liver, breast, and colon.

WORLDWIDE STOMACH CANCER DEATH RATES, 2000

COUNTRY	MALE DEATH RATES PER 100,000	FEMALE DEATH RATES PER 100,000
Japan	53.3	27.8
Russia	37.0	24.4
Germany	17.2	14.8
France	11.0	6.6
USA	5.3	3.7

Occupational Hazards

2,371 Number of Americans who died in 2001 from mesothelioma (white lung), a rare lung cancer related to asbestos exposure. This is a residual effect of long-ago exposure to asbestos, banned in 1990

18th Century in which an association between employment and cancer risk was first reported. Young chimney sweeps who routinely worked naked inside the enclosed chimneys developed scrotum cancer at an alarming rate

19th Century in which a high rate of bladder cancer was observed in chemical-dye workers exposed regularly to benzidine

Cancer's Fat Chance

25–30 Percentage increase in the chance of certain cancers among those who are obese and physically inactive

41,000 Number of new American cancer cases attributed to obesity in 2002

3.2 Percentage of these diagnoses among all new cancer cases

25 The ideal female body mass index (BMI) number

11,000–18,000 Number of American breast cancer deaths this body mass could save every year. Post-menopausal obese women are particularly prone to breast cancer due to high levels of estrogen in fat tissue

2–4 Increased risk of uterine cancer among obese women

40 Percentage of uterine cancer cases in developed countries that can be attributed to obesity

36 Increased percentage risk that an overweight person will develop kidney cancer

84 Increased risk for an obese person

3–4 Number of hours of moderate exercise per week that can decrease the risk of colon cancer as much as 50%

20 Average percentage decrease in breast cancer risk through a similar moderate exercise program among women of all weights

37 The same percentage decrease among women of normal weight

Here Comes the Sun

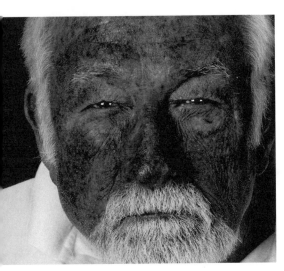

6.9 Death rate for skin cancer in Australia per 100,000 people

3.4 The same rate in the U.S.

1.6 The same rate in Argentina

0.7 The same rate in Japan

Playing Survivor

4 Percentage of U.S. pancreas cancer victims who are still alive after 5 years

14 The same percentage for lung cancer

21 For stomach cancer

52 For ovary cancer

61 For kidney cancer

63 For colon cancer

75 For childhood cancer

86 For breast cancer

96 For prostate cancer

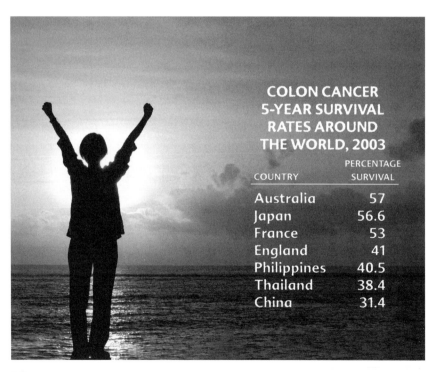

COLON CANCER 5-YEAR SURVIVAL RATES AROUND THE WORLD, 2003

COUNTRY	PERCENTAGE SURVIVAL
Australia	57
Japan	56.6
France	53
England	41
Philippines	40.5
Thailand	38.4
China	31.4

Cancer-causing Agents

According to the World Cancer Report, the most important human carcinogens include tobacco, aflatoxins, and ultraviolet light. Another 20% of cancers are associated with chronic infections, the most significant being hepatitis. Other causative factors are diet, physical activity (or lack thereof), alcohol consumption, and environmental exposures. Deaths from these cancer-causing factors are also found in other chapters:

TOBACCO is positively associated with lung, esophagus, pancreas, bladder, and kidney cancers. See also killer plants and animals in the "Accidents—Flora & Fauna" chapter, COPD in the "Bad Breath" chapter, and cardiovascular disease in the "Broken Heart" chapter.

FOOD CONTAMINANTS (such as aflatoxins naturally occurring in ground grains such as corn and peanuts) contribute to liver cancer, especially in Africa and Asia. See also fungi death from the aflatoxin aspergillus in the "Bugs" chapter.

RADIATION (the most harmful of which is ultraviolet light from the sun) is a primary cause of skin cancer. Survivors of radiation from the atomic bombings in Hiroshima and Nagasaki experienced higher rates of breast, thyroid, and leukemia cancers. For more on war deaths, see the "War" chapter.

CHRONIC INFECTIONS are positively associated with stomach, cervix, liver, lymphoma, Kaposi sarcoma, bladder, and leukemia cancers. See the "Bugs" chapter for hepatitis deaths and HIV/AIDS cancer deaths.

DIET is positively associated with stomach cancer (too much salt); colon, breast, prostate cancers (too much animal fat and protein); mouth, lung, cervix, and uterus cancers (not enough fruits and vegetables). See also cardiovascular disease in the "Broken Heart" chapter and diabetes and obesity in the "Hormones" chapter.

ALCOHOL can cause cancer of the oral cavity, esophagus, and liver, and may increase the risk of breast and colon cancer. See also cirrhosis of the liver in the "Bad Plumbing" chapter and alcohol-use disorders in the "Drugs" chapter.

ENVIRONMENTAL EXPOSURES

(such as air pollution) contribute to lung cancer. See also asbestos-caused death to miners in the "Bad Breath" chapter.

TOP 5 CAUSES OF WORLDWIDE CANCERS

AGENT	PERCENTAGE
Tobacco	30
Diet	30
Chronic infections	18
Alcohol	3
	(4% men, 2% women)
Air, water, and soil pollution	1—4

Most at Risk of Premature Death from Cancer

WORLDWIDE DEATH RATES, 2002
(per 100,000 population)

AGE	MALE	FEMALE
0–4	6.5	6.8
5–14	4.6	4.1
15–29	9.7	7.8
30–44	33.6	36.3
45–59	206.5	161.3
60–69	680.1	398.0
70+	1,434.8	885.5

Main Cause

Lung cancer

Prevention

- DON'T SMOKE
- WATCH WHAT YOU PUT IN YOUR MOUTH
- WASH YOUR HANDS
- DON'T DRINK TOO MUCH ALCOHOL
- LIMIT SUN EXPOSURE
- GET REGULAR MEDICAL EXAMINATIONS

Brok
h

#2 Cause of premature death in the world
2002 (under age 70)

#2 Cause of premature death in the USA
2001 (under age 75)

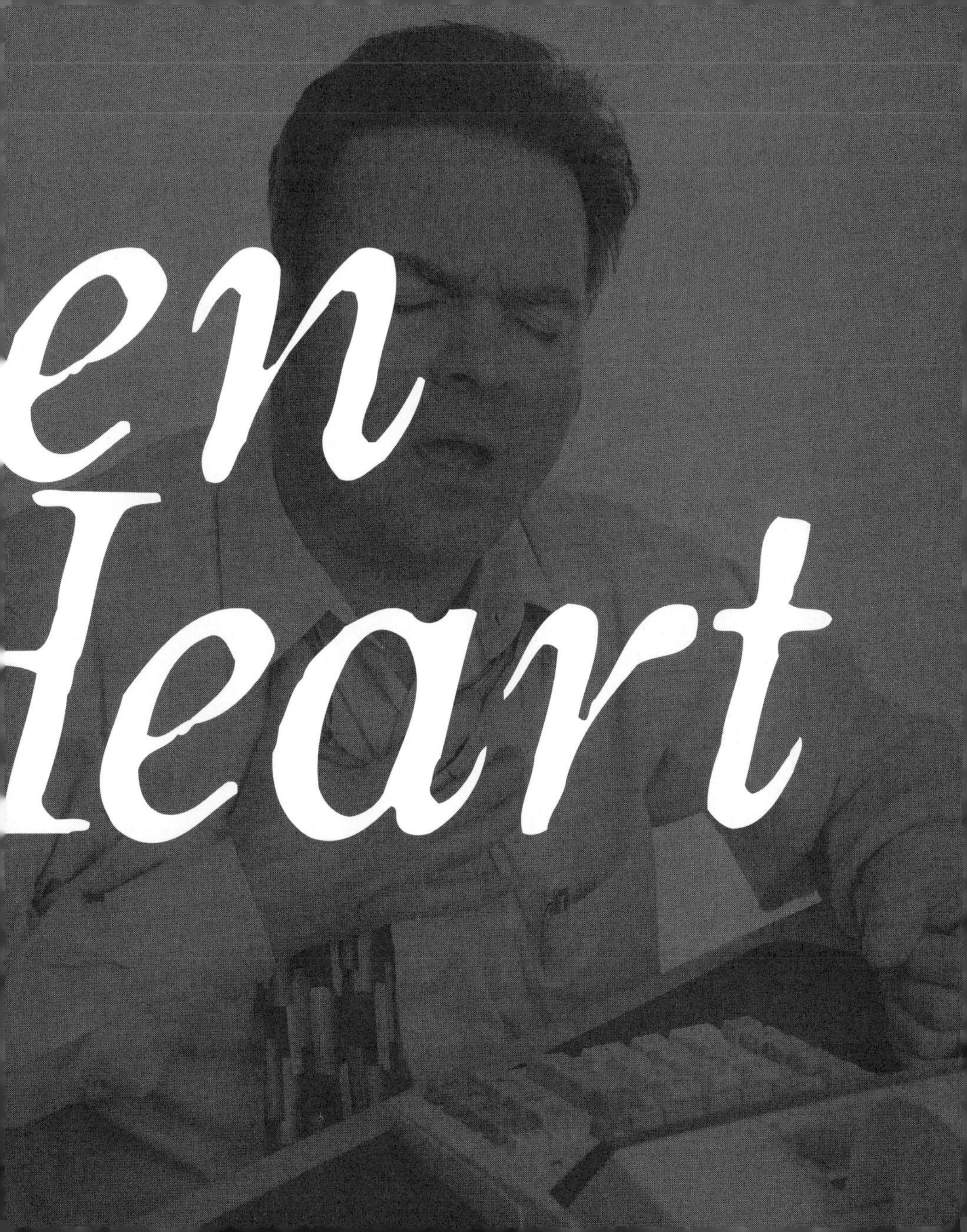
en
Heart

QUESTION: Are you more likely to die sitting in an airplane or crashing in one? **ANSWER: Sitting**

An air-travel passenger is 2 times more likely to develop blood clots than one who is not traveling. 8,842 died in the U.S., in 2004, from either a pulmonary embolism (PE) or arterial embolism and thrombosis (DVT) versus 800 who die annually, on average, in air-traffic accidents.

Q Are you more likely to be killed by a shark or by hemorrhoids?

A: Hemorrhoids

14 people in the U.S. died of hemorrhoids in 2004 versus the fewer than 3 per year on average who die from shark attacks.

Q Which condition causes more accidents among older drivers: bad heart or diabetes? **A: Diabetes**

Older people in at-fault crashes were only 1.15 times more likely to die with a heart condition than those with no medical condition versus 1.58 for those who had diabetes.

Q Is the heart or the liver the most transplanted organ? **A: Neither**

The organs transplanted the most in 2002 were #1 kidney, #2 liver, #3 heart, #4 lung, and #5 pancreas.

Q At what age in the U.S. does heart attack become the #1 cause of death? **A: Age 45–54 for men versus 75+ for women**

When you're young, you're more likely to die of accident, murder, suicide, cancer, bugs, or hormones before your heart goes.

Q What month in the U.S. are you more likely to die of narrowing coronary arteries? **A: January**

Of the 494,382 ischemic heart disease deaths in the U.S. in 2002, the most (47,406 deaths) occurred in January.

Q Which European diet is least likely to lead to heart attack: French coq au vin, German bratwurst, or Spanish paella? **A: French**

In 2000, the French died from acute myocardial infarction at a rate of only 42.60 per 100,000 population versus 62.60 in Spain and 81.8 in Germany. By comparison, the USA's 192,895 heart attack deaths were at a rate of 68.3 per 100,000.

Q Are you more likely to die in the U.S. from varicose veins or crashing your car into a deer?

A: Varicose veins

In 2001 in the U.S., 183 people died from varicose veins versus 150 who died in a deer-caused car crash.

Q What's more dangerous: clogged arteries from sitting and eating fatty foods or falling? **A: Falling**

In the U.S. in 2001, 15,019 people died from falls versus 14,086 from atherosclerosis (clogged arteries).

Broken Heart World Death Rates
by WHO Region (per 100,000 population)

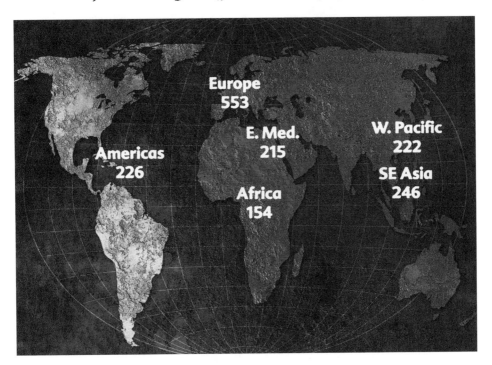

Europe
553

E. Med.
215

W. Pacific
222

Americas
226

SE Asia
246

Africa
154

BROKEN HEART DEATHS, 2002—ALL AGES

Americas (incl USA):
1,926,612

USA: **926,999***

Europe: **4,856,772**

E. Mediterranean: **1,079,633**

Africa: **1,035,691**

W. Pacific: **3,816,582**

Southeast Asia: **3,910,970**

* USA totals are for 2001.

Heart Disease, Heart Failure, Stroke, and Circulatory Disease Deaths Worldwide, 2002

Disease	Deaths
Narrowed coronary arteries (ischemic heart disease)	7,168,113
Loss of blood to the brain (cerebrovascular diseases)	5,493,698
High blood pressure (hypertensive heart and renal disease)	906,873
Inflammatory heart diseases	401,532
Rheumatic heart disease	327,669
Other cardiovascular diseases	2,357,039
TOTAL	**16,654,924**

THE HEART is remarkably dependable. Encased in a typical body, it'll beat 37,868,311 times a year for a total of 2,650,781,781 beats for more than 70 years. It's hard to get a heart to stop doing its job. Even when stabbed, shot, or abused with artery-clotting fat, the heart will try to keep a hearty beat going. But it isn't indestructible.

BEAT GOES ON?

It's a mortal shock for the faithful heart to turn faithless. You have to keep the love alive if you want your heart to keep beating for you. Put down that pork chop and lace up your running shoes. Don't fib to your heart now, because we'd hate to have to defib you later.

Note: All deaths cited are for 2001 in the U.S. and 2002 in the world, unless otherwise noted

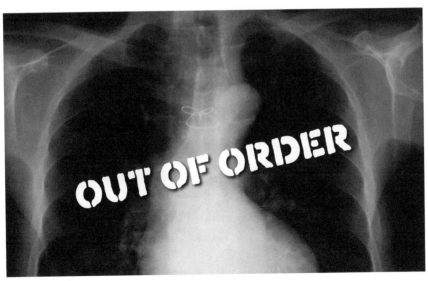

Quick & Dead Summary for the U.S.

1 Rank of cardiovascular malfunction
in U.S. deaths among all age groups

2 Rank of cardiovascular disease in deaths
of people under age 75

926,999 Number of deaths by "broken heart"
in a total of 2,416,425 deaths

14,086 Number of deaths from cholesterol deposits
in the major arteries or atherosclerosis

9,533 Number of circulatory-disorder deaths from
pulmonary embolism or arterial embolism and thrombosis

3,209 Number of circulatory-disorder deaths
from phlebitis and thrombophlebitis

183 Number of circulatory-disorder
deaths from varicose veins

THE TOP 5 MOST LETHAL CARDIOVASCULAR AND CEREBROVASCULAR DISEASES IN THE U.S.

RANK	TYPE OF DISEASE	NUMBER OF DEATHS
1	Narrowed coronary arteries (ischemic)	502,189
2	Loss of blood to brain (cerebrovascular)	163,538
3	Inability to pump blood (heart failure)	56,934
4	Heart muscle inflammation (cardiomyopathy)	26,863
5	High blood pressure (hypertensive)	24,689

Heart of the Matter

300 Weight in grams of an average healthy heart (about 10.5 ounces)

2 Number of fists put together that equal the size of the average adult heart. For a child, one of your fists is approximately equal to the size of your heart

6 Number of quarts of blood in an average adult body

3 Number of times per minute blood circulates completely through the body

72 Rate per minute of a typical human heartbeat

Top 5 Major Risk Factors for Heart Disease and Stroke

1. High blood pressure
2. Tobacco use
3. High blood cholesterol
4. Obesity
5. Diabetes

Heart rate is directly related to the activity level and size of the organism. As moderately large animals, humans have a moderately slow heart rate—not nearly as slow as the gray whale (9 beats per minute) nor as fast as the shrew (600 bpm) or hummingbird (1,200 bpm)

Out of Circulation

99,000 Approximate length in miles of arteries, veins, and capillaries in an adult circulation system. A middle-size child has about 60,000 miles

10 Number of the tiniest capillaries that could fit inside the width of a human hair

96/62 Average blood pressure of an adult of the Yanomamo tribe from the Venezuelan rain forest.

Yanomamos follow an ancient lifestyle, eating fruits, vegetables, nuts, roots, and only a small amount of meat

100/70 Blood pressure below which the chance of stroke or heart attack remains small

125/80 Blood pressure of a normal adult in the U.S. Blood pressure is an indication of the arteries' health, which is directly related to the chance of stroke or heart attack

Artery Having Fun Yet?

Artery walls are supposed to be flexible like a garden hose: When your heart pushes blood into them, they expand slightly and then squeeze back into normal size, giving your blood an extra push along its journey. Artery walls are supposed to be smooth and unobstructed so your blood can flow easily through them.

The problem is keeping arteries healthy. When cholesterol, fats, and lipids form a plaque on the insides of artery walls, cells get less oxygen, the heart works harder, blood pressure rises, and the bloodstream trickles down to dangerous, sometimes fatal levels. More dramatically, chunks of the plaque can break off and float down the bloodstream until they lodge in a narrow spot. If they block blood to the brain, it's a stroke; if they block blood to the heart, it's a heart attack.

The solution? The advice you may already have heard: Stay away from tobacco smoke, avoid saturated and trans fats, exercise regularly and vigorously, eat fruits and vegetables, eat meat sparingly if at all, learn to deal with stress, and keep "bad" cholesterol levels low.

200,000 Estimated maximum number of people who die each year in the U.S. from pulmonary embolism, caused when a blood clot breaks loose and lodges in the pulmonary artery. The most conservative estimate is 50,000

90 Percentage of pulmonary embolism cases that are a result of deep vein thrombosis (DVT) in the legs, known colloquially as "economy class syndrome," since blood pooling and clotting is a hazard of constricted sitting on long flights and dehydration from dry air and alcohol consumption

50 Percentage of DVT cases in which symptoms are subtle or imperceptible: They include tenderness, discoloration, and swelling in the affected leg

8,627 Number of U.S. deaths from pulmonary embolisms

Be Still, My Heart

1 in 2 Odds of dying of a heart-related problem if you make it to 70 years of age worldwide

1 in 28 Odds of dying of heart disease or stroke in the coming 12 months for a typical woman over 70 worldwide

1 in 4 Proportion of Americans with some sort of cardiovascular disease (70,100,000 total), according to the American Heart Association

570 Percentage increase in chance of dying prematurely from any two of three controllable risk factors (high blood pressure, high cholesterol, and smoking) among people with a history of heart attack or stroke. With no history, the chances merely double

430 Percentage increase in death risk if a person with a history of heart attack or stroke had only 1 of the 3 risk factors

46 Percentage reduction in heart disease among elderly men when they were

among the top 25% consumers of dark green and yellow vegetables when compared with the bottom 25%. They also had a 70% lower rate of cancer

3—4 Number of orgasms per week that halve the risk of a major heart attack or stroke

1 Rank of West Virginia in death rate from heart disease and stroke

2—5 Respective ranks of Pennsylvania, Mississippi, Oklahoma, and Florida

1 Rank of Alaska in lowest death rate from heart disease and stroke

2—5 Respective ranks of Utah, Colorado, Minnesota, and New Mexico

1 Rank of Europe in number of heart disease and stroke deaths

1 Rank of Europe in percentage of older population

WORLD REGION BROKEN HEART DEATH RATES

(per 100,000 population, % population age 60+)

WORLD REGION	MALE	FEMALE	TOTAL
Europe	7.5	11	18.5
Americas	5.0	6.3	11.3
W. Pacific	5.1	5.9	11.0
SE Asia	3.6	4.0	7.6
E. Mediterranean	2.8	2.9	5.7
Africa	2.1	2.6	4.7

WORLD BROKEN HEART DEATH RATES BY AGE, 2002

(per 100,000 population)

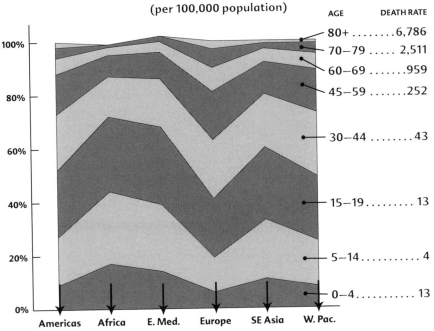

AGE	DEATH RATE
80+	6,786
70–79	2,511
60–69	959
45–59	252
30–44	43
15–19	13
5–14	4
0–4	13

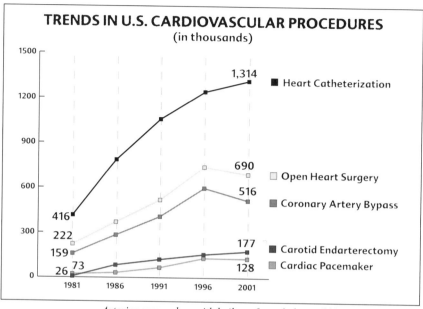

TRENDS IN U.S. CARDIOVASCULAR PROCEDURES
(in thousands)

- 1,314 ■ Heart Catheterization
- 690 □ Open Heart Surgery
- 516 ■ Coronary Artery Bypass
- 416
- 222
- 159
- 73
- 26
- 177 ■ Carotid Endarterectomy
- 128 ■ Cardiac Pacemaker

1981 1986 1991 1996 2001

Arteries gummed up with built-up fatty cholesterol block
oxygen from heart tissue, damaging or killing it

Heart Attack

1 Position of ischemic heart disease as primary cause of broken heart deaths

20 Average interval in seconds between heart attacks in the U.S.

94 Average interval in seconds between U.S. heart attack deaths

3 in 5 Overall odds of surviving a heart attack. Younger victims have better odds

90–95 Percentage chance of surviving a heart attack when the patient makes it to the hospital

4Es Mnemonic by which medical personnel remember the most likely triggers of a heart attack: "Exertion, Eating, Excitement, and Exposure to cold"

30 Time in minutes after being deprived of oxygen-rich blood that heart tissue begins dying. Chewing an uncoated aspirin on the way to the hospital can reduce the damage

1 in 4 Proportion of heart attacks that are "silent"—occurring without identifiable symptoms. Sometimes they don't show up until tests reveal their damage after the fact

1 in 5 Odds of your life ending via heart attack

7–9 a.m. Likeliest 2-hour time of the day to have a heart attack. The second most risky 2-hour period

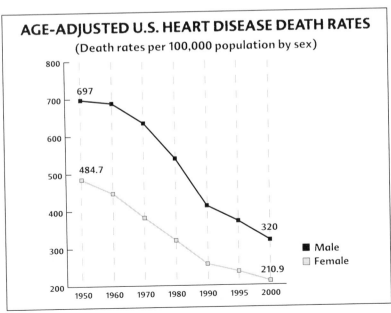

AGE-ADJUSTED U.S. HEART DISEASE DEATH RATES
(Death rates per 100,000 population by sex)

- ■ Male
- □ Female

is from 11 p.m. to 1 a.m. Monday is the riskiest day; Saturday, the second

1 to 41 Ratio of female to male heart attacks before age 44. Although the incidence is uncommon, a young female heart attack victim is twice as likely to die as her male counterpart

1 to 1.7 Ratio of female to male heart attacks after age 65

1 in a million Risk, for a 45-year-old man with none of the mentioned factors, of having a heart attack in the next hour

10 in a million Risk, for a 45-year-old man with significant risk factors, of having a heart attack in the next hour

2 times Factor by which to multiply your 1-hour heart attack risk if you have engaged in brisk

Life Can Be So Unfair

While unapologetic smoker Bette Davis lived well into her retirement years, running guru Jim Fixx died of a heart attack at age 52 during his daily jog. With a series of bestselling books, Fixx had brought jogging to mainstream America in the 1970s. So why the early death? Most experts believe that Jim did extend his life through exercise; before taking up running at 35, he was an overweight smoker, and his father had died of a heart attack at age 43. Some forms of genetic heart disease are hard to predict and control, but even without modern statins, Fixx might've extended his life even longer if he had followed up with cholesterol checks.

walking, sex, or an equally strenuous activity in the past 2 hours. If the sex was preceded by a heavy meal and lots of alcohol, the risk is slightly higher. But if you regularly exercise (e.g., 30 minutes in a gym 3 times a week), the increased risk is insignificant

U.S. ISCHEMIC HEART DISEASE (NARROWING OF THE CORONARY ARTERIES) DEATH RATES
(per 100,000 population by race & sex)

WHITE MALES	WHITE FEMALES	BLACK MALES	BLACK FEMALES
195.8	185.3	138.9	135.2

Ischemic heart disease kills more men than women; more whites than blacks

Stroke

2 Rank of stroke (also known as cerebrovascular disease) among U.S. circulation-related deaths, for a total of 163,538

45 Average interval in seconds between strokes in the U.S.

5 Average interval in minutes between U.S. stroke deaths

U.S. CEREBROVASCULAR DISEASE (STROKE) DEATH RATES
(per 100,000 population by race & sex)

WHITE MALES	WHITE FEMALES	BLACK MALES	BLACK FEMALES
46.6	74.0	44.6	56.9

Strokes kill more women than men; more whites than blacks

Catherine II (the Great) (1729–96) was a strong, decisive, and fearless leader of the Russian empire. Because she was controversial, political enemies invented many rumors about her, some of them concerning her death. As grand as she lived her life, her passing was neither scandalous nor noble. Like Elvis Presley and Judy Garland, she died while sitting on her toilet, from a stroke.

2 Number of stroke types coming from reduced blood flow to the brain. An ischemic stroke is caused by a blockage in an artery that supplies the brain; a hemorrhagaic stroke, by ruptured blood vessels within the brain

5 Time in minutes after being deprived of oxygen-rich blood that brain tissue starts dying, resulting in permanent brain damage and possibly death

22 Percentage reduction in incidence of stroke among men who ate three servings of fruits and vegetables per day

$53.6 Estimated annual "direct and indirect" cost in billions of strokes in the U.S., according to the American Heart Association. This amount is the equivalent of the U.S. trade deficit for the month of March 2005. With it, you could fund NASA for a year, buy a fleet of a hundred Boeing 747s, provide every citizen of Seattle with a new Subaru Outback, and still have a few billion left over

19 of 42 Number, in a Japanese study of men who had strokes while having sexual intercourse, who were engaged in extramarital relations

1/2 Relative stroke risk between light smokers

(fewer than 10 cigarettes a day) versus heavy smokers (more than 40)

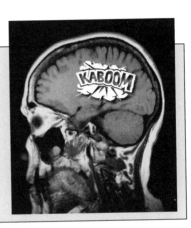

Warmonger Attila the Hun died a rather unceremonious death on his wedding night. After drinking heavily and retiring for a night of feisty lovemaking, his nose started bleeding, a symptom that can indicate a brain aneurysm. If so, then a hemorrhagaic stroke killed a guy who a hundred armies couldn't.

Heart Failure

3 Rank of heart failure among circulation-related deaths in the U.S. Over time, the heart gradually

becomes less efficient at pumping blood. To compensate, it may expand, grow more muscle, and/or

U.S. HEART FAILURE (INABILITY TO PUMP BLOOD) DEATH RATES (per 100,000 population by race & sex)			
WHITE MALES	WHITE FEMALES	BLACK MALES	BLACK FEMALES
16.9	27.1	11.6	15.8

Heart failure kills more women than men; more whites than blacks

pump faster. Blood vessels may constrict to keep blood pressure up, and the body may reduce blood flow to other organs to keep the brain and heart alive

56,934 Number of U.S. deaths from heart failure. Treatments can include a pacemaker, a bypass, or in extreme cases, a transplanted heart

18 Number of days Lewis Washkansky lived after receiving the first heart transplant. Still, the 1967 operation, conducted by surgeon Christiaan Barnard in Cape Town, South Africa, was considered a success in that Washkansky died of pneumonia and not the transplant itself

2 Number of years that 81% of heart transplant patients now live past; 87% make it past the 1-year milestone

3 Ranking of hearts in the most-transplanted-organ list

U.S. TRENDS IN HEART TRANSPLANTS

(Number of transplants per year)

Year		Count
1968	♥♥♥	23
1970	♥	10
1975	♥♥	22
1980	♥♥♥♥	57
1985	♥♥♥♥♥♥♥♥	719
1990	♥♥♥♥♥♥♥♥♥♥♥♥♥	2,107
1995	♥♥♥♥♥♥♥♥♥♥♥♥♥♥♥	2,363
2000	♥♥♥♥♥♥♥♥♥♥♥♥♥♥	2,199
2003	♥♥♥♥♥♥♥♥♥♥♥♥♥	2,057

DISPOSITION OF DONATED ORGANS IN THE U.S., 2002

ORGAN	NUMBER DONATED	% TRANSPLANTED	% DISCARDED	% USED FOR RESEARCH
Kidney	12,040	80.4	10.6	1.8
Lung	9,938	16.3	0.4	0.2
Liver	6,018	82.5	3.1	3.4
Pancreas	4,771	30.4	7.0	1.5
Heart	4,436	49.2	0.2	0.1
Intestine	4,070	2.6	<0.1	<0.1

Cardiomyopathy

4 Rank of cardiomyopathy in the number of heart-related U.S. deaths, a total of 26,863 deaths. These are diseases of the heart muscle itself, including abnormal enlargement

1,000 Weight in grams of an extremely diseased heart (more than 2 pounds)

U.S. CARDIOMYOPATHY (HEART MUSCLE INFLAMMATION) DEATH RATES
(per 100,000 population by race & sex)

WHITE MALES	WHITE FEMALES	BLACK MALES	BLACK FEMALES
10.9	7.9	14.9	10.1

Cardiomyopathy kills more men than women; more blacks than whites

U.S. HYPERTENSIVE HEART DISEASE (HIGH BLOOD PRESSURE) DEATH RATES (per 100,000 population by race & sex)			
WHITE MALES	WHITE FEMALES	BLACK MALES	BLACK FEMALES
6.4	9.2	15.9	16.2

Hypertensive heart disease kills more women than men; more blacks than whites

High Blood Pressure

5 Rank of hypertensive heart disease in heart-related deaths. High blood pressure can come from obesity; heavy drinking; overuse of salt; mineral deficiencies in potassium; calcium, or magnesium; chronic stress; smoking, and insulin difficulties. It can lead to heart attack and heart failure, stroke, kidney failure, blindness, and gangrene

24,689 Number of U.S. deaths from high blood pressure

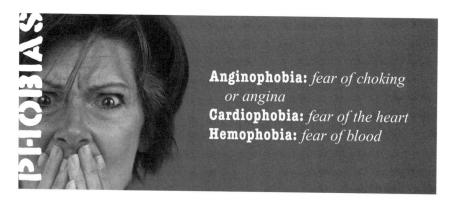

Anginophobia: *fear of choking or angina*
Cardiophobia: *fear of the heart*
Hemophobia: *fear of blood*

Most at Risk of Premature Death from Broken Heart

WORLDWIDE DEATH RATES, 2002
(per 100,000 population)

AGE	MALE	FEMALE
0–4	11.8	14.7
5–14	3.8	4.4
15–29	13.2	11.9
30–44	53.6	32.1
45–59	316.8	187.1
60–69	1,143.8	790.6
70+	3,684.3	3,612.5

Main Cause

Heart disease

Prevention

- WATCH WHAT YOU PUT IN YOUR MOUTH
- EXERCISE (in moderation if you have a heart condition)
- GET REGULAR MEDICAL EXAMINATIONS

Acci

#5 Cause of premature death in the world
2002 (under age 70)

#3 Cause of premature death in the USA
2001 (under age 75)

dents

QUESTION: What day is the worst to be on the road with a bad driver? **ANSWER: Saturday**

Number of U.S. fatal crashes was highest at 7,036 on Saturdays in 2003.

Q When's the deadliest time to go for a walk? **A: 6–9 p.m.**

Dusk is the most deadly 3-hour period for pedestrians on U.S. roadways.

Q If you're a young man, how much more likely are you to die in a motor vehicle accident versus being murdered with a gun?

A: Almost 3 times

In 2002 the firearm homicide rate for 15–24-year-old males was 10.6 per 100,000 versus 28.2 for those who died in a motor vehicle accident.

Q If you're a black man, are you more likely to be murdered or die in a car accident? **A: Murdered**

In 2002, black males had a homicide rate of 38.4 per 100,000 versus 21.5 for motor vehicle accidental deaths.

Q At the age when you're least likely to die, how much more

likely are you to die from an accident than cancer? **A: 2.5 times**

In 2002, accidents killed Americans aged 5–14 at a rate of 6.6. Cancer killed the same age group at a rate of 2.6 per 100,000.

Q Which job is statistically more lethal: police officer or logger?

A: Logger

In 2003, 104 loggers died at a rate of 131.6 per 100,000 loggers (71% from being struck by an object) versus 126 police who died at a rate of 20.9 (51% from transportation accidents and 49% from homicide).

Q Are you more likely to die while working as a postal carrier or as a convenience store clerk?

A: Postal carrier

In 2003, 35 of the 3,425,840 U.S. convenience store clerks were shot and killed (a rate of 1.03 per 100,000). Meanwhile, 10 of the 344,900 mail carriers died—mostly in driving incidents (a rate of 2.9 per 100,000).

Q Are you more likely to die from an organ transplant or a legal execution? **A: Organ transplant**

In 2001, of 3,021 medical-error and surgery-complications deaths—72 were from organ transplants. That year 63 people were executed.

Q At what age are you most likely to die from a fall? **A: Age 65+**

In 2003 in the U.S., 83% of home accident deaths from falls occurred to Americans age 65+.

Accident World Death Rates
by WHO region (per 100,000 population)

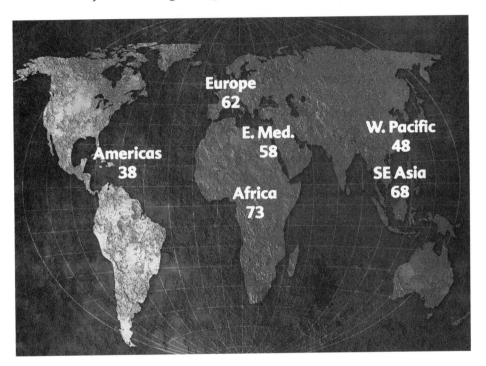

ACCIDENT DEATHS, 2002 — ALL AGES

Americas (incl USA): **320,799**

USA: **108,756***

Europe: **546,807**

E. Mediterranean: **293,391**

Africa: **487,944**

W. Pacific: **826,950**

Southeast Asia: **1,080,324**

* USA totals are for 2001.

Accident Deaths Worldwide, 2002

Type of Accident	Deaths
Road traffic	1,191,732
Falls	392,689
Drownings	384,560
Poisonings	354,606
Fires	310,566
Other unintentional injuries (including "Flora & Fauna," "Nature," & "Sports")	927,870
TOTAL	**3,562,023**

MANY dangers are simply beyond our control. A defective toaster shoots out a lethal spark. A drunken driver careens into our lane. A rotten floorboard gives way. A surgeon slips, a bridge collapses, a train derails, a maniac detonates a stick of dynamite, a distracted teen driver calls someone on her cell phone . . .

STUFF HAPPENS

Yet Freud claimed, "There are no accidents," and he had a point: Many "accidental" deaths are in fact quite predictable—and preventable. Drive badly, madly, or drunk, and the last thing to go through your mind could be the dashboard. Smoke in bed, and you may wake aflame. Leave off the motorcycle helmet, and your noggin might never fit in one again. Maybe there should be a better term than *accident* for betting your life and losing: When you take an unnecessary risk, it's no accident if the worst case turns up.

TOP 10 MOST LETHAL U.S. TRANSPORTATION ACCIDENTS BY MODE

RANK	TRANSPORT MODE	VICTIM	ANNUAL DEATHS
1	Car	Occupant	14,946
2	Foot	Pedestrian	6,071
3	Truck or van	Occupant	3,739
4	Motorcycle	Rider	3,042
5	Airplane	Occupant	918
6	Bicycle	Rider	792
7	Off-road vehicle	Rider	751
8	Boat	Occupant	413
9	Heavy transport	Occupant	374
10	Animal	Rider	116

Note: All deaths cited are for 2001 in the U.S. and 2002 in the world, unless otherwise noted.

Quick & Dead Summary for the U.S.

108,756 Number of U.S. accidental deaths

24 Percentage of U.S. accidental deaths occurring to people 75 and over

43,788 Number of U.S. accidental deaths involving motor vehicles

15,019 Number from falls

14,078 From accidental poisoning

5,555 From suffocation, including choking

3,309 From fires

3,281 From drowning

3,021 From medical and surgical complications

2,752 From contact with machinery, sharp objects, explosions, and other nonliving forces

1,100 From contact with nature

13,353 From other causes

Road Traffic, Fall, Poison, Fire, Drown, Other

U.S. MOTOR VEHICLE FATALITY RATE TRENDS 1910–2001

(per 100,000 population)

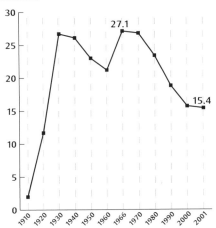

Since 1966, safety improvements have dramatically decreased the rate of traffic deaths. With the introduction of mass-produced cars, U.S. motor vehicle death rates had significantly risen from 1910 to the late 1930s. During World War II, rates dropped because of gas rationing and the absence from U.S. streets of most high-risk young male drivers. But after the war they picked up again through the 1960s, leading to legally mandated safety standards, including seat belts and air bags.

My Way, the Highway

14,164 Estimated number of U.S. lives saved by seat belts in 2002

80 Minimum estimated percentage of drivers and passengers using seat belts

35.29 Motor-vehicle-crash death rate per 100,000 residents in Wyoming, making it the #1 state in 2002

2, 3, 4, 5 Respective rankings of Mississippi, Montana, South Carolina, and West Virginia in motor-vehicle-crash deaths per capita. States with the worst rankings tend to be rural with many 2-lane highways, high speed limits, lots of space between populated areas, and a lower compliance in wearing seat belts

49

7.14 Motor-vehicle-crash death rate per 100,000 residents in Massachusetts, giving it the country's lowest ranking (50)

49, 48, 47, 46 Respective rankings of Rhode Island, New York, New Jersey, and Connecticut in traffic deaths per capita. States with the best safety records tend to have more cities and freeways, and a higher rate of seat belt use

30 Percentage of pedestrian deaths that could be prevented if city traffic were slowed by 3.1 mph, according to an Australian study

58,195 Number of Americans who died in the 2 decades of American involvement in Vietnam

1¼ Approximate time in years it takes American traffic deaths to equal that total

9 Percentage rate of increase in fatal auto accidents in the week following a well-publicized suicide, according to a study correlating California newspapers and traffic statistics

72 Percentage of world road-traffic-accident deaths experienced by males

90 Percentage of worldwide traffic deaths that occur in low- and middle-income countries. Africa has the highest rate of road traffic deaths (29 per 100,000), and Europe has the lowest (15). The majority do not occur in private cars, but among pedestrians, bicyclists, motorcyclists, and passengers on public transportation

2/3 Ratio of road-traffic deaths in New Delhi involving buses and trucks

15 Rate of road-traffic-accident deaths per 100,000 males in the U.S. in 1999

9.4 Rate of death per 100,000 American females that same year

TOP 10 MOST DANGEROUS COUNTRIES FOR DRIVING
(reported between 1992 and 2002, excluding Africa,
India, China; per 100,000 males)

RANK	COUNTRY	# MALES KILLED	DEATH RATE
1	El Salvador, 1999	2,119	41.7
2	Dominican Republic, 1998	2,812	41.1
3	Brazil, 1995	38,051	25.6
4	Colombia, 1998	8,917	24.2
5	Kuwait, 2000	363	23.7
6	Venezuela, 2000	5,198	23.1
7	Latvia, 2001	562	22.7
8	Republic of Korea, 2001	10,496	21.9
9	Thailand, 1994	12,411	21.0
10	Costa Rica, 2000	719	20.1

TOP 10 SAFEST COUNTRIES FOR DRIVING
(reported between 1992 and 2002, excluding Africa,
India, China; per 100,000 males)

RANK	COUNTRY	# MALES KILLED	DEATH RATE
1	Malta, 2001	19	4.3
2	Macedonia (formerly Yugoslavia), 2000	110	5.1
3	Singapore, 2001	201	5.2
4	United Kingdom, 1999	3,479	5.6
5	Tajikistan, 1999	246	5.6
6	Armenia, 2000	2,332	5.6
7	Sweden, 2000	548	5.7
8	Israel, 1998	345	5.9
9	Bahamas, 1995	17	6.1
10	Georgia, 2000	344	6.2

TOP 10 SAFEST U.S. CITIES FOR DRIVING, 2002
(per 100,000 Population)

RANK	CITY	NUMBER KILLED FROM MOTOR VEHICLE CRASHES	DEATH RATE
1	Glendale, CA	5	2.51
2	Overland Park, KS	4	2.52
3	Fort Wayne, IN	6	2.86
4	Moreno Valley, CA	6	2.98
5	Spokane, WA	7	3.57
6	Irvine, CA	6	3.70
7	Minneapolis, MN	14	3.73
8	Grand Rapids, MI	8	4.07
9	Garland, TX	9	4.10
10	Norfolk, VA	10	4.18

TOP 10 MOST DANGEROUS U.S. CITIES FOR DRIVING, 2002
(per 100,000 Population)

RANK	CITY	NUMBER KILLED FROM MOTOR VEHICLE CRASHES	DEATH RATE
1	Louisville, KY	69	27.45
2	Knoxville, TN	44	25.34
3	Tampa, FL	71	22.53
4	Orlando, FL	38	19.62
5	Miami, FL	69	18.41
6	Kansas City, MO	78	17.59
7	Atlanta, GA	73	17.18
8	Phoenix, AZ	232	16.91
9	San Bernardino, CA	32	16.70
10	Birmingham, AL	39	16.29

WORST DAYS AND TIMES TO BE ON THE ROAD
(U.S., 2003)

DAY OF THE WEEK	TIME OF DAY	# FATAL CRASHES
Saturday	Midnight to 3 a.m.	1,228
Sunday	Midnight to 3 a.m.	1,208
Friday	9 p.m. to midnight	1,094
Saturday	9 p.m. to midnight	1,079
Saturday	6 p.m. to 9 p.m.	1,034

2:1 Ratio of fatal U.S. traffic accidents between males and females

89 Rate of driver involvement in fatal crashes per 100,000 licensed drivers in the most dangerous age group—males aged 16–20. The rate for female drivers age 16–20 is 39

47 Rate of male driver involvement in fatal crashes age 25–34. That rate will decrease to 30 by age 55–64, but then creep up to 33 after age 69

12 Average number of minutes that will pass before another traffic fatality occurs in the U.S.

12–3 a.m. Deadliest 3-hour period on the deadliest nights of the week, Saturday and Sunday

6–9 p.m. Deadliest time to be a U.S. pedestrian

1 Rank of September as the month with the most fatal U.S. car crashes in 2002

1 Rank of "tree/shrubbery" as the fixed object most likely to be hit in a fatal U.S. motor vehicle crash, 2002 (3,258). Other frequent targets include "culvert/curb/ditch" (2,385), "pole/post" (1,997), "embankment" (1,308), "guardrail" (1,093), and "bridge" (397)

Fashion Victim

The mother of modern dance, Isadora Duncan, died as dramatically as she lived. As she drove home after a night out in Paris, a long, flowing scarf she was wearing became entangled in the back wheel of her roadster, flinging her from the car. Although people rushed to aid her, she was already dead on the road, choked to death by her own scarf.

1 Rank of pedestrian as the "nonfixed object" most likely to be hit in a fatal U.S. motor vehicle collision, 2002 (4,464). Other frequent movable targets include bicyclists (650), parked motor vehicles (453), trains (231), and animals (158)

$2^1/_4$ Increased chance of death from vehicle rollover among SUVs over sedans. In 2003, the top-heavy behemoths were responsible for more than a third of U.S. rollover deaths, killing 2,579 drivers and passengers

1 Percentage of U.S. auto fatalities resulting from collisions with animals or animal-drawn vehicles in 1932

0.2 The same percentage in 2003

8 Percentage of U.S. auto fatalities from collisions with trains in 1928

0.7 The same percentage in 2003

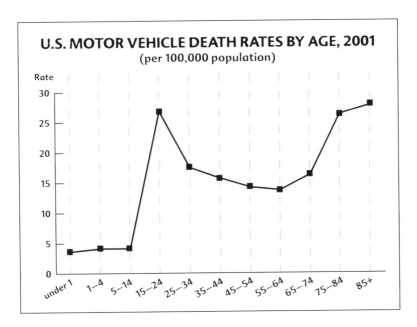

U.S. MOTOR VEHICLE DEATH RATES BY AGE, 2001
(per 100,000 population)

TOP 5 BAD-DRIVER BEHAVIOR CAUSING KNOWN FATAL U.S. MOTOR VEHICLE CRASHES, 2003

RANK	BEHAVIOR	NUMBER OF FATAL ACCIDENTS
1	Swerving out of lane or off-road	18,781
2	Speeding	11,990
3	Under the influence of alcohol or drugs	6,313
4	Failure to yield	4,604
5	Inattention or distraction	3,730

The Plane Truth

0.02 Average U.S. death rate in 2000–2002 from scheduled airline travel per 100 million miles. This compares favorably to almost every other kind of travel: auto (.79), bus (.03), and train (.03)

266 Number of crew members and passengers who died in four commercial planes hijacked by terrorists on September 11, 2001. This accounted for half of the U.S. large and commuter airline plane crashes and nearly half of its 544 fatalities that year

Plane & Fancy

Several celebrities have died in or around helicopters. One of the most notable victims was actor Vic Morrow on the set of *The Twilight Zone* movie in 1982. During one of the final shoots of Morrow's segment, following a frighteningly loud special-effects explosion that was simulating a battle, a helicopter in the scene got too close to Morrow and two child actors, Renee Chen and My-ca Le. Renee was struck and killed by the foot of the helicopter. The helicopter blades decapitated both Morrow and My-ca. The incident spawned more stringent child labor laws in the movie industry.

Another equally horrifying celebrity helicopter death was that of comedienne/traffic gal Jane Dornacker. While reporting live for New York City's WNBC radio, her helicopter crashed into the Hudson River. Millions of listeners heard the motor rev and Dornacker screaming, "Hit the water, hit the water!" as the copter went down. Dornacker died on the way to the hospital; the pilot survived.

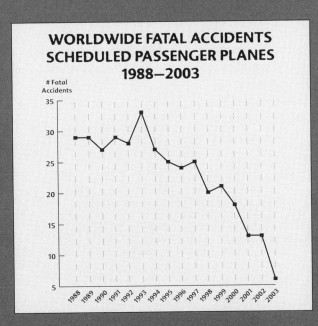

WORLDWIDE FATAL ACCIDENTS SCHEDULED PASSENGER PLANES 1988–2003

Fatal Accidents

FATAL U.S. CIVIL AVIATION ACCIDENTS AND DEATHS
1999–2003

YEAR	LARGE AND COMMUTER AIRLINES		ON-DEMAND AIR TAXIS		OTHER PLANES	
	# FATAL ACCIDENTS	# DEATHS	# FATAL ACCIDENTS	# DEATHS	# FATAL ACCIDENTS	# DEATHS
1999	7	24	12	38	340	619
2000	4	97	22	71	345	596
2001	8	544	18	60	325	562
2002	0	0	18	35	345	581
2003	3	24	19	45	351	626

Going Down?

30 Average number of U.S. elevator and escalator deaths per year. About half of the deaths occurred to workers trying to repair or maintain an elevator

17,100 Average number of injuries

1 Number of deaths per 100 million miles traveled on elevators

5 Number of deaths per 100 million miles traveled on stairs

Killer Job!

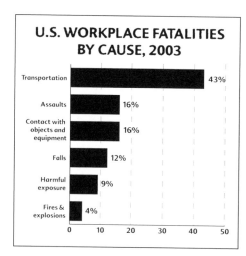

U.S. WORKPLACE FATALITIES BY CAUSE, 2003

Cause	Percentage
Transportation	43%
Assaults	16%
Contact with objects and equipment	16%
Falls	12%
Harmful exposure	9%
Fires & explosions	4%

4.3 U.S. fatal work injuries per 100,000 workers in 2001

4.0 Death rate for 2003, down from a 10-year high of 5.4 in 1994

5,559 Number of workers killed on the job in 2003

50 Percentage of workers killed between the ages 20 and 44

TOP 5 U.S. FATAL AT-WORK INJURIES BY INDUSTRY, 2003
(per 100,000 workers)

RANK	OCCUPATION	# ACCIDENTAL DEATHS	ACCIDENTAL DEATH RATES
1	Agriculture, forestry, fishing, and hunting	707	31.2
2	Mining	141	26.9
3	Transportation and warehousing	805	17.5
4	Construction	1,126	11.7
5	Wholesale trade	191	4.2

TOP 5 U.S. FATAL AT-WORK INJURIES BY SELECTED OCCUPATIONS, 2003
(per 100,000 workers)

RANK	OCCUPATION	# ACCIDENTAL DEATHS	ACCIDENTAL DEATH RATES
1	Logging	104	131.6
2	Aircraft pilots and flight engineers	113	97.4
3	Farmers and ranchers	329	39.3
4	Driver/sales workers and truck drivers	861	26.7
5	Construction laborers	289	25.1

59

Accidental Death Begins at Home

33,100 Number of U.S. accidental deaths occurring at home in 2003

2,800 Number of U.S. drowning victims in 2003

700 Number of those drownings that occurred at home

AGE GROUP MOST AT RISK OF IN-HOME DEATHS

83% or 7,500 of **fall** deaths were ages **65+**

65% or 1,500 of **fire** deaths were ages **45+**

51% or 5,800 of **poison** deaths were ages **25–44**

50% or 1,100 of **choking** deaths were ages **75+**

50% or 1,000 of **suffocation** deaths were ages **0–4**

43% or 130 of natural **heat** or **cold** deaths were ages **75+**

38% or 270 of **drowning** deaths were ages **0–4**

30% or 120 of **firearm** deaths were ages **25–44**

56% or 3,400 of **"other causes"** were ages **75+**

The Gravity of the Situation

15,019 Number of U.S. fatalities from falls

2,570 Number from falling on the same level

1,462 From falling down stairs or steps

834 From falling from one level to another

734 From falling off beds, chairs, or other furniture

580 From falling out of buildings

564 From slipping, tripping, and stumbling

439 From falling off ladders and scaffolding

7,830 Number of other, unspecified falls

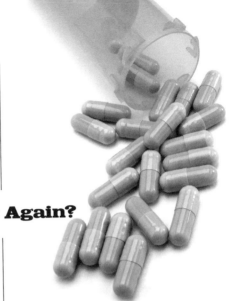

How Many Was That Again?

14,078 Number of accidental U.S. poisoning deaths, compared with 5,191 poisoning suicides

1 Rank of overdose by narcotic and mood-altering drugs, both legal and not, in accidental poisoning deaths (6,509)

2 Rank of medicine for epilepsy, Parkinson's, etc., at 763 deaths

656 Number of accidental annual deaths from gases and vapors (e.g., carbon monoxide)

3 to 2 Proportion of annual accidental deaths from alcohol overdose to that of aspirin and other over-the-counter painkillers

Take My Breath Away

5,555 Number of accidental U.S. suffocation deaths

742 Number of U.S. deaths from inhaling food, a fraction of the number who die from inhaling non-food items (3,021)

422 Number of U.S. deaths from vomit and other "gastric" contents

456 Number of accidental strangulations in bed

279 Number of accidental deaths from other strangling or hanging. A significant number of both "accidental" and "suicidal" hangings (one researcher estimated at least 31% among adolescents) are the result of "autoerotic asphyxiation," a dangerous attempt at achieving a better orgasm by cutting off oxygen to the brain

76 Number of deaths from being trapped in a low-oxygen environment or as a result of a cave-in

Tennessee Williams, noted playwright, choked to death while inhaling something from a nose spray bottle. He had apparently placed the cap in his mouth, and the suction of his sniff sucked the cap down his throat, asphyxiating him.

Where There's Smoke

3,309 Number of U.S. deaths from fires

2,570 Number of U.S. fire deaths that were residential

TOP 5 CAUSES OF U.S. RESIDENTIAL FIRE DEATH

RANK	DEATH SOURCE	NUMBER KILLED
1	Cigarettes and other tobacco products	750
2	Cooking equipment	310
3	Heating and cooling equipment	220
4	Candles	200
5	Electrical wiring and plugs	190

Spontaneous Human Combustion

Stories of people mysteriously going up in flames have appeared in legend, fiction, and even Temperance tracts of the nineteenth century. Novelists from Herman Melville to Charles Dickens have recounted tales of characters who spontaneously combust. Often, the victims described were heavy imbibers of alcohol—the posited theory being that the high alcohol in the blood fueled the flames.

Scientists have found that, indeed, abusers of alcohol, tobacco, and other drugs are disproportionate victims of the phenomenon—but not for the reasons that nineteenth-century chroniclers put forth. Two Florida investigators pored through dozens of purported cases and found none that couldn't be explained otherwise. Most commonly, a smoker becomes unconscious from alcohol, sleeping pills, or a heart attack and drops a cigarette. It begins smoldering and eventually sets them on fire, where their body fat is "wick"-ed into the clothes like wax from a candle. Like a candle's, the flame is contained and controlled, with the heat flowing upward toward the ceiling, covering it with greasy soot from the burning fuel, which then suddenly combusts.

TOP 5 U.S. SOURCES OF FIRE DEATH

RANK	DEATH SOURCE	NUMBER KILLED
1	Building structure fire	2,673
2	Melting material, including clothing	183
3	Out-of-control fire, not in a building	61
4	Controlled fire inside (e.g., fireplace)	44
5	Controlled fire outside (e.g., campfire)	41

In Over My Head

3,281 Number of U.S. drowning deaths

1,054 Number who drowned in "natural water"—lakes, rivers, ponds, and oceans

596 Number who drowned in swimming pools

322 Number who drowned in bathtubs

64 Percentage of under-5-year-olds who drowned in and around the home in a bathtub (per the U.S. Consumer Products Safety Commission in a study from 1996 through 1999)

13 Percentage of under-5-year-olds who drowned in 5-gallon buckets

12 Percentage of under-5-year-olds who drowned in a spa or hot tub

3 Percentage who drowned in the toilet

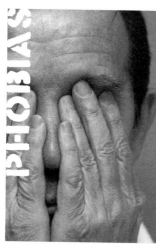

PHOBIAS

Acrophobia: *fear of heights*
Agyrophobia: *fear of crossing streets*
Aichmophobia: *fear of pointed objects*
Amaxophobia: *fear of car rides*
Ambulophobia: *fear of walking*
Amychophobia: *fear of being scratched*
Aviophobia: *fear of flying*
Catapedaphobia: *fear of jumping*
Climacophobia: *fear of stairs*
Cremnophobia: *fear of precipices*
Cyclophobia: *fear of bicycles*

TOP 5 MEDICAL-ERROR DEATHS

RANK	ERROR	DEATHS INCLUDED IN CHAPTERS
1	Failure to rescue	Accidents (transportation, falls, etc.), Suicide, Murder, Broken Heart
2	Postoperative infection	Bugs
3	Adverse drug events	Accidents, Drugs
4	Postoperative pulmonary blood clot	Bad Breath
5	Bedsores	Bad Framing

Paging Dr. Stumblebum

33,321,784 Number of U.S. patients admitted to a community hospital

1,191,276 Number of U.S. patients who died in a hospital or medical center

44,000 to 195,000 Range of estimates of annual U.S. deaths from in-hospital medical errors. Most of these deaths are included in other chapters

3,021 Number of U.S. deaths attributed directly to medical errors and complications from surgery

2,041 Number of these deaths resulting from surgical operation or procedure such as implant, bypass, transplant, organ or limb removal, reconstructive surgery, etc.

475 Number from other medical procedures such as kidney or urinary catheterization, dialysis, shock therapy, and radiotherapy

277 Number from adverse drug events

Contact with Inanimate Objects

2,752 Number of U.S. fatalities from being caught, crushed, or blown up

853 Number of those resulting from striking or being struck by an inanimate object (football, bat, pole, etc.—for more details see "Sports")

802 Number caused by an accidental firearms discharge

648 Number caused by inadvisable contact with a machine or its parts

Shocked, Bitten, and Burned

1,100 Number of U.S. deaths resulting from forces of nature (for more details see "Nature")

431 Number of U.S. deaths from electrical current, radiation, temperature, and pressure

47 Among the electricity deaths, the number caused by small appliances such as toasters and hair dryers

221 Number of U.S. deaths from being bitten, struck, stung by, or crushed by venomous and non-venomous animals and plants (for more details see "Flora & Fauna")

Tran Quoc Dong, a martial arts teacher in Vietnam, chose to celebrate International Workers Day in 2003 with his family gathered around the karaoke machine. As Tran took his turn, the microphone shorted, electrocuting him and sending him flying across the room, where he hit his head on a bed. He died instantly from massive brain damage, the world's only known victim of karaoke.

137 Number of U.S. deaths from overexertion (for more details see "Sports")

114 Number of U.S. deaths from heat and hot substances such as tap water and coffee

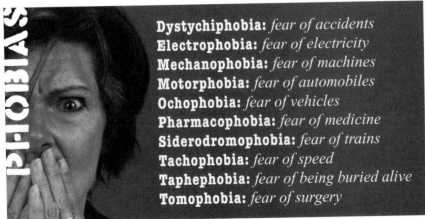

PHOBIAS

Dystychiphobia: *fear of accidents*
Electrophobia: *fear of electricity*
Mechanophobia: *fear of machines*
Motorphobia: *fear of automobiles*
Ochophobia: *fear of vehicles*
Pharmacophobia: *fear of medicine*
Siderodromophobia: *fear of trains*
Tachophobia: *fear of speed*
Taphephobia: *fear of being buried alive*
Tomophobia: *fear of surgery*

Flora & Fauna

QUESTION: What's more dangerous, a deer or your bathtub?

ANSWER: Bathtub

If you are 20 or older in the U.S., you're 2 times more likely to drown in the bathtub. 100 people die in collisions with animals annually versus 322 who died in the bathtub in 2001 (of which 108 were 19 or younger).

Are you more likely to die in the U.S. of a spider bite or by lightning? **A: Lightning**

In 2001, 44 people in the U.S. died from lightning versus 4 from spider bites.

In the U.S., what's deadlier, a bear or shark? **A: Bear**

Over the past 100 years in the U.S., bears have killed 1.3 humans per year (50% in Alaska), while sharks have killed only 52 people in 333 years.

What non-human mammal kills most in the U.S.? **A: Horse**

Of all U.S. encounters with animals in 2001, 79 animal riders fell or were thrown and died (mostly riding horses) versus 25 who died from dog bites.

What non-human mammal kills most in the world? **A: Dog**

Man's best friend is responsible for an average of 25 deaths per year from dog attacks in the U.S. and about 50,000 per year in the world, including deaths from rabies, usually caused by a dog bite.

If you work with animals, should you worry more about cattle or horses? **A: Cattle**

16 U.S. workers died from encounters with cattle versus 12 from horses in the U.S., 2001.

If you live in Florida, are you more likely to be killed by a shark or an alligator? **A: Alligator**

Alligators have killed 12 since 1948, while sharks have killed 12 since 1670.

If you live in Japan, are you more likely to die eating fugu or not eating? **A: Not eating**

In 2000 in Japan, 186 people died from eating disorders, mostly anorexia, while 50 died eating puffer fish.

In the world, are you more likely to die from a coconut falling on your head or from an attacking hippo? **A: Hippo**

Hippos cause an estimated 200 annual deaths worldwide, versus 150 from falling coconuts.

STALKING

tigers, ravenous sharks, vengeful bees, stampeding buffalo, slithering snakes, flesh-eating plants: Deadly flora and fauna inhabit our nightmares. Instincts bred over millennia have taught us to fear claws, teeth, and stingers. For most of us, it's an outdated fear, once crucial to our survival but now as irrelevant as our appendix, tailbone, and wisdom teeth, but with an emotion this deep, we do what we can to make sense of it. Many of our most popular fantasies, movies, and books, even trips to the zoo, are attempts to satisfy those ancient, primitive fears. But as we fixate on what has become fiercely improbable, it distracts us to the real dangers from the familiar flora and fauna around us.

A tiger seems like more of a danger than a mouse or rat—yet rodents are great carriers of fatal diseases. Spiders and bees inspire deeper fear than mosquitoes, though mosquitoes kill many more thousands of people. Encountering a mountain lion on a deserted path seems more terrifying than encountering a deer on the highway, but the deer is more likely to kill you. In children's stories, the big, bad wolf is more ferocious than the three little pigs, but in real life pigs attack and kill many more people than wolves do. Perhaps we're slowly adapting. Perhaps in the far future, the humans who will have survived are the ones who find their scariest nightmares inhabited not by killer bees, but killer beef. Perhaps smoldering cigarettes will be the scariest monster in future horror films. Until that time, though, we'll have to depend on our puny conscious, rational minds for that self-protective function.

STALKING THE WILD AND WOOLLY

Quick & Dead Summary for the U.S.

221 Number of deaths recorded by the Centers for Disease Control in 2001 from contact with animate mechanical forces and venomous animals and plants

65 Number of those deaths from being bitten or struck by other mammals

45 Number from being struck by or against another person (see "Sports" chapter for more information)

43 From hornets, wasps, and bees

25 From being bitten or struck by a dog

9 From being bitten or stung by nonvenomous insects and other arthropods

7 From venomous snakes and lizards

5 From venomous spiders

22 From other causes

Killer Plants and Animals

2,100,000 Estimated number of annual world-wide deaths caused by tobacco—mainly from smoking (see chapters "Bad Breath," "Broken Heart," "Cancer," "Bad Birth," and "Suicide" for more information)

1,800,000 Estimated number of annual world-wide deaths from diarrhea, caused primarily from contact with animal feces (see "Bugs" chapter for more information)

1,200,000 Estimated number from malaria and dengue fever caused by mosquito bites (see "Bugs" chapter for more information)

55,000 Estimated number of worldwide deaths from rabies—caused by

rabid-animal bites (see "Bugs" chapter for more information)

50,000 Estimated minimum number of deaths from venomous snake bites per year in the world

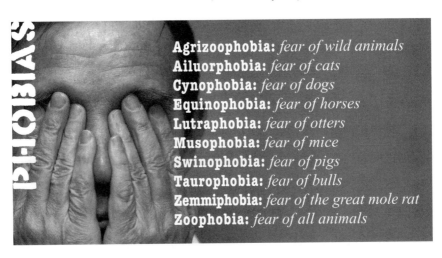

PHOBIAS

Agrizoophobia: *fear of wild animals*
Ailuorphobia: *fear of cats*
Cynophobia: *fear of dogs*
Equinophobia: *fear of horses*
Lutraphobia: *fear of otters*
Musophobia: *fear of mice*
Swinophobia: *fear of pigs*
Taurophobia: *fear of bulls*
Zemmiphobia: *fear of the great mole rat*
Zoophobia: *fear of all animals*

Fauna

Mammals

Bears

133 Number of people killed by bears of all kinds in North America during the past century. Roughly half the bear fatalities took place in Alaska. Bear encounters have increased in the latter half of the century because more people are working, camping, and hiking in bear territory

3 to 1 Odds that the bear will be the victim in a fatal human-bear encounter. Of the 472 significant bear confrontations reported in Alaska, 11% resulted in the death of the human, while 33% resulted in the death of the bear

55 Number of deaths from bears in Alaska between 1900 and 2002: 1 from a polar bear, 6 from black bears, and 48 from grizzly bears

48 Number of people killed by sloth bears in India from 1989 to 1994. Although sloth bears are shy and mostly eat termites and plants, they react aggressively when surprised by humans

Bison

2 Number of people killed in Yellowstone Park by bison between 1979 and 1994. Another 54 people were seriously wounded by headbutts and gorings to the thighs, buttocks, and midsection. Tourists often venture close to the placid-looking animals, unaware that bison are unpredictable, moody, heavy, and surprisingly fast

1 Rank of the African (or Cape) buffalo, according to big-game-hunter folklore, in killing hunters among their "big five" trophy animals (buffalo, elephant, lion, rhino, and leopard). Instead of running away when injured, buffalo have a reputation for wheeling around and charging

10 Estimated number of seconds it took for a Kenyan buffalo in 2004 to fatally gore wildlife artist Simon Combes while he was walking with his wife and a friend. Combes specialized in painting wild fauna, including buffalo. The 2 women threw objects at the buffalo to scare it off, but Combes died at the scene

Cattle

1 Rank of death from heart disease, heart failure, stroke, and circulatory disease in the world and in the U.S. High blood cholesterol is a primary cause of death and is often caused by a

high-fat diet (for more information see the "Broken Heart" chapter)

1 Position cattle occupy in fatal animal-caused work injuries in the U.S. Between

U.S. CONSUMPTION OF BEEF AND MILK VERSUS HEART DISEASE DEATH RATES			
	1980	2002	DECLINE
Whole milk (per capita consumption)	16.5 gallons	7.3 gallons	55%
Beef (per person)	72 pounds	65 pounds	10%
Heart disease (rate of death per 100,000 population)	412.1	240.4	41%

1992 and 1997, 375 worker fatalities were associated with animals, 141 caused by cattle

2 Percentage of the American cattle population that are bulls

---

WORLDWIDE DEATHS FROM VARIANT CREUTZFELDT-JAKOB DISEASE, 1996–2000

(from eating beef contaminated with BSE)

COUNTRY	# OF DEATHS
British Isles	130
France	6
Canada	1
Italy	1
USA	1

---

50 Percentage of the 141 U.S. cattle-related deaths caused by bulls. Cows are more placid but can turn aggressive when calving

14 Number of human deaths from 1924 to 2004 during the annual running of bulls in Pamplona, Spain

24,000 Number of bulls killed for sport every year in Spain during bullfighting season (March to October)

240 million Estimated number of cattle slaughtered for meat each year worldwide

Cats (Big)

80 Average number of people killed every year by tigers who stalk the mangroves of southern India. In the 1930s, the tigers killed 1,000–1,300 people annually

2 Number of faces that prevent tiger attacks. Since tigers hunt by sneaking up behind prey, the Indian government issued masks to villagers in 1986. By wearing a mask on the backs of their heads, villagers confused the tigers enough to dramatically decrease attacks. The masks have become less effective as tigers have figured out the illusion

436 Number killed by a notorious tigress in Champawat, India, early in the twentieth century. Her bad teeth, damaged by a bullet, limited her to hunting slower animals such as humans. Her average of one person every three days was ended in 1937 by Colonel Jim Corbett, a specialist in hunting human-eaters

1,300 Estimated number of men, women, and children killed by 12 man-eating cats that were shot by Corbett over 35 years, including a leopard that had reportedly killed 400 people in Panar. Corbett later became a conservationist and wildlife photographer

18 Number killed by leopards in India's Maharashtra State in 2002

2,000 Estimated number of people killed and eaten by a pride of lions in the Njombe District of Tanganyika (now Tanzania) between 1932 and 1947, when the last 15 members of the pride were hunted down and killed. Apparently the family matriarch had been unable to hunt normal prey and passed on the taste for human flesh to her offspring and descendants

500 Minimum estimated number killed by lions from 1989 to 2004 in Tanzania

80 Percentage decline in African lion population in the past decade, from 50,000 to 10,000

17 Number of confirmed deaths from mountain lion attacks in the U.S. and Canada from 1890 to 1990

Cats (House)

70 million Estimated number of pet cats in the U.S. An additional 10 million are feral

0 Number of U.S. fatalities from cat scratch fever in 2001, 2002, and 2003

1 Number of U.S. fatalities from cat scratch fever in 2004

14 Average number of annual U.S. fatalities from toxoplasmosis, contracted from contact with cat feces, from 2001 through 2004 (for more information see "Parasites" in the "Bugs" chapter)

71 Percentage of cats placed in animal shelters that will typically be put to death

Mystery writer Edgar Allan Poe is said to have died after an election-day drinking binge on his way to meet his fiancée. Although Poe had a history of alcohol abuse, he showed no signs of intoxication when he was admitted to the hospital. In 1996, however, researchers in the *Maryland Medical Journal* theorized a new possible cause of death. His symptoms, they said, point to rabies. Poe was a known pet collector, with several cats and other animals. Because there was no autopsy, his death—like many of his short stories—may have to remain a mystery.

Deer

150 Estimated annual deaths in car crashes caused by deer on U.S. roadways. The collisions also cause 29,000 human injuries

7,400,000 Estimated number of deer killed by hunters each year

56 Number of people shot and killed by deer hunters in North America in 2001 (including other hunters, innocent bystanders, and self-inflicted accidents)

Two were killed with a bow and arrow, and one by a muzzle-loader

1,300,000 Estimated number of deer that die in the 1.5 million collisions between deer and motor vehicles that occur each year in the U.S. Despite the carnage, the deer population continues to increase, totaling about 33 million today

Dogs

60 million Estimated number of domestic dogs living in U.S. households

25 Average annual number of U.S. deaths from nonrabid dog bites between 1999 and 2001

75 Percentage of U.S. dog attacks nationwide that occur on their owners'

property, 58% of these dogs were unrestrained

31 Percentage of U.S. dog attack fatalities attributed to pit bulls in the 1980s and 1990s. Rottweilers contributed 18%, and German shepherds were third with 11%

0 Number of laws broken in Indiana if your dog attacks somebody—whether friend, foe, or postal

carrier—while he or she is on your property

2 Average number of annual rabies fatalities in the U.S. between 2001 and 2004. Wild animals accounted for 93% of all rabies cases, and cats were twice as likely to carry it as dogs

50,000–60,000
Estimated number of rabies deaths worldwide. India and Bangladesh account for more than half

Elephants

1 Rank of elephants among all captive animals in killing their keepers in zoos and circuses

17 Number killed by captive elephants in the U.S. between 1983 and 2000

1 Number of elephants lynched in the Deep South. Big Mary, a circus elephant weighing five tons, killed her trainer in Kingsport, Tennessee in 1916. Because of her

size, the lynch mob commandeered a derrick car from a railroad to hang her

67 Percentage decrease in wild elephants in Sri Lanka during the twentieth century. As in most elephant habitats worldwide, human encroachment and hunting is taking a huge toll

60 Number of Sri Lankans killed by wild elephants in a typical year

110 Number of Sri Lankan elephants killed by people in a typical year

300 Number of people killed by elephants in India in a typical year

5–10 million Population of African elephants in 1930

600,000 Population of African elephants in 1989, the year they were added to the endangered-species list

US $8,500 Fee for a guaranteed elephant kill charged by hunting guides in Zimbabwe

US $12 billion Earnings by Zimbabwe in 2004 for allowing hunters to shoot their game

Gorillas

98 Percentage of genes shared by humans and gorillas

2 Number of animals that are known to prey on gorillas: leopards and humans

600 Population of mountain gorillas in the rain forest of east central Africa

5,000 Number of lowland gorillas remaining in their habitat, a drop of more

---

Alexander I of Greece was crowned king in 1917 after French and British troops deposed his father, Constantine I. Alexander's reign didn't last long. Three years into it, he was bitten by his pet monkey. The bite became infected and he died of blood poisoning. After that, the throne went back to Alexander's father.

than 60% in the last decade. Blame the fashion of killing them for "bushmeat" and the Ebola virus

750 Number of gorillas wiped out in one sanctuary by the Ebola virus in the Congo Republic, nearly a third of the sanctuary's total population

Hippopotamuses

1 Rank of the hippo among the most dangerous animals in Africa, more than the crocodile, elephant, and lion. The herbivore is aggressive, foul-tempered, and unafraid of people

200 Estimated number of people killed by hippos each year, on land and in the water

75 Percentage of "great white hunter" Spencer Tyron's body that was left after a run-in with a hippo on Lake Rukwa, Tanzania. A bull hippo overturned his

100 Number of humans killed by Ebola in the Congo Republic between January and March 2003. Medical researchers blamed the deaths on the consumption of infected gorilla meat

dugout canoe and bit off Tyron's head and shoulders

10,000 Estimated number of hippos killed by armed factions in the Congo's civil war since 1994

20 Width in inches of the swath of grass a hippo can "mow" with its wide, muscular lips. A hippo hikes 2 to 6 miles each night to grasslands, where it can eat 88 pounds of grass and return to the river before sunrise

Horses

1.7 Percentage of U.S. households that own horses. This compares to 4.6% with birds, 31.6% with cats, and 36.1% with dogs

116 Number of Americans who died in 2001 while riding horses or in horse-driven vehicles. Of these, 79 fell or were thrown off a horse; 13 collided with a motor vehicle; 5 collided with another horse or a pedestrian; and two collided with a stationary object

104 Number of fatal work injuries in the U.S. between 1992 and 1997 associated with equine animals (which includes horses, ponies, mules, burros, and donkeys)

50,000 Estimated number of the 30 million horse owners who typically end up in an emergency room each year for some kind of horse-related accident

Nobel Prize–winning author William Faulkner loved his horses more than writing, he claimed. In June 1962, his horse startled and threw him to the ground. From that point, Faulkner suffered excruciating back pain that inspired him to drink heavily. When he died from a fatal heart attack a few weeks later, his doctors blamed the injury, pain, and drinking. Other famous people who died from horse injuries include Genghis Khan, Pope Urban VI, William the Conqueror, Alexander III of Scotland, and Cambyses II of Persia.

Kangaroos

60 Percentage of vehicle/animal collisions in Australia that involve a kangaroo. Some motorists attach "roo bars" to their vehicles in the hope of minimizing vehicle damage

2.2 Percentage of kangaroo-related accidents in which a human died, in a study with 46 patients at Royal Perth Hospital

67 Percentage of a typical kangaroo's weight situated in the lower half of its body. They tend to bounce off bumpers when struck instead of flying through windshields—a major reason why hitting one is not as deadly as hitting a comparably sized deer

1 Total documented number of humans killed by kangaroo attacks in the last 100 years. A hunter died in 1936 when he tried to rescue his dogs during a battle. Kangaroos are strong kickers, and their sharp hind toenails can disembowel an opponent. Luckily, despite a rise in kangaroo attacks as humans encroach on their habitat, they tend to run away from confrontation

Monkeys and Chimpanzees

2 Number of monkey virus strains that merged to create HIV. Chimpanzees surround groups of monkeys and rip them to shreds to eat on the spot. Two separate strains of simian immunodeficiency virus (SIV)

combined when chimps ate red-capped mangabeys and spot-nosed guenons at the same sitting. The virus probably spread to humans as hunters ate infected chimps, sometime before 1930 when the disease was first described

31,200,000 Estimated number of worldwide AIDS/HIV deaths since the virus's inception through the end of 2005 (more about AIDS/HIV in the "Bugs" chapter)

Rats

20 million

Estimated deaths due to the fourteenth-century bubonic plague, transmitted by rats to humans via fleas

70 Number of known rat-borne diseases, including bubonic plague, typhus, and leptospirosis. Researchers believe there may be many more

362 Number of deaths in Thailand in 2000 from leptospirosis, a bacterial illness spread by rat-urine-contaminated water or food. No deaths were reported in the U.S.

23 Number of deaths in Thailand in 2000 from typhus, a bacterial disease transmitted by lice and fleas from rats to humans

1 Number of deaths from typhus in the U.S. in 2000

7 Number of worldwide deaths from rat bite fever between 1996 and 2001. Two U.S. fatalities—one each in Florida and Washington State—were reported in 2003

30 to 70 Number of offspring a typical rat can

produce in a year during an average 3-year lifespan

35 million Estimated number of rats sold in markets in Asia's Mekong River markets annually. Rats are considered a delicacy, cooked over a charcoal fire

3.4–23.6 million Estimated range of annual rat killings in research labs. How lowly rats are regarded is indicated by both the high number and that nobody bothers keeping an accurate count

Rhinoceroses

2 Number of wildlife-park personnel killed by rhinos in Africa in the last 10 years. Rhinos can be aggressive but rarely kill people, partly because most are closed up in heavily guarded parks. The rhino's scary-looking horn is made of compacted fur, so it most often kills with its teeth or feet

$40,000 Price paid per kilo for a rhino horn according to the International Rhino Foundation. The horns are used in traditional Asian medicine as a spurious antifever medication and for ceremonial dagger

handles in Yemen and Oman. Poachers leaving the animal dead after removing its horn have driven the rhino to near extinction

5 Number of currently existing rhino species, of the dozens that once roamed the earth. All five species

WORLD RHINO POPULATIONS

SPECIES	# IN EXISTENCE, 2005
Javan	60
Sumatran	300
Indian	2,400
Black	3,610
White	11,100

are considered endangered, two critically so

90 Percentage decline in number of rhinos since 1970

178 Number of rhino poachers killed in Zimbabwe by 1996, after the government instituted a shoot-to-kill policy in 1984

Swine

1,900 Number of American workers hurt by swine between 1992 and 1997, out of 75,000 animal-occupational-related injuries

0 Number of U.S. animal workers killed by swine during that same period

47 Pounds of pork consumed by the average American in 2001

12 Average number of annual cases in the U.S. between 1997 and 2001 of trichinosis (caused by eating undercooked pork containing the *Trichinella* worm—not to be confused with trichuriasis, caused by a whipworm), according to the CDC. None resulted in death

38 Number of fatalities from a pig-borne strain of *Streptococcus suis* in China's Sichuan Province as of August 2005. Humans acquired it from contact with pigs or from eating contaminated pork that had not been properly cooked

100 Number of Malaysian deaths in 1998–99 after

265 people got sick from febrile encephalitis. Pigs are efficient transmitters of disease to humans, responsible for incubating the leap from chicken flus to human flus. Other sometimes-fatal pig-borne illnesses include E. coli, erysipelas, brucellosis, and leptospirosis

2 million Estimated number of feral pigs in Texas, the descendants of escapees from farms over the last 4 centuries. Besides wreaking an estimated $52 million per year havoc on crops and carrying diseases, including brucellosis, pseudorabies, and tuberculosis, they are aggressive and can cause fatal car accidents. Because of their low-riding weight distribution, their bulky bodies tend to end up under cars when hit, seriously undermining drivers' steering control

$7 Bounty offered by Van Zandt County, Texas, for a matching pair of feral hog ears in 2004. Residents traded in 2,000 sets before the county's $14,000 budget ran out, having little effect on the problem

Wolves

6 Number of documented cases in which wolves are believed to have killed humans in North America before 1900

0 Cases of humans killed since 1900 by wolves that were both wild and healthy. Of the few wolf attacks in both Europe and North America, all were attributed to either rabid wolves or wolf-dog hybrids

2,500 Estimated number of wolves in the 48 contiguous states. They are protected to regulate the populations of deer, elk, and other animals

Birds

Death Most Fowl

8 Number of Asian countries reporting cases of avian flu in bird populations as of early 2004

20 million Estimated number of fatalities from the 1918 Spanish flu, passed from birds to humans (for more information on the flu, see the "Bad Breath" chapter)

100 million Estimated number of chickens, turkeys, ducks, and geese that either died of avian flu or were exterminated to prevent its spread from late 2003 to early 2004

4 Number of countries as of June 2005 with officially confirmed human deaths from avian influenza A (H5N1), the most deadly type of bird flu. The countries are Cambodia, Indonesia, Thailand, and Vietnam

6 Number of worldwide confirmed human deaths from the virus in 1997, when it first appeared, out of 18 people infected

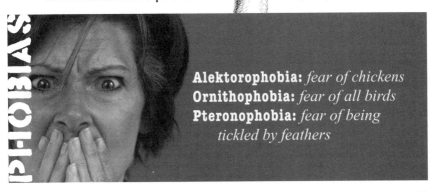

PHOBIAS

Alektorophobia: *fear of chickens*
Ornithophobia: *fear of all birds*
Pteronophobia: *fear of being tickled by feathers*

1 Number of worldwide human deaths from H5N1 in 2003

6,000 Estimated number of migrating geese that died from avian flu in China's Qinghai Province in 2005. This is the largest number of wild birds killed by the disease to date

Chickens

54 Pounds of meat from chickens that the average American consumes in a year

253 Number of eggs eaten in the U.S. per capita in 2001

25 Percentage of poultry in the U.S. that carries *Salmonella enteritidis.* The bacteria causes one of the most common and widely distributed food-borne diseases and is most often contracted by consuming feces-contaminated poultry, eggs, meat, or milk

1.4 million Estimated number of salmonella cases annually in the U.S. according to the World Health Organization (WHO) in 2005

580 Number of annual deaths attributed to salmonella in the U.S. (see the "Bugs" chapter for more information)

45 Salmonella's percentage of the lab-confirmed 84 food-borne illnesses in the U.S., 2004

224,000 Estimated number of victims of a 1994 salmonellosis outbreak after a tanker truck for Schwan's ice cream hauled salmonella-infected liquid eggs and didn't clean the truck adequately afterward. The company distributed contaminated ice cream to all 48 contiguous U.S. states

Reptiles

Alligators

3,000 Pounds of force exerted per square inch of an alligator's bite

1 million Estimated number of alligators in Florida

327 Number of documented alligator attacks in Florida since 1948, the year the state began keeping track

15 Number of human deaths in Florida from alligator attacks

Crocodiles

52 Average number of humans killed by crocodiles each year in Zambia

12 Number of deaths caused by saltwater crocodiles in northern Australia between 1975 and 1988. The saltwater crocodile is the largest of all living reptiles, capable of taking animals up to the size of an adult-male water buffalo in the water or on land

200 Estimated annual number of deaths caused by crocodiles, hippos, and lions in Kruger National Park, South Africa. Deaths from the jaws of crocodiles are extremely hard to verify, since the reptiles often feed once a person is dead from other means

10.6 Land speed in miles per hour of the fastest crocodile on record. The average speed of a crocodile is about 7 mph. They can't travel for long at this speed, so odds are that you can outrun them

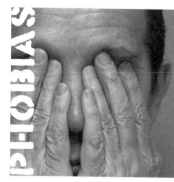

PHOBIAS

Batrachophobia: *fear of amphibians*
Bufonophobia: *fear of toads*
Herpetophobia: *fear of reptiles*
Ophidiophobia: *fear of snakes*
Ranidaphobia: *fear of frogs*

Gila Monsters

2 Number of venomous lizards in the world. The Gila monster, a native of the U.S. Southwest deserts, is one. The Mexican beaded lizard is the other

8 Number of deaths attributed to captive Gila monsters from 1878 to 1954

0 Number of deaths attributed to wild Gila monsters from 1878 to 1954

Komodo Dragons

12 Number of deaths from the bite of the Komodo dragon in the last century. Komodo dragons are not venomous, but they do have some of the world's most dangerous bacteria in their mouths. Without medical attention, victims can get infected and die

6,000 Estimated number of Komodo dragons in Indonesia, the only place where they live in the wild

Snakes

600 Minimum number of venomous snake species in the world. This is out of approximately 3,000 snake species overall. Most venomous snakes are found in warm, tropical locations

90 Number of venomous snake species in Australia, the only continent where venomous snakes outnumber nonvenomous ones

7 Number of venomous snake species in Western Europe

50,000–125,000 Estimated range of annual snakebite deaths worldwide, from the 500,000 to 2.5 million people who are bitten

Types of Poisonous Snakes

There are three different types of poisonous snakes in the world:

PROTEROGLYPH snakes possess fixed fangs and inject their victims with neurotoxic venom, which attacks the nervous system. Death results because the victim can no longer breathe.

SOLENOGLYPH snakes fold their fangs into their mouths. They deliver hemotoxic venom through their bite, which attacks the circulatory system, destroying blood cells, damaging arteries and veins. Death results from internal bleeding.

OPISTHOGLYPH snakes have fangs in the rear of their mouth. They are primarily nonvenomous with two major exceptions: the boomslang and the twig snake, which are both lethal to humans.

Most Dangerous Snakes in the World

The most dangerous snake in the world is whatever venomous snake is in front of you at the time. By region, the deadliest snakes are:

NORTH AMERICA—Western and Eastern diamondback rattle-snakes. Their venom is highly toxic, they sport large venom glands, they are prevalent throughout much of the U.S., and they aren't as shy as some of the other venomous North American snakes.

AFRICA—saw-scaled viper, Egyptian cobra, puff adder, and black mamba.

ASIA—common cobra, Russell's viper, and krait.

8,000 Estimated annual bites by venomous snakes in the U.S. From all snakes, people get about 45,000 bites per year

40 Percentage of U.S. snakebite victims with high blood-alcohol levels

12 Largest number of snakebite deaths per year in the U.S. from 1960 to 1990

95 Percentage of U.S. snakebite

fatalities caused by dia-mondback rattlesnakes

1/25th Portion of a second that it takes a rattlesnake to strike

3,000 Estimated annual number of snakebites in Australia

2 Typical annual number of fatalities from venomous snakes in Australia. Most Australians live in cities, and most venomous snakes live in unpopulated regions

Rattlesnake XING

Most Toxic Snakes in the World

1. **Inland taipan** (Australia)
2. **Australian brown snake** (Australia)
3. **Malayan krait** (Southeast Asia)
4. **Taipan** (Australia)
5. **Tiger snake** (Australia)
6. **Beaked sea snake** (South Pacific & Indian Ocean)
7. **Saw-scaled "carpet" viper** (Africa & Middle East)
8. **Coral snake** (North America)
9. **Boomslang** (Africa)
10. **Death adder** (Australia & New Guinea)
11. **Black mamba** (Africa)
12. **Bushmaster** (Central & South America)
13. **King cobra** (South Asia)
14. **Fer-de-lance** (Central & South America)
15. **Sharp-nosed pit** (China & Southeast Asia)

Cleopatra, the charming queen of Egypt, was said to have been killed by an asp hidden in a basket of figs. Although what looked like two bite marks were found on her arm, a snake was never discovered in the sealed mausoleum where she died.

Poison Arrow Frogs

170 Estimated number of species of poison arrow frogs in Central and South America

1 Minimum number of drops from the deadliest known poison arrow frog (*Phyllobates terribilis*) that can stop your heart from beating. The toxins come from consumed ants; a frog transforms their toxic chemicals into a poison excreted from its skin. Without a supply of ants, frogs lose their toxicity

0 Number of human deaths caused each year by

poison arrow frogs. Although the poison has been used in warfare, the American tribes that use it now do so for hunting only

The poison from the most toxic frogs in South and Central America can't seep into the skin of a human just by touch; an abrasion must be present. Tribes that still use frog poison on their darts or spears avoid any risk of contamination by skewering a frog to the ground and wiping the tips of their darts on its back. For less toxic frogs, they may slowly roast the creature and catch the concentrated toxic "drippings" to use on their weapons.

Insects and Bugs

Ants

89 Number of known bull ant species, 88 of which can be found in Australia. Bull ants are particularly fearsome, possessing long, powerful jaws, a venomous bite, and an aggressive attitude. They defend their nests by streaming over any passerby, biting from one end while delivering painful stings from the other

4 Number of human deaths in Tasmania between 1980 and 1999 from jack jumper bull ant bites. Generally, the bites are not deadly unless the victim is allergic enough to go into anaphylactic shock

25 Percentage of the 324 emergency injections of adrenaline for anaphylactic shock by the Royal Hobart Hospital in Australia from 1990 to 1998 that were triggered by bull ant stings. This compares to 13% for honeybee stings

12 Number of Americans who die each year after being stung by fire ants, a virulent species from Brazil that landed in Mobile, Alabama, from a ship's hold in 1930 and has since colonized the Southern states. As of 2000, at least 80 people have died outdoors from stings, and 3 have died indoors

50 Minimum percentage of residents in fire ant territory that will be stung at least once this year. About 1% of the population is hypersensitive enough to the stings to be in jeopardy of death

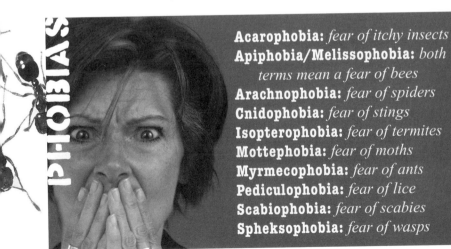

PHOBIAS

Acarophobia: *fear of itchy insects*
Apiphobia/Melissophobia: *both terms mean a fear of bees*
Arachnophobia: *fear of spiders*
Cnidophobia: *fear of stings*
Isopterophobia: *fear of termites*
Mottephobia: *fear of moths*
Myrmecophobia: *fear of ants*
Pediculophobia: *fear of lice*
Scabiophobia: *fear of scabies*
Spheksophobia: *fear of wasps*

Assassin Bugs

8–15 Continuous time in minutes that an assassin bug will feed on a sleeping victim

16,000 Average annual number of deaths between 2000 and 2002 by assassin bugs in Central and South America. These creatures, which strike at night and feed on blood, are known as kissing bugs because they often latch onto a victim's lips, eyelids, or ears. They inject their saliva into the skin, which acts as an anesthetic but also can kill people who are allergic. The worst potential for damage is that the South American version defecates into the wound after feeding, often transmitting a microbial parasite that causes Chagas' disease (see "Parasites" section of the "Bugs" chapter for more information)

1 Number of U.S. deaths in 2002 from the kissing bug

Bees, Hornets, and Wasps

46 Average annual number of U.S. fatalities between 1999 and 2001 from hornets, wasps, and bees. Besides anaphylactic shock, the collective poison from 30 wasp stings or 200–300 honeybee stings can be

---

Victor Leslie, a former European president of the Sega game company, was enjoying a bowl of ice cream at a picnic in 2002. Unbeknownst to him, so was a wasp. When he scooped the wasp into his mouth, it stung him on the tongue. He collapsed and died within minutes. He had never been stung before and had no idea he had an allergy that would so quickly kill him.

enough to kill a person
if untreated

1 Approximate percentage
of humans who are allergic
to insect stings

7 Number of U.S. deaths
from 1985 to 2004 from
Africanized bees

175 Number of Mexican
deaths from Africanized
bees during the same period

The Sting's the Thing

Many people can't tell a honeybee from a hornet or yellow jacket. So the gentle honeybee—which gives honey, pollinates most of our fruits and vegetables, and almost never stings if away from its hive—gets slandered regularly, making life less sweet for beekeepers everywhere. Here's a quick look at common stinging insects.

Honeybees are the only stinging insects in America that have to make a life-or-death commitment to stinging, because their stingers rip off their bodies, killing them. Unlike wasps and bees, they live in huge, permanent colonies (60,000–100,000 members) in hollow trees, wall openings, or in man-made bee boxes.

Wasps include hornets and yellow jackets. They're often brightly striped and live in small colonies, either underground or hanging like a small piñata from a branch or overhang.

Wasps are meat-eating predators that hunt down other insects (and, on picnics, bits of your hot dog).

Bumblebees are big, fuzzy, and gentle, the sheepdogs of the bee world, living up to their original name, humblebee. They "buzz" the flowers as they collect pollen and nectar, which is especially useful for self-pollinating plants such as tomatoes.

Fleas

90 Percentage death rate of those exposed to plague during major epidemics in the sixth, fourteenth, and seventeenth centuries. The plague was passed to people by fleas; the fleas got it from infected rats

137 million Estimated number of people who died during the aforementioned epidemics. Cities were decimated; once-thriving villages became ghost towns, inhabited only by the rotting corpses of their former residents

1 Percentage death rate for endemic typhus, a disease you can contract by scratching a flea bite. The flea doesn't directly transmit the disease; instead, it defecates next to the bite, then your fingernails drag the infected flea poop into the bite. People usually recover uneventfully from its fever and chills, but deaths do happen among the elderly, the medically vulnerable, or the hapless people who are allergic to sulfa drugs and are mistakenly treated with them

Lice

40 Percentage death rate for lice-borne epidemic typhus. Though endemic typhus (see above) is relatively harmless, epidemic typhus is pretty deadly even though it is spread in a similar way, particularly in refugee camps and other lice-filled places where people are tightly compacted without adequate bathing facilities

1 Number of U.S. deaths from louse-borne typhus in 2004. None were recorded in 2001, 2002, or 2003

105 Typical temperature in degrees Fahrenheit for a high, 6-day fever that comes with trench fever, another lice-caused disease. The name comes from the World Wars, when it was passed among frontline troops in the trenches. It's also known as shinbone disease, because that's where its muscle and bone pain often centers. The symptoms can cycle through multiple recoveries and recurrences. Still, trench fever is almost never fatal

0 Number of serious or potentially fatal diseases you can contract from that scourge of the grammar school classroom, head lice

Ticks

3 Number of potentially fatal human diseases carried by American ticks: Lyme disease, Rocky Mountain spotted fever, and three flavors of ehrlichiosis

3 Number of American tick species most likely to spread these diseases: deer tick, American dog tick, and lone star tick

4 Percentage death rate among those 600–800 people who catch Rocky Mountain spotted fever each year. Before antibiotics, the mortality rate was closer to 30%

2–10 Percentage mortality rate for human granulocytic ehrlichiosis and human monocytic ehrlichiosis. Isolated cases of the most recently discovered variation, *Erlichia ewingii,* have only recently been discovered in Missouri, Oklahoma, and Tennessee, so little is known about its mortality rate

0–1 Percentage mortality rate for Lyme disease. In a small number of cases, victims experience chronic arthritic and neurological symptoms

23,763 Number of Lyme disease cases reported to the CDC in 2002. Only 19,804 Lyme disease cases were reported in 2004

6 Number of U.S. deaths from Lyme disease in 2004, the same number reported in 2002. There were 2 cases in 2001 and 4 in 2003 (see "Bacteria" section of the "Bugs" chapter for more information)

12 Number of U.S. deaths from tick-borne spotted fever in 2003. There were 6 deaths reported in 2001 and 2004, and 10 in 2002

20 Number of deaths attributed to the toxic bite of the Australian paralysis tick

Lyme disease got its name from the town of Lyme, Connecticut, where the disease was discovered after 51 residents came down with a mysterious arthritis and rash between 1975 and 1977.

Mosquitoes

28 Number of serious diseases that are transmitted to humans by mosquitoes, including encephalitis, dengue, yellow fever, West Nile disease, and malaria

1,222,180 Number of deaths reported by the World Health Organization from malaria in 2002

700 million Number of people infected with a mosquito-borne disease annually

4 Percentage mortality rate in the U.S. for West Nile disease in 2004. Of the 2,539 cases reported, 100 people died

<1 Percentage of people who will die after being bitten by a West Nile–infected mosquito; 20% will experience mild-to-severe flulike symptoms, 80% will experience no symptoms whatsoever

18,565 Number of deaths reported by the World Health Organization from dengue fever in 2002. About half the world's population lives in dengue risk areas, and 50 million people contract the mosquito-borne disease each year. About 1 in 10 are hospitalized, which decreases dengue's mortality rate to 1–2%—if untreated, death may claim 40–50% of dengue's victims

Centipedes and Millipedes

8 Number of reported deaths from those multi-legged critters in South America in 2000: 3 each in Brazil and Venezuela, 1 each in Argentina and Peru.

Neither carries diseases that can be transmitted to humans, but centipedes have venom glands that can make their bite dangerous for an allergic victim

Scorpions

1,500 Minimum number of known scorpion species

25 Number of scorpion species dangerous to humans

2 Number of scorpion species native to North America whose toxin can kill a human

1 Number of deaths recorded by the CDC in the U.S. from scorpion bites in the

year 2000. Some other estimates put the annual number of deaths as high as 122

Spiders

170,000 Minimum number of known spider species

2 Number of spider species in the U.S. with poison toxic enough to kill a person: the brown recluse and the female black widow

0 Number of verified U.S. deaths from brown recluse spiders. In fact, medical literature records a total of only 10 possible bites. While their poison is lethal, their fangs

are not large and strong enough to pierce skin

2,786 Number of people bitten by black widow spiders in the U.S. in 2000

2,944 By brown recluse spiders

273 By tarantulas

12,643 By all other spiders

5 Number of U.S. deaths from all spider bites in 2000

The Most Dangerous Spiders in the World

ATRAX FORMIDABILIS Northern funnel-web, aka tree-dwelling funnel-web. This spider comes from Australia, and although its venom is toxic, it lives in remote wooded areas and rarely comes in contact with humans.

PHONEUTRIA Banana spider, aka Brazilian wandering spider. From Central and South America, usually found nesting in leaves. It would rather run than bite when confronted with a human, but it will defend itself. Not usually lethal, the banana spider's venom still causes a great deal of pain.

SICARIUS Six-eyed crab. Native to Africa and South America. It's poisonous but rarely comes in contact with humans. Its habitat is in remote areas where it nests in the sand.

PHONEUTRIA NIGRIVENTER Brazilian "armed" spider. Found in Brazil, it has the most active neurotoxin in its venom of all spiders in the world. Although some deaths have been reported, it injects venom into only about a third of all its bites. Contact with this spider is more often nothing more than a scare.

LOXOSCELES Brown recluse, aka fiddleback. This little spider, found worldwide, hunts down its prey instead of lying in wait in its web. This may be why the recluse has sometimes been found in between sheets, in shoes, and in clothes. This sort of proximity to humans means painful and serious sores from bites, not usually lethal.

The Most Dangerous Spiders in the World

LATRODECTUS Widow spider, aka black widow, red-back widow, katipo, karakurt, shoe-button, brown widow. This group of spiders, which include the much feared black widow in the U.S., can be found from North America and Africa to Europe and Australia. The mature female is the spider to watch out for as her venom is dangerous. With the advent of antivenom, deaths have become rare. From 1726 to 1943 there were 1,291 recorded black widow bites in the U.S. and just 55 deaths.

ATRAX ROBUSTUS Sydney funnel-web. From 1927 to 1980, 13 deaths were officially attributed to this Australian spider. There's an average of 30 to 40 bites annually; about 10% have enough toxin to require antivenom. Prior to antivenom, an adult was often dead within 24 hours, a small child in just hours. The Sydney funnel-web venom is so powerful that researchers are now using it to create potent, effective, and safe pesticides.

LOXOSCELES LAETA Chilean recluse. More toxic than its North American recluse cousin, it has been implicated in several deaths each year in South American countries.

Marine Animals

Cones and Snails

10 Number of deaths worldwide between 1889 and 1967 from marine cones, sea snails that live on coral reefs. These mollusks can pierce the skin and inject poison through barbs that act like harpoons. The geographer cone is most likely to cause a quick death—among divers, it's nicknamed the cigarette cone because the grim joke is that you have about enough time to smoke a cigarette before it paralyzes you permanently. One researcher says, "A sting from *Conus geographus* is equivalent to eating a lethal dose of badly prepared Japanese puffer fish while a cobra is biting you"

15,387 Number of worldwide deaths from schistosomiasis, a tropical disease from parasitic worms that live in the digestive system of freshwater snails. The infected snails poop out multitudes of the worms' tiny larvae, which can penetrate the skin of waders, swimmers, or bathers. The larvae travel through the body, causing deadly mischief in the kidneys, lungs, liver, intestinal tract, bladder, brain, and/or spinal column (for more information see the "Parasites" section of the "Bugs" chapter)

Electric Eels

600+ Minimum number of eel species, most of which are harmless

0 Percentage of "electric eels" that are truly eels. This is part of a family that includes other electric fish such as the ghost fish and knife fish. Its closest relative is the catfish

600 Number of volts in the jolt of an electric eel, about 5 times the shock of a finger stuck in a U.S. wall outlet. It's probably not fatal, absent other medical issues. But it can incapacitate, and if you're in the water, there's a decent chance of drowning

PHOBIAS

Ichthyophobia: *fear of fish*
Ostraconophobia: *fear of shellfish*
Potamophobia: *fear of rivers and moving water*
Selachophobia: *fear of sharks*
Thalassophobia: *fear of the sea*

Fish

1,000 Estimated species of venomous fish in the world. These include certain species of shark, catfish, weever fish, scorpion fish, stonefish, and stingray

200 Number of jellyfish species known to be venomous. The result of a sting can range from mild skin irritation to death

67 Number of people who died between 1984 and 1996 as a result of being stung by a box jellyfish (*Chironex fleckeri*), also known as the sea wasp, found in Australian and Asian waters. Covering the skin with a thin, tough outer layer, such as women's panty hose, prevents most if not all stings

13 Number of dorsal fins on a reef stonefish, the most venomous fish in the world—yet the few deaths attributed to stonefish have not conclusively been proven

10,000 times Toxicity of the blue-ringed octopus's venom when compared to cyanide. Its tetrodotoxin is also found in the deadly puffer fish

2 Number of Australian deaths ever associated with the profoundly poisonous blue-ringed octopus

Poisonous Fish

500 Minimum number of fish species that can kill if eaten. They're particularly well-represented in the Pacific Ocean

50 Average number of annual Japanese fatalities from puffer fish poisoning. Puffers (also known as fugu, blowfish, toadfish, globefish, and balloonfish) contain tetrodotoxin, the most potent neurotoxin known, in the skin and many of the internal organs. If not prepared correctly, puffers can cause death within hours of consumption

26 Number of people who died in Guatemala in 1987 after eating clam soup in which the shellfish were toxic

1 million Number of times a fish such as the

shark or swordfish can accumulate methylmercury above the levels found in the waters in which they live

27 Amount in tons of mercury compounds that were dumped into the Minamata Bay by the Chisso Corporation from 1932 to 1968

1,000 Estimated number of deaths in the 1950s attributed to consuming fish from Minamata Bay

Sharp-Toothed Fish

20 Average number of fish in a school of hunting piranha

12 Number of people who died from U.S. shark attacks from 1970 through 2000

11 Number of worldwide fatalities due to unprovoked shark attacks in 2000, a record year for shark attack fatalities

7 Number of recorded fatal shark attacks around the world in 2004. There were only 4 in 2002 and 3 in 2003. Some estimates are higher, with an average annual death toll of 25 to 30 worldwide

50 Estimated number of unprovoked shark attacks in U.S. waters in 2000

30 The same number for 2004. Increased beach safety awareness may be responsible

80 Percentage of all shark species that are threatened with extinction

99 Percentage decline in the white-tipped shark

WORLDWIDE CONFIRMED UNPROVOKED SHARK ATTACKS, 1580–2003

TERRITORY	# OF ATTACKS	# OF DEATHS	LAST FATALITY
Australia	282	132	2003
Africa	255	67	2003
Asia	114	53	2000
Pacific/Oceania Islands (not including Hawaii)	115	48	2003
U.S. (excluding Hawaii)	737	38	2003
Central America	57	31	1997
South America	89	21	2002
Antilles & Bahamas	57	19	1972
Europe	39	18	1984
Hawaii	96	14	1992
New Zealand	44	9	1968
Bermuda	4	0	
Other	20	6	2003
Total	**1,909**	**456**	

population over the
last 50 years due, in large
part, to overfishing to
feed humans' hunger for
shark fin soup

30–100 million
Estimated number of
sharks killed by people each
year, according to the
National Marine Fisheries

U.S. COASTAL SHARK ATTACKS AND FATALITIES ON RECORD 1670–2003

STATE	# OF ATTACKS	# OF DEATHS	LAST FATALITY
Florida	489	12	2001
Hawaii	96	14	1992
California	80	6	2003
South Carolina	46	3	1883
North Carolina	25	4	2001
Texas	24	3	1962
Oregon	16	1	1974
New Jersey	15	5	1926
Georgia	9	0	
Delaware	5	1	1698
New York	5	0	
Virginia	4	1	2001
Alabama	4	0	
Massachusetts	3	2	1936
Louisiana	2	0	
Connecticut	1	0	
Mississippi	1	0	
Washington	1	0	
Other	7	0	
Total	**833**	**52**	

Sea Snakes

169 Number of species of sea snakes in the world, the vast majority of marine reptilian species

32 Number of those species found in the waters around Australia

<10 Percentage of sea snakes that inject venom into a human during a bite. Most avoid human company and don't inject venom when they bite defensively

150 Estimated number of annual deaths worldwide from sea-snake bites, about 3% of all sea-snake bites

Flora

99 Number of poisonous plants listed in Cornell University's Poisonous Plants Database. Toxic to both humans and most animals, these include all the famous names: death angel mushrooms, poison hemlock, oleander, tobacco, poison oak, poison ivy, and wisteria

Mushrooms

6 Number of death cap mushroom species found in North America. The death cap is responsible for 95% of all North American mushroom-related deaths

14 Number of deaths from poisonous mushrooms in North America between 1985 and 1996

85,000 Number of officially reported "exposures" to poisonous mushrooms in North America during the same period

Algae

1/160,000 Strength of the active ingredients in cocaine compared with that of the toxin responsible for paralytic shellfish poisoning (PSP), occurring when shellfish consume certain plankton algae before being eaten by humans

9 Number of suspected hospitalizations in 2001 from an outbreak of PSP in Washington State

Fungi

100,000 Minimum number of different mold fungi in the world. Fungal infections are usually minor, but can lead to death in those with compromised immune systems. However, toxic mold in damp buildings has caused serious illness and death when inhaled by otherwise healthy individuals. Fungus-related illnesses can come from a variety of sources, from feces to decaying organic matter in soil

27 Number of infants who became seriously sick due to mold following floods in the Cleveland area in 1993

9 Number of infants who died from those molds

Claudius, fourth emperor of Rome, had a difficult life. With a limp, speech impediment, and reputation for dim-wittedness, he was constantly staving off assassination attempts by those he trusted. His fourth wife (and niece), Agrippina, finally succeeded where others had failed. She slowly took power from the infirm emperor and had him adopt her son, the infamous fiddled-while-Rome-burned Nero. Then, she fed Claudius poisonous mushrooms. After Claudius' long and excruciating death, Nero was crowned emperor.

PHOBIAS!

Anthophobia: *fear of flowers*
Botanophobia: *fear of plants*
Dendrophobia: *fear of trees*
Hylophobia: *fear of forests*
Lachanophobia: *fear of vegetables*
Mycophobia: *fear of mushrooms*

8 Poison Plants May Be Lurking in Your Garden

AUTUMN CROCUS: Bulbs can trigger severe nervousness, vomiting

BLEEDING HEART: Leaves and roots can kill

FOXGLOVE: Leaves can trigger erratic pulse, confusion, upset digestive system, death

IRIS: Stems under the soil can upset digestive system

LARKSPUR: Seeds and young growth can trigger depression, upset digestive system, death

LILY OF THE VALLEY: Flowers and leaves can trigger erratic heart beat, upset digestive system, confusion

MONKSHOOD: Roots can upset digestive system, cause severe nervousness

RHUBARB: Leaves can cause convulsions, coma, death

Nature

QUESTION: If you live in Mexico, what's more dangerous—an electrical storm or a sunny day?

ANSWER: Sunny day

376 Mexicans died of melanoma in 2001 versus 223 from lightning.

Which U.S. state has the highest number of deaths from lightning? **A: Florida**

Out of the 66 deaths from lightning in the U.S. in 2002, 10 were in Florida and 6 in Texas.

What's more dangerous, an electrical storm or your bed? **A: Bed**

551 people died in the U.S. in 2002 falling out of bed versus 66 who died from lightning.

What's deadlier, cold or heat? **A: Cold**

Average annual deaths in the U.S. between 1999 and 2001 were 646 from excessive natural cold versus 398 from heat.

Which killed more, the deadliest earthquake in the world or the Spanish flu? **A: Flu**

830,000 died in the worst earthquake in China in 1556 versus 20+ million who died worldwide of the flu in 1918–19.

How much deadlier for Indians was the 2004 tsunami versus the 1971 India-Pakistan war?

A: 5 times

Of the 227,000 who died in 2004 in the Indonesia tsunami, 16,383 deaths were in India versus 3,241 Indians killed in action (KIA) in the war with Pakistan.

What kills more, earth, wind, or fire? **A: Fire**

Average annual U.S. deaths from 1999 to 2001 were 3,344 from smoke, fire, and flames versus 77 from cataclysmic storms and 36 from earthquakes.

What was deadlier, China's 1976 earthquake or Mao Tse-tung?

A: Mao

The Tanshan earthquake killed 655,000 versus 7.7 million who died in China's Cultural Revolution.

SOME of Mother Nature's homicides are sadly predictable. For example, we know that a certain number of mostly vulnerable older people will die from the heat waves and cold snaps that recur year after year. We expect a certain number of deaths from severe storms, hurricanes, and tornadoes. We know that the ground will rumble, water will rise, mud will slide, and lightning will strike.

A BAD MOTHER?

Because so many of these things happen regularly and on a small scale, the deaths become nonlocal news only when they reach some abnormal level of disaster. Part of the problem is that it's hard to say what "normal" levels of natural disasters look like.

Any "typical" year can give atypical results. A major flood, earthquake, tsunami, or volcano eruption can change everything. For example, between 1999 and 2001, the U.S. averaged just 18 annual flood deaths. Then, in 2005, Hurricane Katrina killed more than 1,800 people. A strong earthquake in California or China could likewise skew Mother Nature's hit list. So while our statistics are typical, don't be fooled into thinking they're predictive. When the sky falls, not even little chickens will be safe.

Quick & Dead Summary for the U.S.

1,100 Number of deaths recorded by the Centers for Disease Control in 2001 from exposure to forces of nature

599 Number of those deaths from cold

300 Number from heat   **54** From cataclysmic storms

44 From lightning   **35** From floods

28 From earthquake and other earth movements

40 From other causes

Nature—Born Killer?

39,073 Number of people killed by natural and human-caused disasters worldwide in 2001, a figure about twice as high as the year before. Still, both figures were well below average

62,000 Average number of annual worldwide nature deaths in the 1990s

50 Percentage of disaster fatalities that occur in countries with the lowest levels of industrial development

2/1 Ratio of American men to women as fatal victims of nature

Asteroid Rage

100 Percentage of dinosaurs that were killed worldwide, according to a leading theory, when an asteroid struck Mexico's Yucatán Peninsula at the end of the Cretaceous period 65 million years ago

2,000 Number of square miles of Siberian forest flattened in 1908 by an asteroid. Witnesses 37 miles away were thrown to the ground, but there were no known human fatalities

4 billion Estimated number of meteorites that fall to earth each day, according to NASA. Most are minuscule, but together they'd total several tons

ASTEROID HARMFULNESS

SIZE OF ASTEROID/METEOR	FREQUENCY OF CONTACT WITH EARTH'S ATMOSPHERE	POTENTIAL HARM
Dust to bowling ball	Continually	If not burned up as a "shooting star," slight damage
Automobile	Twice monthly	Atomic-bomb-like explosions in upper atmosphere
Blue whale	Every few centuries	Powerful shock wave 100 miles in all directions
The Titanic	Every few hundred centuries	In ocean, a deadly tsunami; on land, a major earthquake
.5 mile (.8 km)	Every 200– 500,000 years	A continent-wide calamity
1 mile (1.6 km)	Every million years	Worldwide calamity
2 miles (3.2 km)	Every 10 million years	Human extinction

1 Number of people known to have been struck by a meteorite

600 Number of known comets and asteroids that are potential disasters to earth as of October 2002

Elizabeth Hulitt Hodge of Sylacauga, Alabama, was relaxing in her sitting room on November 30, 1954, when an 8-pound space rock crashed through the roof, smashing her radio and giving her a bruising wallop on the hip. She was otherwise uninjured; the rock is now housed at the Smithsonian.

That's Cold!

10,000 Estimated number of worldwide deaths from snowstorms between 1947 and 1980

2 to 1 Ratio of Americans who died from hypothermia (599 exposure-to-cold deaths) versus those who died from hyperthermia (300 exposure-to-heat deaths) in 2001

30,000 Average number of Britons who die each winter from exposure to cold. According to the BBC, this is more than in either Finland or Russia and is due to a lack of preparation for cold weather.

1/2 Ratio of these U.K. cold-weather deaths from strokes and heart attacks brought on by thickened blood from lowered body temperatures

1/3 Ratio of the deaths brought on by respiratory diseases. Flu accounts for only 1 in 10 of the deaths, and hypothermia proper, only about 1 in 60

689 Average annual U.S. hypothermia deaths between 1979 and 2002

66 Percentage of hypothermia-related U.S. deaths that occur to males

52 Percentage of hypothermia victims over 65. Alcoholics, drug users, the homeless, heart patients, and the chronically ill are also at increased risk

1 Rank of Alaska among all states in hypothermia death rates (3.0 people per 100,000). North Dakota and New Mexico are tied for #2 with an 0.9 rate, and Montana is #3 with a 0.8 rate

71 Percentage of U.S. hypothermia deaths in the four coldest months (November through February)

TOP 5 MODERN U.S. RECORD COLD SPOTS

RANK	LOCATION AND DATE	TEMPERATURE (DEGREES F)
1	Prospect Creek, Alaska January 23, 1971	-80
2	Rogers Pass, Montana January 20, 1954	-70
3	Peter's Sink, Utah February 1, 1985	-69
4	Yellowstone Park, Riverside Ranger Station, Wyoming, February 9, 1933	-66
5	Maybell, Colorado February 1, 1985	-61

Some Like It Hot

14,802 Number of people who died in France during a record heat wave in August 2003 in which temperatures soared to 104° F and stayed high for 2 weeks. The heat wave killed more than 20,000 others throughout Europe

1,500–2,000 Estimated number of heat-caused deaths during a typical U.S. summer. The numbers of deaths are higher around the world in places where air-conditioning is scarce

1,260 Number of deaths during one 24-hour period in New York City in July 1966—well above the daily average of 490. Besides causing fatal hyperthermia, stifling heat can trigger heart attacks, strokes, and other afflictions

TOP 5 MODERN U.S. RECORD HOT SPOTS

RANK	LOCATION AND DATE	TEMPERATURE (DEGREES F)
1	Greenland Ranch, California July 10, 1913	134
2	Lake Havasu City, Arizona June 29, 1994	128
3	Laughlin, Nevada June 29, 1994	125
4	Waste Isolation Pilot Plant, New Mexico, June 27, 1994	122
5	Steele, North Dakota July 6, 1936	121

307 Increased number of deaths that occur in a sweltering New York City summer when compared with the average number of deaths in its other seasons

129 Number of excess deaths during an average summer in Philadelphia

0 Number of extra summer deaths among residents of Phoenix, Arizona, and Miami, Florida, in a typical summer. Thanks to heat-friendly building designs and an acclimated population, people in warmer climates are better equipped to survive heat waves

2 times Increased rate of heat-related deaths by 2020, to 3,000–4,000, in the 15 biggest U.S. cities alone, according to a UN study

2.5–10.4 Range of increase in degrees Fahrenheit of the earth's average temperature by the end of the century, projected by the Intergovernmental Panel on Climate Change

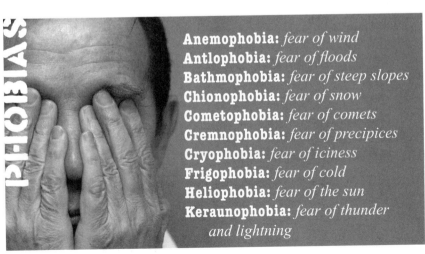

PHOBIAS

Anemophobia: *fear of wind*
Antlophobia: *fear of floods*
Bathmophobia: *fear of steep slopes*
Chionophobia: *fear of snow*
Cometophobia: *fear of comets*
Cremnophobia: *fear of precipices*
Cryophobia: *fear of iciness*
Frigophobia: *fear of cold*
Heliophobia: *fear of the sun*
Keraunophobia: *fear of thunder and lightning*

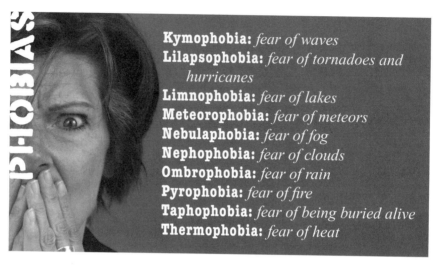

PHOBIAS

Kymophobia: *fear of waves*
Lilapsophobia: *fear of tornadoes and hurricanes*
Limnophobia: *fear of lakes*
Meteorophobia: *fear of meteors*
Nebulaphobia: *fear of fog*
Nephophobia: *fear of clouds*
Ombrophobia: *fear of rain*
Pyrophobia: *fear of fire*
Taphophobia: *fear of being buried alive*
Thermophobia: *fear of heat*

Drought

24 million Estimated number of deaths in China's drought and famine of 1907

3 million Number who died from drought in India, 1900

1.5 million Number who died from drought in India, 1965–67

600,000 Number who died from drought in Sahel, Africa, 1972–75

137,100 Number of all World Health Organization-reported African starvation deaths in 2002 (see "Starvation" chapter for more info)

35 Estimated percentage of the world's starvation deaths that occur in Africa

14 million Estimated number at risk of starvation in Lesotho, Malawi, Mozambique, Swaziland, Zambia, and Zimbabwe

850 million Estimated number in tons of topsoil that blew off America's southern Plains in 1935 alone. Poor farming methods, combined with a drought that spread over 75% of the country, created a "Dust Bowl" that displaced tens of thousands of farmers and their families

Shakin' All Over

12 million Estimated number of earthquakes worldwide in a typical year

100 Estimated number of these earthquakes that cause significant damage and disruption

TOP 10 MOST MURDEROUS EARTHQUAKES

RANK	PLACE	YEAR	MAGNITUDE	DEATHS
1	Shansi, China	1556	8.0	830,000
2	Tanshan, China	1976	7.5	655,000
3	Aceh, Sumatra	2004	9.0	283,000
4	Aleppo, Syria	1138	N/A	230,000
5	Xining, China	1927	7.9	200,000
6	Damgahan, Iran	856	N/A	200,000
7	Gansu, China	1920	8.6	200,000
8	Ardabil, Iran	893	N/A	150,000
9	Kanto, Japan	1923	7.9	143,000
10	Ashgabat, Turkey	1948	7.3	110,000

Misleading Death Numbers

After the San Francisco earthquake and fire of 1906, the fatality count was deliberately lowballed by city authorities. According to the U.S. Geological Survey, the city's official fatality figure of 700 dead was probably more accurately 2,100–2,800.

Over Our Heads

10,000 Number of floods spilling onto formerly dry land worldwide in a typical year

1 Rank of floods as the twentieth century's costliest U.S. disasters in terms of lost lives and property damage

8,891 Number of U.S. flood deaths reported between 1913 and 1980

6,000 Estimated number of drowning victims from a hurricane that struck Galveston, Texas, in 1900, the deadliest natural disaster in U.S. history

1,836 Estimated number of deaths caused

by Hurricane Katrina after the August 2005 storm slammed into Louisiana and Mississippi

90 Percentage of hurricane fatalities who die from drowning

Landslides

180,000 Estimated number killed in the worst landslide in history, in Kansou, China, in 1920

30,000 Estimated number killed in landslides and flash floods after heavy rain along Venezuela's north coast in 1999

18,000 Estimated number killed by landslide in Huascarán, Peru, from a massive 1970 earthquake. A landslide 8 years earlier in the same place killed 4,000

$688 million Damages, adjusted for inflation, of the most costly landslide in U.S. history. In 1983, a massive landslide dammed the Spanish Fork River, creating a new lake with the town of Thistle, Utah, at the bottom. In honor of the lost town, the new body of water was named Thistle Lake

26 Number killed in the U.S.'s deadliest landslide. Half a mountain slid into Montana's Madison Canyon, burying a campground and damming the Madison River. Only seven bodies were recovered—the rest are presumed buried under tons of dirt and rock

25–50 Estimated number of U.S. landslide casualties in a typical year

What Makes Land Slide?

Powerful pressure from an earthquake or lava flow can cause a mountain to loose a deadly barrage of dirt and stone. It can also come from erosion or construction undermining the underpinnings of the mountain's structure. However, sometimes just water and gravity can be enough—supersaturated soil from thaws or rainstorms can produce just the grease it takes to let things slide.

Lightning Strikes

1,000,000 Amount of energy in volts a lightning strike may contain. If the amperage is also high, it's called a "hot" strike, because its heat can set fire to flammable materials. A "cold" strike is just as dangerous: its high-volt, low-amperage effect is more explosive than incendiary

50,000 Average temperature of a lightning strike in degrees Fahrenheit

1/10 Speed in seconds of a hot lightning strike. Cold strikes are even quicker. Both travel in a bolt that's about the diameter of a quarter or half-dollar

20 Distance in miles from a storm cloud that a "positive giant" lightning bolt can hit. These clear-sky strikes can contain 3–4 times more energy than a normal bolt and give credence to the advice that you seek cover long before a storm actually overtakes you

100,000 Estimated number of annual thunderstorms worldwide

834 Number of worldwide reported lightning deaths in 2000. Many countries,

The golf course may be the last place you want to be during a thunderstorm. Ask Lee Trevino, who was struck by lightning during the 1975 Western Open: "There was a thunderous crack like cannon fire and suddenly I was lifted a foot and a half off the ground. 'Damn,' I thought to myself, 'this is a helluva penalty for slow play.'"

Trevino's advice about surviving a lightning storm? "Hold up a 1-iron and walk. Even God can't hit a 1-iron." Don't really try it. He was, of course, just joking.

% LIGHTNING STRIKE LOCATIONS

(compiled from 1959 to 1994 statistics in which location was reported)

45% Open fields & nongolf recreation areas

23.3% Under trees (not including golf)

13.3% Water (boating, fishing, swimming)

8.3% Golf course, including under trees

5% On farm, operating heavy equipment

4% Proximity to telephone receiver or lines

1.1% Proximity to radio, TV, transmitter, antenna

including large nations such as China, don't report this figure to international authorities. Of the countries that did, Thailand accounted for 24% of these deaths, Mexico for 23%, and Brazil for 15%

25 million Estimated number of annual lightning strikes in the U.S.

1 Rank of Florida as the state with the most lightning-related injuries and deaths, accounting for more than twice as many casualties as any other state. Rounding out the top 5 are Michigan, Texas, New York, and Tennessee

3,500 Estimated average number of lightning strikes in Florida every day

73 Average number of Americans killed each year by lightning over the last thirty years

4 to 1 Ratio of men to women in chances of a lightning strike. Men account for 82% of the humans hit, and 84% of the fatalities, probably because men are more likely to be out in boats and fields brandishing metal objects

10 Percentage of lightning victims who are struck dead by the experience. Of the people who survive, 70% suffer long-term residual effects, mostly of the brain and nervous system, including problems with sight and hearing

4 p.m. Most likely time of day to get struck by lightning. Two-thirds of lightning casualties occur between noon and 4 p.m., with 4 being the peak time. To further increase your chances, go golfing (the top lightning sport) on Sunday (the top day) in July (the top month) in Florida (the top state)

If lightning is the weapon of a vengeful God, He may have taken issue with Mel Gibson's *The Passion of the Christ*. While filming outside Rome, lightning struck Jim Caviezel, the actor who played Jesus. The film's assistant director, Jan Michelini, was also struck by the same bolt; oddly, he had also been hit earlier in the filming when lightning struck his umbrella in Matera, Italy. And you thought human critics were tough!

Tsunami!

100 Minimum number of miles that a tsunami's wavelength can measure. (A typical ocean wave might have a wavelength of 150 meters.) A tsunami has a long wavelength with a short amplitude (height), a meter or less. On a ship at sea, you may barely feel the slight upward "hump." It isn't until the wave hits the resistance of a continental shelf that it bunches up in height

DEADLIEST TSUNAMIS IN HISTORY

YEAR	LOCATION	NUMBER OF DEATHS
2004	Indonesia, Sri Lanka, India, etc.	227,000
1410	Greece, off Crete's north coast	100,000
1782	South China Sea	40,000
1883	Krakatau, Indonesia	36,500
1498	Nankaido, Japan	31,200
1707	Tokaido, Nankaido, Japan	30,000
1896	Sanriku, Japan	26,400
1868	Northern Chile	25,700
1792	Japan, Kyushu Island	15,000
1771	Japan, Ryukyu Trench	13,500

10 Depth in meters above which a typical tsunami travels through the ocean. Once thought to travel through deep water, a tsunami actually stays close to the surface

TSUNAMI HAZARD ZONE

IN CASE OF EARTHQUAKE, GO TO HIGH GROUND OR INLAND

100 Height in feet of the wave that hit Hokkaido Island in Japan in 1993, roughly as tall as a 10-story building. The wave crashed over specially built tsunami walls and washed away all the island's wooden structures and many of its people

2 Number of Japanese words that were combined to create the name: tsu (harbor) and nami (wave); a slightly more accurate name than the old term tidal wave

DECEMBER 2004 TSUNAMI DEATHS

Indonesia 166,320
Sri Lanka 38,195
India 16,383
Thailand 5,322
Somalia 298
Myanmar 90
Maldives 82
Malaysia 68
Tanzania 10
Bangladesh 2
Kenya 1
Estimated Total 226,771

4 Number of major causes of tsunamis. Besides earthquakes, there are also exploding underwater volcanoes, and even (as discovered in the 1950s) major underwater landslides. Add the wild card of asteroid impact on the oceans, and you've got every reason to stay far away from the coasts

450 Speed in miles per hour at which a tsunami can travel in deep water, with little loss of energy until it hits a coast

Volcanoes Erupt

15 Height in miles of the largest known volcano in the solar system. Measuring 335 miles wide, Olympus Mons on Mars is three times taller than Mount Everest

20 Distance in miles that a volcano has been known to spew deadly hot rocks. Ash and fumes can cover 100 miles or more

1,500 Approximate temperature in degrees Fahrenheit of the pyroclastic lava flows that can spew out of volcanoes

100–150 Approximate speed in miles per hour of the pyroclastic flow

92,000 Estimated number killed by the deadliest known

The Death of Pliny the Elder

Curiosity, plain and simple, killed Pliny the Elder. That and a volcano. According to his nephew Pliny the Younger, the Elder Pliny began sailing across what is now the Gulf of Napoli toward Pompeii as soon as he saw that Mount Vesuvius was erupting. The boat was showered with stones from the eruption, but still he sailed onward to get a closer look. He landed and camped the night. The next morning, as ash and smoke engulfed his camp, his crew members fled, but Pliny the Elder stayed and was asphyxiated.

DEADLIEST VOLCANOES IN HISTORY

YEAR	LOCATION	# OF DEATHS	CAUSE OF DEATH
1815	Tambora, Indonesia	92,000	eruption, famine
1883	Krakatau, Indonesia	36,000	resulting tsunami
1902	Mount Pelée, Martinique	30,000	pyroclastic lava
1985	Nevado del Ruiz, Colombia	25,000	mudflows
1792	Unzen, Japan	15,000	collapse, tsunami
1586	Kelut, Indonesia	10,000	mudflows
1783	Lakagigar (Laki), Iceland	9,000	famine
79	Vesuvius, Italy	3,360	lava, ash

volcano, which hit Tambora, Indonesia, in April 1815. Only 10,000 died in the initial eruption—the rest were killed by the famine that resulted when their fields were burned and inundated

3,360 Number killed when Vesuvius destroyed Pompeii and Herculaneum in AD 79. It has erupted three dozen times since then

Winds of Destruction

74 Minimum constant speed in miles per hour of a tropical storm's winds to qualify as a hurricane. If the winds fall below 38 mph, it is downgraded to a "tropical depression." Hurricanes are called typhoons in the western Pacific, and cyclones in the Indian Ocean

20–40 Diameter in miles of a typical hurricane's eye. The calm within the center

of the storm can fool people into a complacency right before the wind hits again, going the other direction. In fact, being hit with this "eyewall" is what can cause the most damage

300 Miles in diameter of a typical hurricane

2 Typical time in weeks that a hurricane can survive over open water. Once it hits land, it begins to dissipate

80 Percentage of tornadoes that strike between noon and midnight

695 Number killed in a single U.S. tornado, which touched down in Missouri, Illinois, and Indiana in 1925

They Call the Wind Maria?

Because several tropical storms can occur at the same time, hurricanes are given names to avoid confusion. Hundreds of years ago, storms in the West Indies were named according to the most recent saint's day in the Catholic liturgical calendar, but at the end of the nineteenth century a male meteorologist in Australia began giving hurricanes women's names. After a storm of protest from women's groups in the 1970s, the U.S. Weather Service began alternating between male and female names, using six rotating lists for the Atlantic and a different six lists for the Pacific. The names on each list are assigned alphabetically for each letter except Q, U, and Z. Names of particularly destructive and/or deadly storms are retired forever from the lists, so we'll never again see a hurricane named Katrina, Andrew, Hattie, Juan, Fifi, Elena, Betsy, Inez, Camille, Fabian, or any of 60-some retired names.

DEADLIEST WINDSTORMS IN THE TWENTIETH CENTURY

YEAR	TYPE	LOCATION	DEATHS
1970	Cyclone	Bangladesh	300,000–500,000
1991	Cyclone	Bangladesh	138,000
1998	Hurricane	Central America	11,000
1900	Hurricane	Galveston, Texas	8,000–12,000
1928	Hurricane	Lake Okeechobee, Florida	2,500–10,000
1991	Typhoon	Philippines	6,000
1958	Typhoon	Japan	5,000

Sports

Q UESTION: What's more dangerous, a kayak or sailboat?

ANSWER: Kayak

60 annual deaths related to canoes and kayaks
versus 9 from sailboats in the U.S., 2001.

Q Which professional sport is the
most dangerous? **A: Motor sports**

37% of all 1992–2002 professional athletic
deaths were associated with automobile or
motorcycle racing (such as driving or flagging).

Q How many occupations had
higher death rates than professional athletes in 2003? **A: Five**

Loggers, pilots, farmers, driving salespersons,
and construction workers had higher death rates
than professional athletes. But athletes experienced
more fatalities per capita at 22 per 100,000
than police and sheriff's patrol officers at 20.9.

Q What's the most dangerous
amateur sport? **A: Football**

High school football average annual
deaths (11 per year) are almost 3 times
higher than basketball deaths (4 per year).

Q What's deadlier when you're
5–14, your bicycle or asthma?

A: Asthma

77 young male bicyclists died in 2002 from being hit
by cars versus 123 that age who died of asthma.

Q Who's more likely to die, a bull
in Spain or an old American?

A: Bull

24,000 out of 100,000 bulls bred for the
bullring die each year in Spain versus 15,113
out of 100,000 85-year-old Americans who
died in 2001 from all causes of death.

Q What's riskier when you're
15–24, going for a walk or
eating too much candy? **A: Walking**

269 male pedestrians age 15–24 died in
2001 versus 85 who died from diabetes.

Q If you go for a walk, are you
more likely to be killed facing
or with your back to traffic? **A: Back**

5.7% of all U.S. pedestrians killed or injured
were walking with traffic in 2003 versus
3.9% walking against.

SPORTS
make us stronger, faster, and healthier. Most animals play, hunt, and fight to become better at surviving; the human animal has done the same since before recorded history. So when we think of death, the athlete is not the first image to pop into our minds; rarely do we visualize the sudden deaths of healthy young people in great shape.

The Centers for Disease Control does not separately categorize death by sports, although most such deaths are included under accidents. Many athletes who die after exertion—second only to being hit by something or someone as a cause of death in sports—do so from undetected physical weaknesses, undiscovered Achilles' heels of which sudden death may be the first clear symptom.

It's easy to take the wrong lessons from sports death statistics. The reality is that the small number of deaths that result from exercising come nowhere near the overwhelming number of deaths that come from not exercising. Good physical condition helps protect us from many serious risk factors for heart disease, diabetes, depression, osteoporosis, high blood pressure, and stroke. If the average sports enthusiast spent as much time playing sports as he did watching them, we'd be a healthier species indeed.

SUDDEN-DEATH PLAY-OFFS

Quick & Dead Summary for the U.S.

137 Number of deaths recorded by the Centers for Disease Control (CDC) from overexertion and privation, most often exercise-related

87 Number of those deaths from lack of food

8 Number from overexertion and strenuous or repetitive movements

1 Number from prolonged stay in a weightless environment

41 Number from unspecified privation

45 Number of deaths from being struck by or against another person

27 Number of deaths of professional athletes according to the Bureau of Labor Statistics

Sports Health Risks

Sports-related deaths are included in multiple categories:

TRANSPORTATION ACCIDENTS are found under "Accidents."

SUDDEN DEATH from preexisting bad-heart conditions is included in the "Broken Heart" chapter.

DROWNING, FALLS, and EXPOSURE (some sports-related) are found under "Accidents."

ASTHMA is in the "Bad Breath" chapter.

KIDNEY (renal) FAILURE (some caused by rhabdomyolysis, a breakdown of the muscle fiber experienced by some marathon runners and weight lifters) is covered in the "Bad Plumbing" chapter.

MALIGNANT LIVER TUMORS (some caused by athletes' use of anabolic steroids to boost performance) are in the "Cancer" chapter.

MOUTH CANCERS (some related to athletes' chewing tobacco) are included with other "Cancer" deaths.

LIGHTNING (some while on the golf course) is included in the "Accidents—Nature" chapter.

EATING DISORDERS are in the "Bad Wiring" chapter.

OSTEOARTHRITIS (some resulting from sports injuries) is in the "Bad Framing" chapter. Most occur later in life.

IRON-DEFICIENCY ANEMIA (some reported in long-distance runners) is found in the "Hormones" chapter.

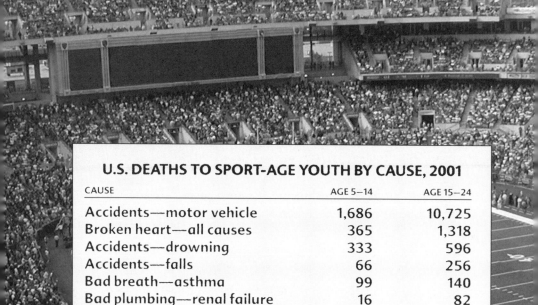

U.S. DEATHS TO SPORT-AGE YOUTH BY CAUSE, 2001

CAUSE	AGE 5–14	AGE 15–24
Accidents—motor vehicle	1,686	10,725
Broken heart—all causes	365	1,318
Accidents—drowning	333	596
Accidents—falls	66	256
Bad breath—asthma	99	140
Bad plumbing—renal failure	16	82
Cancer—liver	15	29
Cancer—lip, mouth, and pharynx	4	29
Accidents—nature (lightning)	3	10
Accidents—struck by or against another person	3	7
Bad wiring—anorexia & bulimia	0	5
Bad framing—arthritis	0	0
Starvation—iron-deficiency-anemia-caused	0	0

The Pros

219 Number of work-related fatalities to U.S. sports professionals from 1992 to 2002. These include professional baseball players, race car drivers, jockeys, and boxers

91 Of the above deaths, number caused by motor vehicle accidents on land (e.g., car or motorcycle races)

47 Number caused by drowning and "other environmental hazards"

25 Number caused by contact with objects or equipment

18 By falls

15 By contact with animals (e.g., horses, bulls, etc.)

8 By contact with feral humans (i.e., homicide, assault)

6 Aircraft-related (e.g., skydiving)

5 In water vehicles (e.g., boat races)

U.S. PROFESSIONAL ATHLETE WORK-INJURY DEATHS, 1992–2002 BY AGE

AGE	# OF DEATHS
20–24	22
25–34	74
35–44	58
45–54	37
55–64	15
65+	9

Risky Business

22 Average on-the-job professional athletic fatality rate per 100,000 athletes from 1998 to 2002. This compares to 4.7 per 100,000 on-the-job deaths of all workers

96 Percentage of pro sports fatalities who were male

84 Percentage of pro sports fatalities who were white

70 Percentage of pro sports deaths between the ages of 20 and 44

Sports Odds

1 in 9 Odds that the dead pro died in Florida

1 in 10 In California

2 in 25 In Indiana

3 in 50 In Louisiana

WHERE DO SPORTS INJURIES OCCUR?

28% .. Home premises
26% .....Sports arena
8% ...... Public street
38% ....Unknown

The Amateurs

30 million Estimated number of U.S. children and teens who participate in some sort of organized sports

3.5 million Estimated number of injuries they suffer each year

21 Percentage of kids' traumatic brain injuries that are the result of sports and recreational activities

1 out of 2 Proportion of kids' head injuries that occur on bicycles, skateboards, or skates

100–200 Range of sports-related sudden deaths per year among U.S. students. Weak hearts cause the majority; asthma and aneurysms make up the bulk of the rest. Although sudden deaths while participating in sporting events are rare, they occur most commonly in high school athletes involved in competitive sports such as track and cross-country and basketball

TOP 5 U.S. MOST DANGEROUS HIGH SCHOOL & COLLEGE SPORTS
(average annual deaths)

RANK	SPORT	HIGH SCHOOL	COLLEGE
1	Football	11	2
2	Basketball	4	1
3	Track & cross-country	3	.2
4	Soccer	2	.2
5	Baseball	1	.3

The A to Z of Sports

Auto Racing

135 Number of accidental fatalities associated with street racing in the U.S. in 2001

37 Percentage of all 219 professional athlete fatalities reported by the U.S. Bureau of Labor Statistics between 1992 and 2002 that resulted from motor racing

0.6 Average annual number of NASCAR racing deaths from 1989 to 2000: 1 death in each of 1989, 1991, 1993, 1997 and 2000, and 2 deaths in 1994, for a total of 7 in 12 years

Baseball and Softball

15,600,000 Estimated number of Americans who played baseball in 2002

13,600,000 Estimated number who played softball

304,543 Number of U.S. baseball and softball injuries

126,000 Number of injuries to players under age 15 serious enough to require hospitalization

1 Rank of baseball as the deadliest sport for children 5 to 14

43 Number of recorded deaths from baseball from 1918 to 1950, making it the deadliest sport at that time

38 Number of deaths suffered by players during unofficial and organized baseball games from 1973

Lou Gehrig's Disease

One of the most famous of sport deaths was that of Lou Gehrig, the baseball player who died from amyotrophic lateral sclerosis (ALS) in 1941 and had his cause of death named after him. Before his death, Gehrig set several major league and American League records and was voted the greatest first baseman of all time by the Baseball Writers' Association.

ALS is nearly always progressive, eventually leading to death. A major risk factor is thought to be environmental (not related to baseball). In 2001, the U.S. Department of Veterans Affairs released a news release declaring veterans who had served in the Gulf War (1990 to 1991) were nearly twice as likely to develop ALS as their nondeployed counterparts, although death rates remain low. Death usually follows diagnosis within 3 to 5 years.

U.S. DEATHS FROM MOTOR NEURON DISEASE (MOST FROM LOU GEHRIG'S DISEASE)
(PER 100,000 POPULATION)

YEAR	DEATH RATE	DEATHS
1995	1.9	5,127
2001	1.9	5,398
2004	1.9	5,663

For more information on ALS see "Other Wiring Issues" in the "Bad Wiring" chapter. For more information on war deaths, see the "War" chapter.

to 1995 from commotio cordis, occurring when a player is hit in the chest with a ball, causing the heart to stop. It primarily strikes children aged 5–15 with no preexisting heart conditions

26 Number of minor league players to die from the game since 1883. Only 2 of these deaths occurred after 1961, due mostly to protective headgear (introduced in 1905, but not enforced until 1971) and better lighting conditions at night games

8 Number of high school players of organized baseball who suffered fatalities because of the game from 1982 to 2004

3 Number of organized-baseball college players who suffered fatalities in that same period

1 Position in baseball history of the death of 21-year-old American James

Creighton Jr. His swing of the massive bat in use in 1862 caused an internal injury, resulting in the first recorded fatality of the game

1 Number of minor league pitchers killed by a batted ball. Charles Harrington was killed in 1902 when a ball he pitched in Midlothian, Texas, was rocketed back and hit him in the stomach. He still managed to throw the batter out at first but died as he prepared to face the next hitter

1 Number of players who've been poisoned during a game. In 1909 a venemous snake bit James Phelps of Louisiana while he was playing the outfield in Monroe, Louisiana; he kept it to himself and his team played on. He died hours after the game ended

1 Number of minor league players killed by lightning during a game. Andy Strong of the Evangeline

League was killed during a June 1951 Louisiana game when lightning struck him. No one else was hurt and the game was called

13 Rank of baseball as a cause of recreation-related hospital visits among Australian children

16 Rank among Australian adults

Look Out Below!

After the Cleveland Indians hit the news for a publicity stunt in 1938, catching balls that had been lobbed off a 700-foot-tall skyscraper in downtown Cleveland, the publicity man for the San Francisco Seals came up with a similar idea the following year. He figured that catching a ball tossed onto the field from the Goodyear blimp would not only beat the Indians' height record, but also make a great season-opening stunt for the San Francisco team. So Seals catcher Joe Sprinz was recruited for the big show.

From the blimp, 800 feet up, came the first ball. It landed on the bleachers and cracked them. The second ball embedded itself in the dirt on the field. Finally, a ball came close enough for Joe to try for it. The ball came down and landed in his glove, bounced up and hit him in the face, split his lip open, broke his upper jaw, and knocked out several of his teeth.

The ball dropped, as did Joe, but the *Guinness Book of World Records* did honor him with the highest-baseball catch ever attempted.

Basketball

28,900,000 Estimated number of American basketball players in 2002

615,546 Number of basketball injuries

94 Number of deaths indirectly attributed to high school and college basketball from 1982 to 2004 (most indirect sports deaths are from exertion or complications)

3 Number of college and high school deaths directly attributed to the game in the same span

Boating

26,626,000 Number of motor- or powerboats in the U.S. in 2002

7,592,000 Number of canoes

617 Number of all boating-accident deaths in the U.S. in 2002

67 Percentage of boating-accident deaths by drowning

33 Percentage of deaths by injury

37 Number of deaths related to canoes and kayaks in 2002 (down from 60 in 2001)

12 To inflatable boats

7 To sailboats

0.2 Rate of death from all boating accidents in the U.S. per 100,000 population each year from 1999 through 2004

1.8 Rate of death from boating accidents per 100,000 boating participants

Boxing

1,700,000 Number of boxing participants in the U.S.

694.7 Injury rate per 100,000 boxing participants

8 Rank of boxing in the top 8 most dangerous sports

6 Percentage of all 219 professional athlete fatalities reported by the U.S. Bureau of Labor Statistics between 1992 and 2002 that resulted from pugilism (boxing, kickboxing, or wrestling)

50 Percentage of boxing fatalities that occur on U.S. soil

90 Percentage of American boxers who suffer a brain injury, making them more susceptible to neurological diseases such as Parkinson's and Alzheimer's

10 Average number of annual boxing deaths worldwide

70 Percentage of those deaths to professional boxers

113 Average number of fights that the Nevada State Athletic Commission authorized per month for the years 2002–3. There are at least 8 ranking boxing organizations that put on hundreds of bouts each year

7.8 Death rate per 100,000 boxers in Nevada as averaged over 281 months, from January 1979 to May 2003

DANGEROUS SPORTS DEATH RATES, 1995

(per 100,000 participants)

SPORT	DEATH RATE
Horse riding and racing	128
Skydiving	123
Hang gliding	55
Mountaineering	51
Scuba diving	11
Motorcycle racing	7
College football	3
Boxing	1.5

The Helmet

The Consumer Product Safety Commission (CPSC) says wearing a helmet can reduce bikers' risk of head injury by 85 percent. But it can't help if you don't wear it properly. Try on several to get the best fit.

Cycling

41,400,000 Estimated number of American cyclists

521,328 Number of cycling injuries

1,200 Number of bicyclists who died at the hands of motorists in 1980

750 Number of bicycle deaths from motorists in 1940

700 Number of bicycle deaths from motorists in 2003

90 Percentage of bicycle fatalities that are male

85 Number of bicycle deaths in August 2001, the deadliest month that year. July was second with 84; January was safest with 39

Diving

51 Number of U.S. water-related occupational deaths to athletes from 1992 to 2002

38 Number that were specifically diver-related

18 Percentage of diver deaths that occurred while diving commercially

Fishing

38,511,000 Estimated number of U.S. freshwater fishermen in 2002

12,240,000 Number of saltwater fishermen

68,743 Number of injuries from fishing

30 Number of deaths related to fishing boats in 2002

Football

10,319,000 Estimated number of U.S. touch football players in 2002

7,400,000 Estimated number of tackle football players, including pickup games, little leagues, school and park leagues, high school, NCAA, and professionals

387,948 Number of U.S. football injuries

22 Number of total deaths attributed to Australian-rules football in Australia from 1968 to 1999. Nine of these were directly attributed to brain injury from

U.S. DIRECT FOOTBALL FATALITIES, 1931–2004

WHERE PLAYED	TOTAL DEATHS
High school	659
Sandlot	177
College	86
Pro and semipro	76
Total deaths	**998**

U.S. INDIRECT FOOTBALL FATALITIES 1931–2004

(heatstroke, lightning, other)

WHERE PLAYED	TOTAL DEATHS
High school	417
Sandlot	106
College	102
Pro and semipro	21
Total deaths	**646**

impact. Most of the others were from arterial complications and previously unidentified heart problems

1 Average number of concussions per every 125 games of Australian football

"There's Murder in That Game!"

Football was not always the genteel game it is today. Once bloodier than modern rugby, the sport was nearly banned from college campuses in 1909 because so many players were being killed—27 in that year alone—and hundreds more seriously injured. Even boxer John L. Sullivan, no stranger to brutal sports, observed, "There's murder in that game!" after watching a Harvard-Yale meeting.

Wrote gunfighter-turned-sportswriter Bat Masterson, another man who didn't flinch from violence: "Football is not a sport in any sense. It is a brutal and savage slugging match between two reckless opposing crowds. The rougher it is and the more killed and crippled, the more delighted are the spectators, who howl their heads off at the sight of a player stretched prone and unconscious on the hard and frozen ground."

Finally, a newly formed Intercollegiate Football Rules Committee was formed under the leadership of the president of Princeton—and future U.S. president—Woodrow Wilson. He actually knew something about the game, having coached a football team while a history professor at Wesleyan University in the 1880s.

Wilson's committee spent 5 months devising rules to make the game less lethal, requiring helmets and prohibiting diving tackles, linked arms on offense, the lifting and carrying of ball carriers, and interference with pass receivers. Most people supported the changes, but many hard-core fans complained that the IFRC ruined the game forever.

Golf

28,300,000 Estimated number of U.S. golfers in 2002

39,470 Number of golf injuries in 2002. These can include direct hits from balls or clubs, slips, falls, animal bites or stings, dehydration, sun exposure, and lightning

9 Number of fatal occupational injuries in the amusement and recreation services industry that occurred at public golf courses in 2002

66 Number of people who died from lightning in the U.S. in 2002

5 Minimum percentage of those lightning victims who were on golf courses (see "Accidents—Nature" for more lightning fatalities)

The world's most dangerous 18-hole golf course is the Konkola Golf Club in Zambia, Africa. Golfers may meet up with a booms-lang, black and green mamba, puff adder, Gaboon viper, or highly venomous spitting cobra in the tall grass. Then there are the crocodiles: as of 2002, 4 caddies had been bitten by crocs while retrieving golf balls. Hippo footprints are most often found on holes 6 and 7, although the only time a golfer was killed by a hippo was when he ran into her leaving the course in his car. (More on death from wild animals can be found in "Accidents—Flora & Fauna").

Hang Gliding

7 Number of U.S. hang-gliding related deaths in 2002

2 Number of deaths in 2003, out of 46 accidents reported

85 Percentage of serious injuries that are the result of takeoff or landing

Hockey–Ice

2,100,000 Estimated number of U.S. ice hockey players in 2002

16,435 Number of hockey-related injuries

7 Number of recorded high school and college ice hockey direct- and indirect-related fatalities between 1982 and 2004

Horse Racing

1,000 Estimated number of working jockeys in the U.S.

16 Percentage of all 219 professional-athlete

fatalities reported by the U.S. Bureau of Labor Statistics between 1992 and 2002 that resulted from working with horses (horse racing) or bulls (rodeos)

Horse Riding

9,500,000 Estimated number of U.S. horse riders in 2002

70,704 Number of horse-riding-related injuries

118 Number of fatal animal-rider accidents

Hunting

24,112,000 Estimated number of American hunters in 2002

805 Number of reported hunting-related nonfatal injuries

93 Number of hunting-related fatalities in 2002

46 Preliminary official number of hunting-related fatalities for 2004. Mandatory orange or visible vests and firearms education are contributing to the decline in fatalities

Lacrosse

11,877 Number of athletes participating in NCAA lacrosse

5 Number of U.S. high school lacrosse-related

deaths between 1982 and 2004

4 Number of college lacrosse deaths in the same period

Mountain Climbing

3,400,000 Estimated number of American mountain climbers in 2002

4,056 Number of injuries suffered by those climbers

200 Estimated number of fatalities on Mount Everest (see "Accidents—Nature" for more information about accidental death due to temperature)

9 Percentage of climbers who died from traumatic accidental death during a climb, per a study published in New Zealand in 2005, based on statistics of 46 serious climbers

Parachuting

TOP 10 COUNTRIES REPORTING PARACHUTE DEATHS, 2000–2001

RANK	COUNTRY	ANNUAL DEATHS
1	USA	24
2	UK	8
3	France	6
4	Australia	4
5	Brazil	4
6	Cuba	4
7	Germany	3
8	Spain	3
9	Scandinavia	3
10	Japan	2

Running

24,748,000 Estimated number of U.S. runners in 2002

29 Number of American high school and college track runners who died of indirect causes from 1982 to 2004

23 Number of American high school and college track-and-field participants who died directly from a track-and-field-related accident in the same span

20 Number of those victims who were high schoolers

Skating and Skateboarding

5,300,000 Estimated number of U.S. ice-skaters in 2002

26,118 Number of ice-skating-related injuries

26,900,000 Estimated number of roller skaters

106,531 Number of their injuries

9,700,000 Estimated number of skateboarders

113,192 Number of their injuries

119 Number of deaths in the U.S. in 2002 from falls

involving ice skates, skis, roller skates, or skateboards

Skiing and Snowboarding

9,600,000 Estimated number of U.S. skiers in 2002

5,600,000 Estimated number of U.S. snowboarders

77 Percentage of skiers who are alpine skiers versus cross-country

63,014 Number of snowboarding injuries

31 Number of skiing deaths

6 Number of snowboarding deaths

Soccer

14,500,000 Estimated number of U.S. soccer players in 2002

173,519 Number of soccer injuries

38,026 Number of NCAA soccer players

37 Number of direct and indirect U.S. high school and college soccer deaths from 1982 to 2004

Swimming

54,700,000 Estimated number of U.S. swimmers in 2002

3,447 Number of accidental drowning deaths in the

U.S. that year (including from boating accidents)

1,333 Number of those drowning deaths that occurred in natural water

7 Percentage of natural-water deaths under age 10

625 Number that occurred in a swimming pool

45 Percentage of swimming-pool deaths under age 10

Tennis

11,000,000 Estimated number of U.S. tennis players in 2002

19,633 Number of tennis injuries

15,819 Number of NCAA tennis players, 2001–2

5 Number of indirect tennis deaths to high school and college tennis players in the 23 years from 1982 through 2004

Volleyball

11,500,000 Estimated number of U.S. volleyball players in 2002

59,225 Number of volleyball injuries

14,222 Number of NCAA volleyball players

92 Percentage of NCAA players who are female

2 Number of U.S. high school and college volleyball deaths from 1994 to 2004

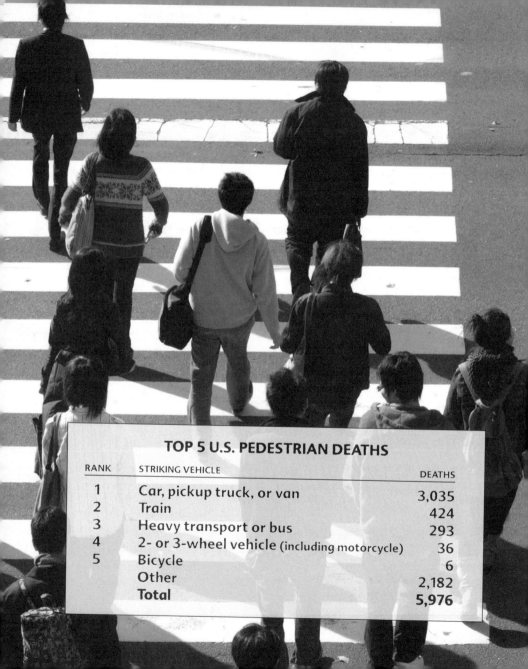

TOP 5 U.S. PEDESTRIAN DEATHS

RANK	STRIKING VEHICLE	DEATHS
1	Car, pickup truck, or van	3,035
2	Train	424
3	Heavy transport or bus	293
4	2- or 3-wheel vehicle (including motorcycle)	36
5	Bicycle	6
	Other	2,182
	Total	**5,976**

Walking

82,183,000 Estimated number of Americans who walked for exercise in 2002

5,976 Number of American pedestrians who were hit and killed by transportation vehicles that year

Wrestling

3,500,000 Estimated number of U.S. wrestlers in 2002

36,702 Number of wrestling injuries

20 Number of wrestling deaths between 1982 and 2004

17 Of those, number who were high schoolers

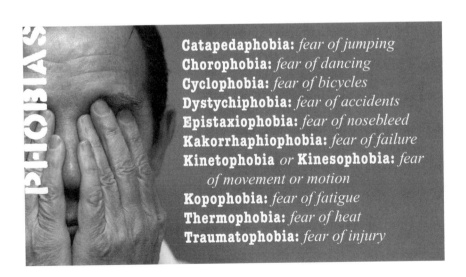

PHOBIAS

Catapedaphobia: *fear of jumping*
Chorophobia: *fear of dancing*
Cyclophobia: *fear of bicycles*
Dystychiphobia: *fear of accidents*
Epistaxiophobia: *fear of nosebleed*
Kakorrhaphiophobia: *fear of failure*
Kinetophobia *or* **Kinesophobia:** *fear of movement or motion*
Kopophobia: *fear of fatigue*
Thermophobia: *fear of heat*
Traumatophobia: *fear of injury*

Most at Risk of Premature Death from Accidents

WORLDWIDE DEATH RATES, 2002
(per 100,000 population)

AGE	MALE	FEMALE
0–4	46.5	46.9
5–14	35.9	25.1
15–29	67.3	28.2
30–44	78.3	29.5
45–59	102.8	43.1
60–69	119.2	60.6
70+	205.5	151.5

U.S. DEATH RATES, 2001
(per 100,000 population)

AGE	TRANSPORT	FALL	DROWN	FIRE	POISON	OTHER
Under 1	3.7	0.6	1.7	1.2		16.6
1–4	4.4	.02	3.0	1.5	0.2	1.8
5–14	4.4	.02	0.8	0.6	0.1	0.6
15–24	27.9	.06	1.5	0.5	3.4	1.6
25–34	18.8	.09	0.9	0.6	6.3	2.0
35–44	17.4	1.4	1.0	1.0	11.2	3.1
45–54	16.0	2.6	0.9	1.1	9.1	4.2
55–64	15.3	4.0	0.8	1.5	3.2	5.3
65–74	17.9	10.0	0.9	2.2	1.6	10.0
75–84	27.9	35.3	1.2	3.4	2.2	30.5
85+	28.9	121.5	1.7	5.7	3.5	115.0

Avoid Being a Premature Death Statistic from Accidents

BE CAREFUL
BE SMART

- WEAR YOUR SEAT BELT AND HELMET
- DON'T DRIVE UNDER THE INFLUENCE
- KEEP YOUR EYES ON THE ROAD AND YOUR HANDS ON THE WHEEL
- WATCH OUT WHEN CROSSING THE ROAD
- WATCH OUT WHEN CLIMBING STAIRS AND LADDERS
- DON'T LEAVE BABIES UNATTENDED
- DON'T SMOKE IN BED
- BE CAREFUL WITH PRESCRIPTION AND OTHER DRUGS
- BE CAREFUL WHAT ELSE YOU PUT IN YOUR MOUTH
- BE KIND TO ANIMALS
- STAY WARM WHEN IT'S COLD AND COOL WHEN IT'S HOT
- DON'T PLAY GOLF DURING A THUNDERSTORM
- DON'T DO SPORTS WITH A BAD HEART

Bad
Bre

#4 Cause of premature death in the world
2002 (under age 70)

#4 Cause of premature death in the USA
2001 (under age 75)

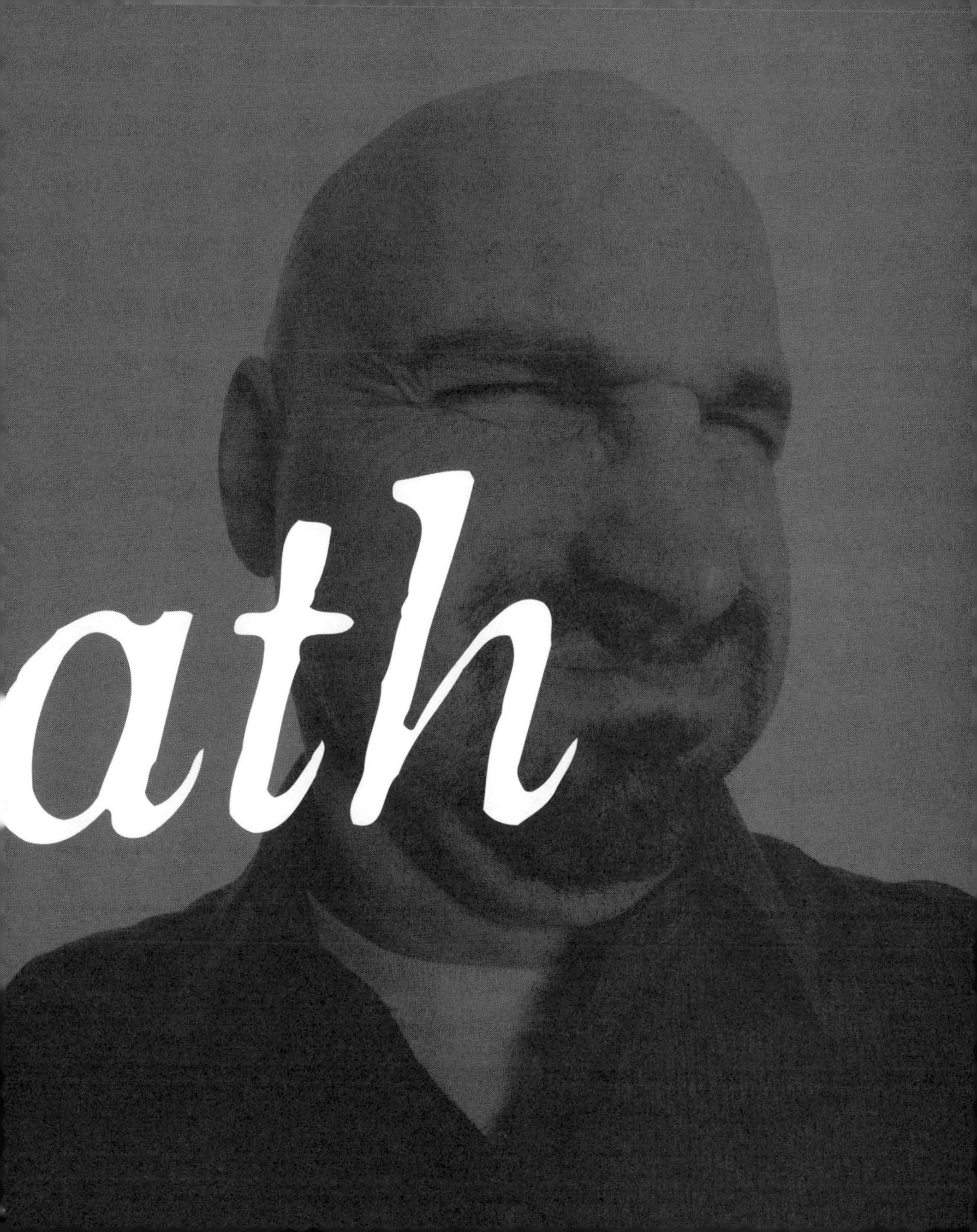
ath

QUESTION: What kills more 15–24-year-old Americans, asthma or HIV? **ANSWER: It's a tie**

The rate of death for both in that age range was 0.4 per 100,000 15–24-year-olds in 2001.

Q Are you more likely to die of asthma in New Zealand or the USA? **A: New Zealand**

New Zealanders die at a rate of 1.7 versus 1.4 per 100,000 respective population.

Q What's the worst month to be asthmatic? **A: March**

March had the highest number of U.S. deaths in 2001 from asthma (412) with January close behind (379). March also had the highest number of deaths from flu, pneumonia, emphysema, and stroke.

Q What killed more British citizens, smoking or World War II?

A: Smoking

Almost 12 times more people have died in the UK from smoking than died in World War II.

Q How much more likely are you to die inhaling food versus marijuana if you're under age 55?

A: 350 times

There were 17,335 deaths in the U.S. in 2003 from pneumonitis (702 under age 55) versus 2 deaths attributed to behavior disorders due to cannabinoids.

Q Which is greater, the amount of air your body takes in or the blood it pumps each day? **A: Air**

Adults, on average, breathe 11,400 liters (3,000 gallons) of air daily versus 6,000–7,500 liters (1,500–2,000 gallons) of blood pumped by the heart.

Q Which donated organ is transplanted more often, the heart or the lungs? **A: Heart**

In the U.S. in 2002, of the 9,938 donated lungs only 16.3% were transplanted versus 49.2% of the 4,436 donated hearts.

Q Which travels quicker, a big-league pitcher's fastball or the particles expelled in your last sneeze? **A: Sneeze**

Power pitchers can throw fastballs at speeds of 95–105 mph (150–170 km/hr) whereas a sneeze can explode at 157.7 mph (252 km/hr).

Bad Breath World Death Rates
by WHO Region (per 100,000 population)

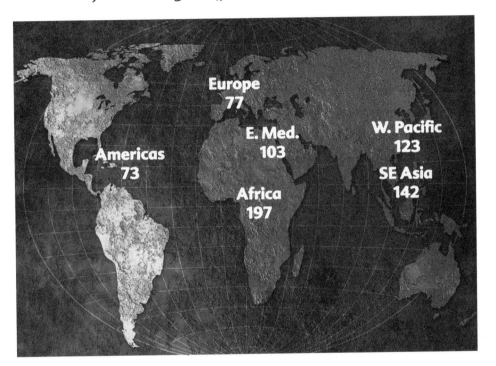

Europe 77
E. Med. 103
W. Pacific 123
Americas 73
SE Asia 142
Africa 197

BAD BREATH DEATHS, 2002—ALL AGES

Americas (incl USA): **625,577**

USA: **230,047***

Europe: **672,410**

E. Mediterranean: **519,899**

Africa: **1,327,622**

W. Pacific: **2,119,876**

Southeast Asia: **2,266,355**

* USA totals are for 2001.

Respiratory Infection and Disease Deaths Worldwide, 2002

Disease	Deaths
Flu, bronchitis, & pneumonia (Respiratory infections caused by bugs)	3,844,724
COPD (chronic obstructive pulmonary disease)	2,745,816
Asthma	239,255
Other respiratory diseases, including black lung and silicosis	711,238
TOTAL	**7,541,033**

WAITING TO INHALE

OUR respiratory system is attacked in various ways:

- Upper (colds) and lower (flu, pneumonia, chronic bronchitis) respiratory-system infections are primarily caused by viruses and bacteria.

- Respiratory diseases (pulmonary disease, or COPD, and asthma) are the result of smoking, toxic environmental exposure, and allergies.

Getting oxygen into our bodies is so vital that even a brief interruption in our breathing is enough to cause a deep, visceral panic; a longer interruption can kill. So it's surprising how cavalier many of us are about our lungs. Flu shot? Why bother! Cigarette? Why not!

How did the very first smoker ever get the idea that gunking up his lungs with burning junk would be a grand idea? That the coughing and wheezing afterward was fun? Maybe that was just primitive ignorance. But how do people today shrug off the well-documented warnings against smoking? For that matter, how do they ignore industrial pollution, the toxic-fume-spewing energy guzzlers in their houses and garages, the ever-increasing cases of asthma, emphysema, and other lung diseases?

This is a look at "bad breath"—not the kind that requires mouth-wash, but the kind that can incapacitate and kill you. Take a deep breath, and let's get some fresh air in here.

~

Following the lead of the World Health Organization and the U.S.

Centers for Disease Control (CDC), this chapter's statistics generally exclude other causes of death from attacks on the respiratory system, such as tuberculosis (see "Bugs") and lung cancer (see "Cancer").

Note: All deaths cited are for 2001 in the U.S. and 2002 in the world, unless otherwise noted

Quick & Dead Summary for the U.S.

230,047 American deaths from respiratory infections and diseases

67 Percentage of those victims over age 75

117,773 Of all respiratory deaths, the number from chronic obstructive pulmonary disease, such as emphysema

62,381 From lower respiratory infections such as flu, pneumonia, and chronic bronchitis

45,624 From other causes including pneumonitis from accidentally inhaling food or gastric content

4,269 From asthma

U.S. DEATHS FROM RESPIRATORY DISEASES VS. INFECTIONS

RANK	CAUSE OF DEATH	NUMBER OF DEATHS
1	Respiratory diseases (COPD, asthma, and other chronic diseases)	167,666
2	Respiratory infections (colds, flu, pneumonia, chronic bronchitis)	62,381

Lung for This World

3 Number of lobes in the right lung

2 Number of lobes in the left lung. This makes room for the heart, which is lodged firmly in between

11,400 Liters of air that you breathe in a typical day

An alveolus

600 million Number of alveoli working inside the lungs to separate air from blood and allow gas to transfer in and out of the bloodstream

100 Surface area of the lungs' alveoli in square meters, about the size of a regulation singles-match tennis court

10–15 Breaths taken per minute by a body at rest

80 Breaths per minute during active exercise

"You should see my alveoli— they're as big as this tennis court!"

Breathing Lessens

Asthma

20 million Americans who suffer from asthma

1.9 million U.S. emergency room visits caused by serious asthma attacks

4,269 U.S. deaths from asthma

150 Percentage increase in U.S. asthma deaths from 1980 to 2001

239,255 Number of worldwide asthma deaths

80 to 1 Odds of dying from asthma over age 85 compared to age 1–14

1 Rank among states of the District of Columbia in percentage of population suffering from asthma (14.2% in 2002)

2, 3, 4, 5 Rank respectively of Oregon, Arizona, Maine, and Connecticut

51 Rank of South Dakota (8.6% in 2002)

2 to 1 Rate of asthma deaths among current and former smokers compared to lifelong nonsmokers

Wheezing Through the Ages

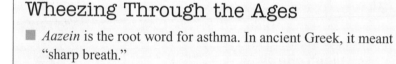

- *Aazein* is the root word for asthma. In ancient Greek, it meant "sharp breath."

- The earliest known reference to asthma was in Homer's *The Iliad*, written no later than the eighth century BC.

- Hippocrates (480–360 BC) was the first to recognize asthma as a medical condition, but thought it primarily an occupational hazard of fishermen, tailors, and metal workers.

- In the second century AD, Claudius Galenus—a Greek doctor who had worked for the medical officer of a gladiator school—wrote extensively about asthma.

ASTHMA DEATH RATES FROM COUNTRIES AROUND THE WORLD, 2000

COUNTRY	DEATHS	DEATH RATES PER 100,000
USA	4,040	1.4
New Zealand	66	1.7
Mexico	2,027	2.0
Australia	430	2.2
Japan	3,257	2.5
Thailand	1,681	2.6

Spunky British Actress

Charlotte Coleman was lively, successful, and asthmatic. She won rave reviews as the redheaded flatmate in the hit movie *Four Weddings and a Funeral*. But in 2001, at the age of 33, she collapsed and died during an asthma attack.

Flu, Colds, and Pneumonia

2 to 3 Number of weeks an infected student can pass the flu to much of his or her school

10 million Number of U.S. flu cases in a typical season

114,000 Number of cases serious enough to require hospitalization

62,381 Number of U.S. lower respiratory infection deaths

1 Rank of March among months for U.S. pneumonia deaths in 2002

Chicken Freezes . . . but So Does Bacon

Frozen food is a relatively recent invention, but seventeenth-century scientist Sir Francis Bacon investigated freezing as a preservative long before TV dinners. In 1626, Bacon stuffed a freshly killed chicken with snow, hypothesizing that a cold temperature could preserve the bird as well as salt. He was right, but in the process he caught a cold, which quickly turned into bronchitis. Bacon died soon after.

A Brief History of the Flu

Fifth Century BC
Historians believe a mutant flu brought down the great civilization of Athens

1918–19
More than 500,000 people in the U.S. and 20–50 million people worldwide die of the "Spanish flu." Nearly 50% were young, healthy adults. The pandemic was named Spanish flu because it was first reported in Spanish newspapers. News reports of the outbreak were suppressed by wartime censorship during World War I. The German army's chief of staff, General Erich Ludendorff, blamed the flu for Germany's loss of the war

1957–58
More than 70,000 people die in the U.S. from the "Asian flu," first identified in China. This pandemic eventually killed 2 million people worldwide

1968–69
More than 34,000 people die in the U.S. from the "Hong Kong flu." This mild pandemic circled the world only one time, killing roughly 1 million people

1976
The U.S. experiences a swine flu scare, labeled a "killer flu," but it never spread beyond Fort Dix, New Jersey

1997
Another "near miss" pandemic when 18 people in Hong Kong become ill from a new flu virus and 6 die. This virus moved from chickens to people but never spread easily from person to person

2003–7
America, and the world, prepare for a new pandemic "bird flu," but as of June 2007 the highly pathogenic avian influenza A (H5N1) epizootic had killed vastly more chickens than humans (191, none in the U.S.)

Diseases

COPD Out

2,745,816 Number of worldwide deaths from chronic obstructive pulmonary disease (COPD). The most common forms are emphysema and chronic bronchitis; the most common cause is cigarette smoking

15–20 Percentage of cigarette smokers who will eventually develop COPD

11.2 million Number of U.S. COPD sufferers

116,242 Number of U.S. COPD fatalities from emphysema

959 Number from bronchitis

4 Median survival time in years for a patient diagnosed with chronic bronchitis. It is not reversible, but can be slowed by avoiding exposure to tobacco and other toxic chemicals

1,042 Number of U.S. lung transplants performed

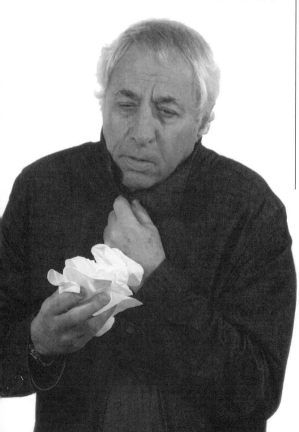

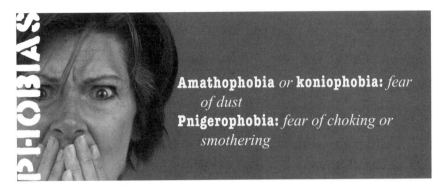

Amathophobia *or* **koniophobia:** *fear of dust*
Pnigerophobia: *fear of choking or smothering*

in a year. This is the only "cure" for COPD

500–600 Average waiting time in days for a suitable lung

25 Percentage of patients on a lung transplant waiting list who actually get one

$257,500 Estimated cost for a lung transplant

$40,900 Average annual maintenance cost after the first year

42 Percentage of lungs still functioning well 5 years after being transplanted

Upchuck and Die

17,301 Number of American deaths from pneumonitis, caused by accidentally inhaling food and stomach acids

70 Minimum age most commonly affected by pneumonitis

Corruption of Miners

367 Number of U.S. deaths caused by black lung disease, infamous for affecting coal miners

5 Percentage of U.S. coal miners currently showing X-ray evidence of black lung damage

2,700 Number of black lung deaths in China

550 Number of U.S. deaths directly attributed to white lung disease, affecting asbestos miners, shipworkers, insulation installers, and others

111 Number of U.S. deaths from other pneumoconiosis, including bauxite lung from the mining and smelting of aluminum

82 Number of U.S. deaths from silicosis, caused by manufacturing, digging, and construction workers' inhalation of silica, the second-most common mineral on earth

36 Percentage decline in U.S. coal workers' pneumoconiosis cases since 1980

43 Percentage decline in silicosis cases in the same period

524 Percentage increase in asbestosis deaths in the same time

Most at Risk of Premature Death from Bad Breath

WORLDWIDE DEATH RATES, 2002
(per 100,000 population)

AGE	MALE	FEMALE
0–4	324.1	317.0
5–14	10.7	14.7
15–29	7.6	10.3
30–44	17.1	14.3
45–59	84.0	58.5
60–69	356.2	228.3
70+	1,389.0	1,102.3

Main Cause

Respiratory diseases and infections
(flu, pneumonia, COPD, asthma)

Prevention

▧ DON'T SMOKE

▧ WATCH WHAT YOU PUT IN YOUR MOUTH

▧ WASH YOUR HANDS

▧ GET ANNUAL FLU SHOT

Bad
Plur

#7 Cause of premature death in the world
2002 (under age 70)

#5 Cause of premature death in the USA
2001 (under age 75)

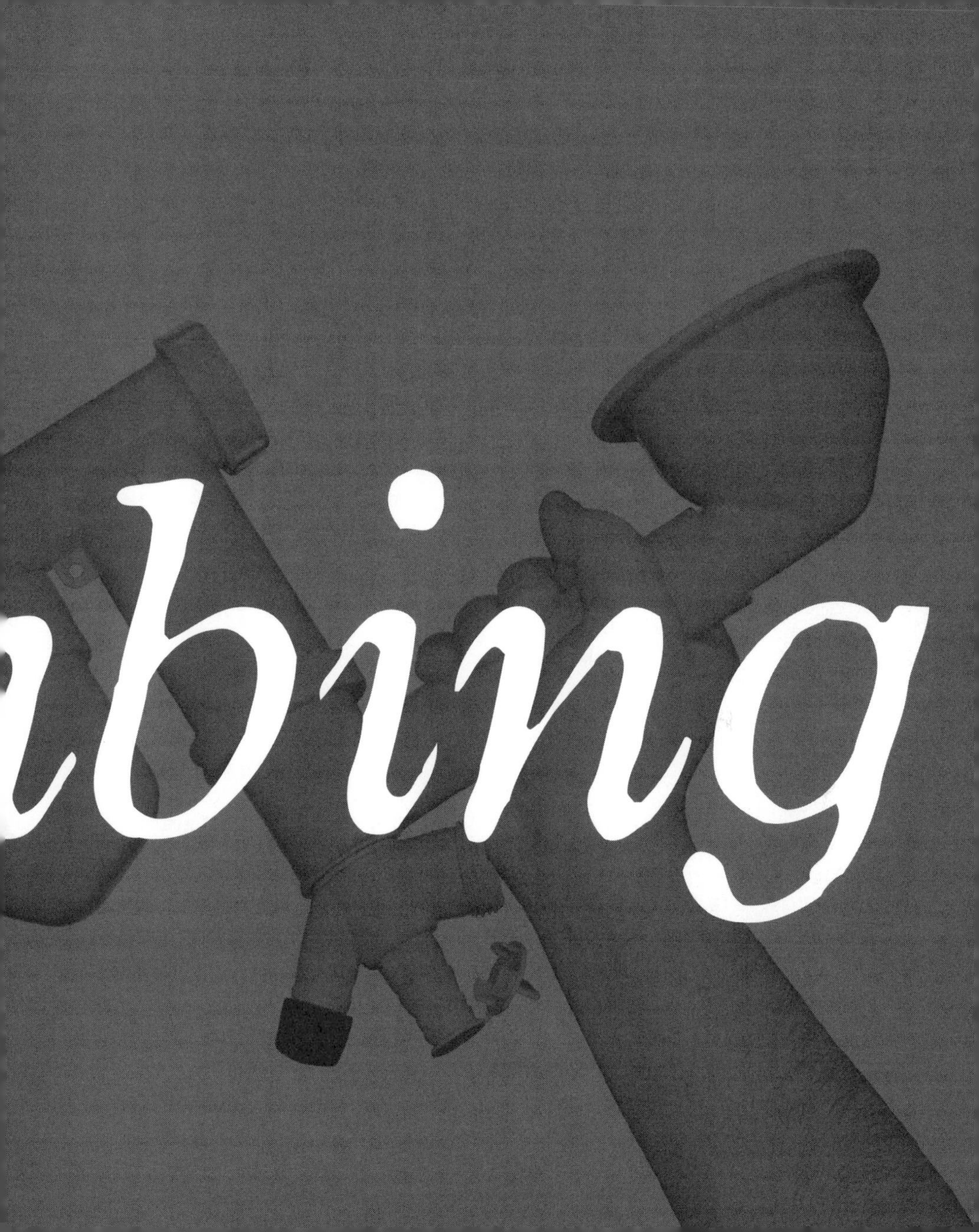
bing

QUESTION: What's deadlier when you're 35–59, irritable bowel syndrome, hot tap water, or spider bites? **ANSWER: If male, spider bites; if female, hot tap water**

Although irritable bowel syndrome kills more people than spiders, it does so later in life. In 2002 in the U.S., 4 men ages 35–59 died from spider bites versus 3 from hot tap water and none from irritable bowel syndrome; 4 women that age died from hot tap water and 3 from irritable bowel syndrome but none from spider bites.

Q What's deadlier, a gassy esophagus or stomach? **A: Stomach**

In 2001, 1,277 died in the U.S. from gastric ulcers versus 692 who died from acid reflux.

Q If kidney stones kill you, are you more likely to die in the U.S. or Mexico? **A: Mexico**

In 2001, 181 Mexicans died from kidney stones at a rate of .17 per 100,000 versus 252 Americans at a rate of .09.

Q Which U.S. state is #1 in deaths from chronic liver disease and cirrhosis? **A: New Mexico is #1 (16.5 per 100,000), followed by Nevada at #2 (14.2).**

Q How much higher are Native American death rates in New Mexico from chronic liver disease and cirrhosis than death rates from all New Mexico residents? **A: More than 156%**

In 2000–2002, the age-adjusted death rate was 45.7 per 100,000 Native Americans versus 17.8 per 100,000 New Mexico residents of all races.

Q What's more likely to kill you, not going to the bathroom or going too much? **A: Not going**

In the U.S. in 2003, 148 people died from constipation versus 51 from diabetes insipidus.

Q Which organ transplant has the highest patient survival rate? **A: Pancreas**

Pancreas transplant patients had a 90.6% 5-year survival rate in 2005 compared to heart transplant patients at 72.8%.

Q How much more likely are you to die from liver scar tissue (cirrhosis) versus heart scar tissue (causing angina pectoris) if you're Japanese? **A: 4 times**

In 2000, 12,018 Japanese died from cirrhosis of the liver versus 2,895 from heart scar tissue (causing angina pectoris).

Q Are you more likely to die of cirrhosis in Japan or the U.S.? **A: Japan**

In 2000, Japanese died at a rate of 9.4 per 100,000 population versus Americans who died at a rate of 7.5.

Bad Plumbing World Death Rates
by WHO Region (per 100,000 population)

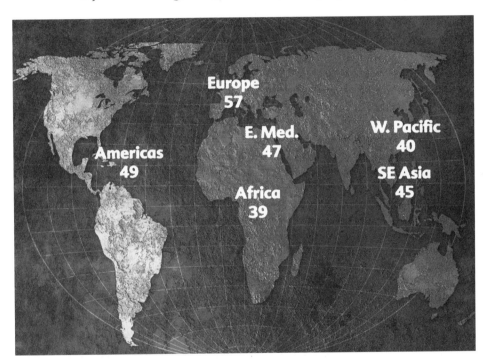

Europe 57

E. Med. 47

W. Pacific 40

Americas 49

SE Asia 45

Africa 39

BAD PLUMBING DEATHS, 2002—ALL AGES

Americas (incl USA): **418,793**

USA: **142,725***

Europe: **496,422**

E. Mediterranean: **234,546**

Africa: **262,495**

W. Pacific: **682,187**

Southeast Asia: **708,639**

* USA totals are for 2001.

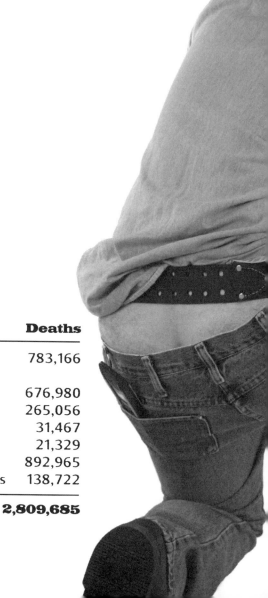

Digestive and Genitourinary Disease Deaths Worldwide, 2002

Disease	Deaths
Cirrhosis of the liver	783,166
Kidney damage (nephritis and nephrosis)	676,980
Peptic ulcer	265,056
Enlarged prostate	31,467
Appendicitis	21,329
Other digestive diseases	892,965
Other genitourinary diseases	138,722
TOTAL	**2,809,685**

THE PROCESS OF ELIMINATION

THIS section has nothing to do with dubious water treatment, polluted water, lead from pipes, or sewage-related diseases. We'll take those up elsewhere. This kind of "plumbing" is in your body from the waist down. Or maybe the waste down, since we're talking about the parts of our bodies that help us separate waste from the food and water we take in: fatal diseases of the stomach, intestines, kidneys, liver, genitals, and urinary tract. Cancers and childbirth-related deaths, though also concerned with these parts of the body, are covered in other chapters. So our process of editorial elimination leaves us here with the process of human elimination.

Note: All deaths cited are for 2001 in the U.S. and for 2002 in the world, unless otherwise noted

Quick & Dead Summary for the U.S.

142,725 Annual deaths from digestive-, urinary-, and genital-related problems

56 Percentage of those over age 75

Bad Plumbing Deaths by Cause:

41,573 Kidney disease/disorder

37,745 Liver-related

25,623 Bowel (intestine/appendix)

14,481 Bladder-related

6,892 Diseases of the pancreas and gallbladder

4,491 Stomach ulcers

972 Genital/reproductive-organ disease and disorders

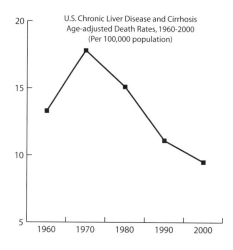

U.S. Chronic Liver Disease and Cirrhosis
Age-adjusted Death Rates, 1960-2000
(Per 100,000 population)

When Digestion Goes Bad

Esophagus

2,112 Number of U.S. non-cancer deaths from diseases of the esophagus (that tube from the back of your mouth to your stomach)

12,530 Number of deaths from esophageal cancer (see "Cancer" chapter)

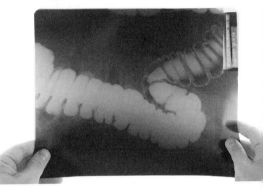

168 Number of deaths from esophagitis, an inflammation, irritation, or swelling of the esophagus. Causes can include acid reflux, ingestion of caustic chemicals, infections, and even getting pills stuck in the throat

15 Number of minutes doctors recommend waiting before lying down to prevent esophagitis, after washing pills down with an adequate amount of liquid

692 Number of U.S. deaths from gastroesopha-geal reflux disease (GERD), in which food and acid back up into the esophagus from the stomach. Besides causing esophagitis, GERD can burn a hole through the esophagus, leaking stomach contents into the chest cavity to fester and decay

85 Percentage of liver cirrhosis patients who also get esophageal vari-ces—like varicose veins in the esophagus—which can rupture and bleed. Rupturing varices are the single most common mechanism in deaths by cirrhosis

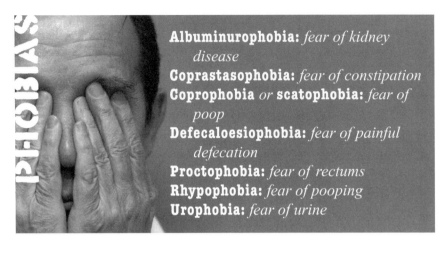

PHOBIAS

Albuminurophobia: *fear of kidney disease*
Coprastasophobia: *fear of constipation*
Coprophobia *or* **scatophobia:** *fear of poop*
Defecaloesiophobia: *fear of painful defecation*
Proctophobia: *fear of rectums*
Rhypophobia: *fear of pooping*
Urophobia: *fear of urine*

Stomach

5 Number of U.S. deaths from dyspepsia (indigestion)

4,491 Number of U.S. deaths from ulcers. It was once thought that ulcers came from stress, but the real culprit is a bacterium called *Helicobacter pylori.* Aspirin, alcohol, tobacco, and other drugs can make us more susceptible

375 Number of U.S. fatalities from an inflamed stomach (gastritis) or duodenum (duodenitis). The duodenum is the gateway from the stomach to the intestines

12,319 Number of U.S. deaths from stomach cancer

3,927 Number of U.S. deaths from noncancerous diseases of the pancreas, a gland that's situated near the stomach and secretes digestive juices into the

Euell Gibbons was a lifelong wild-foods and wilderness enthusiast known for such books as *Stalking the Wild Asparagus* and as a spokesperson for Post Grape-Nuts.

Despite his back-to-nature lifestyle, though, he died from a stomach ulcer. He strongly believed it wasn't his pine-nuts-and-tree-bark diet that led to the ulcer, but the aspirin he took to relieve his arthritis.

intestine through ducts. It also produces insulin

29,803 Number of U.S. fatalities attributed to pancreatic cancer

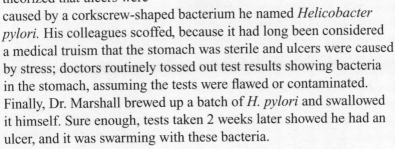

A Good Stomach for Medicine

In the early 1980s, Australian gastroenterologist Dr. Barry Marshall theorized that ulcers were caused by a corkscrew-shaped bacterium he named *Helicobacter pylori*. His colleagues scoffed, because it had long been considered a medical truism that the stomach was sterile and ulcers were caused by stress; doctors routinely tossed out test results showing bacteria in the stomach, assuming the tests were flawed or contaminated. Finally, Dr. Marshall brewed up a batch of *H. pylori* and swallowed it himself. Sure enough, tests taken 2 weeks later showed he had an ulcer, and it was swarming with these bacteria.

The actor/entertainer and world-famous juggler W. C. Fields is the stuff of legend. Known as a curmudgeon, he was also well-known for his alcoholism, which eventually led to bleeding in his stomach, kidney failure, and cirrhosis of the liver.

The Bile Organs

2-5 Range of weight in pounds for a normal human liver. This reddish brown, wedge-shaped organ is unique in that it can re-generate from as little as 25% of itself. It is possible to transplant part of a liver from a healthy donor and have it grow into a full liver

12,207 Number of U.S. deaths from alcoholic liver disease. Because a major function of the liver is to strain out impurities from food and drink, the liver is susceptible to being poisoned

14,828 Number of U.S. fatalities from all other chronic liver disease and cirrhosis

783,166 Number of worldwide deaths from cirrhosis of the liver. The highest rates of death from cirrhosis occur in Europe. The highest adult preva-lence of drinking alcohol in the world is also found in Europe

4,917 Number of Hungarian men who died from chronic liver disease and cirrhosis

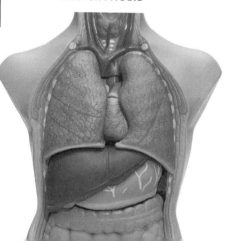

COMPARISON OF U.S. DEATH RATES
FOR LIVER DISEASE & CIRRHOSIS
(per 100,000 population by race & sex)

WHITE MALES	WHITE FEMALES	BLACK MALES	BLACK FEMALES
13.1	7.1	10.4	4.8

1 Rank of Hungary for liver-related deaths in Europe

101.2 Liver-related death rate per 100,000 men in Hungary

59.4 The same rate in Romania, second deadliest in Europe

50.3 The same rate in Slovenia, third

40.4 The same rate in Slovakia, fourth

3,922 Number of U.S. deaths from hepatic failure (meaning of the liver)

392,800 Estimated cost in dollars of a liver transplant in the U.S.

9,000 Number of U.S. liver transplants in a typical year, making it the second most-transplanted organ

1,031 Number of U.S. deaths from other diseases of the biliary system, including the liver, gallbladder and bile ducts (responsible for releasing digestion-aiding bile into the small intestine)

AVERAGE BILLED
COST OF ORGAN
TRANSPLANTS
IN THE U.S.

ORGAN	DOLLAR COST
Intestine	813,600
Heart	478,900
Liver	392,800
Single lung	299,900
Pancreas	270,800
Single kidney	210,000

2,965 Number of U.S. deaths from gallstones and related complications. The gallbladder stores bile from the liver until it's needed to digest fat. This process can be thwarted by hard depos-its of calcium, cholesterol, and bile salts, known as gallstones

13 Weight in pounds of the largest gallstone reported in medical history

The Bowels

28 Length in feet of the human intestine from stomach to anus, long enough to reach the ground from a typical third-story window

23 Length in feet of the "small" intenstine

5 Length in feet of the "large," or wider, intestine

11,865 Number of U.S. deaths from blockages in the mesenteric arteries that supply the intestines with blood (including death from constipation)

5,497 Number of U.S. deaths from inflammations of the intestines

3,428 Of these, number of deaths from diverticulitis, an inflammation of an abnormal pouch in the intestinal wall

5,248 Number of U.S. deaths from bowel obstructions

434 Number of deaths from anal and rectal abscesses. Another 20 die from tears to the anal mucous membrane

428 Number of deaths from appendix difficulties, most notably appendicitis

290 Number of deaths from intestinal

malabsorption, when otherwise well-fed people's bowels can't absorb nutrients

21 Number of deaths from irritable bowel syndrome

Urine Trouble Now

Kidneys and Bladder

39,480 Number of U.S. deaths from inflammatory and noninflammatory kidney disease (nephritis, nephretic syndrome, and nephrosis)

38,784 Number of those deaths resulting from renal failure

489 Number of deaths from bladder infections. Another 14 will die from abnormal narrowing of the urethra, a condition that can make urination difficult and sometimes impossible, causing death

269 Number of U.S. deaths from kidney stones

2 Worldwide rank of nephritis and nephrosis as cause of death from bad plumbing, following cirrhosis of the liver

676,980 Worldwide death toll from these diseases

16.0 Death rate of Chinese males per 100,000 from nephritic syndrome

13.1 The same death rate among U.S. males

4.7 The same death rate among Slovenian males

3.9 The same death rate among Hungarian males. There is no apparent correlation between cirrhosis death rates, alcohol consumption, and nephritic syndrome death rates

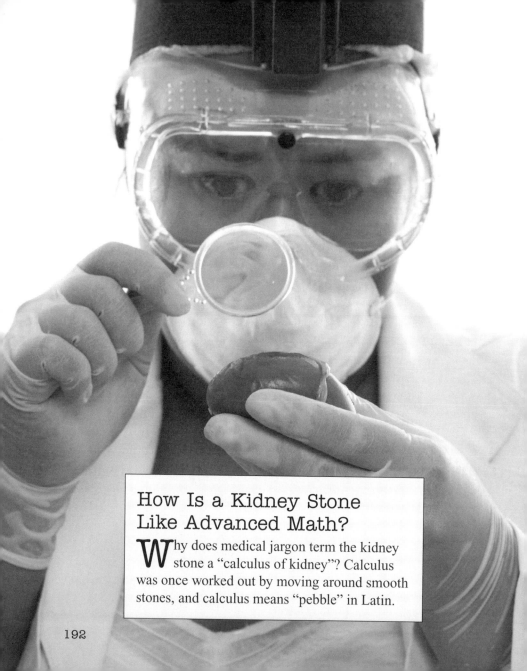

How Is a Kidney Stone Like Advanced Math?

Why does medical jargon term the kidney stone a "calculus of kidney"? Calculus was once worked out by moving around smooth stones, and calculus means "pebble" in Latin.

Danish astronomer Tycho Brahe was a proud man. While at university, he lost part of his nose in a duel with a fellow student; for the rest of his life he wore a metal replacement nose. His death was also one of proud correctness. He had failed to go to the lavatory before a long formal dinner, at which he consumed quite a lot of wine. He was too embarrassed to excuse himself during the meal; his bladder ruptured, killing him.

The Naughty Bits

Boy Parts

439 Number of U.S. deaths from enlarged prostate. Although prostate cancer is more deadly (see "Cancer" chapter), enlarged prostate is much more common

90 Percentage of men over 80 with an enlarged prostate, leading to an oft-repeated medical truism: "All men will have an enlarged prostate if they live long enough"

8 Number U.S. deaths from orchitis and epididymitis—

which sound as if they should be entries in a flower show, but in fact are respectively an inflammation of one or more testicles and of the epididymis (the tube

that connects the vas deferens with the testicles). Like orchitis, orchids get their name from the Latin word for testicles, because that's what their bulbs resemble

2 Number of U.S. males who died from hydrocele and spermatocele. Both are lumps in the scrotum. Hydroceles are sacks filled with fluids, and spermatoceles are cysts. Considering that testicular cancer, much more deadly, also appears as a scrotal lump, these are just 2 more reasons to engage in periodic male self-examination

Girl Parts

127 Number of U.S. deaths from inflammatory diseases of the pelvic organs. For the more deadly problems (for example, cancers, STDs, complications from childbirth) with female organs (see chapters "Cancer," "Bugs," and "Childbearing")

8 Number of U.S. deaths from menopausal disorders

3 Number of U.S. deaths from endometriosis, in which the tissue that normally lines the uterus grows in other areas of the body

Most at Risk of Premature Death from Bad Plumbing

WORLDWIDE DEATH RATES, 2002
(per 100,000 population)

AGE	MALE	FEMALE
0–4	18.1	24.6
5–14	3.7	5.5
15–29	8.6	8.1
30–44	26.2	14.7
45–59	88.8	51.3
60–69	185.9	119.1
70+	446.1	348.4

Main Cause

Problems with liver and kidneys

Prevention

- DON'T DRINK TOO MUCH ALCOHOL
- WATCH YOUR DIET
- WASH YOUR HANDS
- GET REGULAR MEDICAL EXAMINATIONS

Horr

#9 Cause of premature death in the world
2002 (under age 70)

#6 Cause of premature death in the USA
2001 (under age 75)

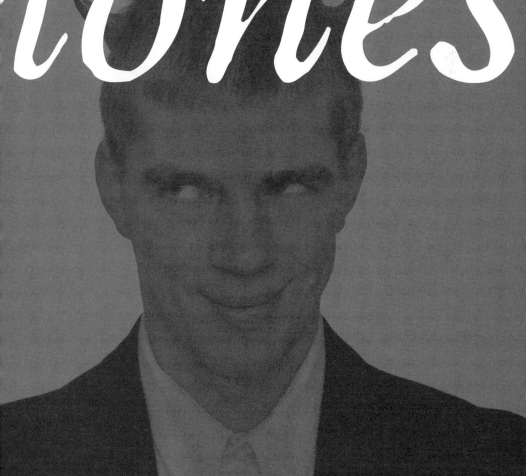

QUESTION: What's more likely to kill you, sugary soda pop or salty steak? **ANSWER: Steak**

> The odds of an American male dying from a heart attack in his lifetime is 1 in 20 versus 1 in 67 from diabetes.

Are you more likely to die from not sleeping or sleeping too much? **A: Sleeping too much**

> In the U.S., 5 people died in 2001 from narcolepsy versus 3 from insomnia.

Are you more likely to die if you have too much or too little pituitary growth hormone? **A: Too little**

> Although both diseases are rare, 83 people in the U.S. died of growth hormone deficiency versus 17 who died of an excess in 2001.

Is a man's peak testosterone age also when he is at highest risk for murder? **A: Yes**

> Male testosterone levels hit their peak at age 17, and the age when men have the highest rate for murder is 15–29.

Are you more likely to die choking on food or being fat?

A: Being fat (if you're under age 50)

> If you're 45–59 in the U.S. you're 4 times more likely to die from obesity than choking, but that changes as you age. When you're 75–79, you're nearly 3 times more likely to die choking.

How much more likely are you to die of pancreatic disorders versus pancreatic cancer? **A: 4 times**

> In the world, 986,837 people died from diabetes (a pancreatic disorder) versus 229,399 who died of pancreatic cancer.

Which is more frequently lethal, the female or male sex organs?

A: Male

> In the U.S. in 2004, 29,632 males died of afflictions to the sex organs (98% from prostate cancer, with only 3 deaths from hormonal testicular dysfunction) versus 27,051 females (54% ovarian cancer, 25% uterine cancer, 14% cervical cancer, with only 2 deaths from hormonal ovarian dysfunction).

Hormone World Death Rates
by WHO Region (per 100,000 population)

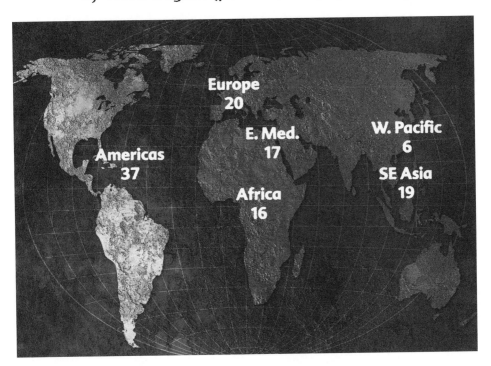

HORMONES DEATHS, 2002—ALL AGES

Americas (incl USA): **314,564**

USA: **102,369***

Europe: **174,571**

E. Mediterranean: **83,926**

Africa: **105,490**

W. Pacific: **243,363**

Southeast Asia: **243,363**

* USA totals are for 2001.

Diabetes and Other Endocrine Disorder Deaths Worldwide, 2002

Disease	Deaths
Diabetes	986,837
Glandular disorders excluding cancer (pancreas and thyroid, etc.)	242,704
TOTAL	**1,229,541**

THE WORD

hormones is often used to explain and even brush aside our moods, feelings, and behavior. But it can be disconcerting to realize that our endocrine systems are constantly dosing us with powerful chemicals and mind-altering substances. Hormones regulate our growth, gender development, immune systems, and blood sugar. They prepare us for fight-or-flight decisions. They help keep us besmitten even when our adorable offspring are squalling and ill-tempered. They keep us sexually attracted to our mates. But hormones also have their downside. Is it really necessary for teens to get so many of the love-crazy and broodiness hormones? Do we really need those cyclical hormones that accentuate our moodiness, prickliness, competitiveness, aggressiveness, mean-spiritedness, and depression?

And that's just when things are working well. When our glands over- or underproduce hormones, it means all kinds of trouble. In fact, it can kill us. Some of our glandular difficulties are out of our control. Some are not. Some can be mitigated with medication. Some can't. It's what makes living in our bodies one gland adventure after another.

MAJOR ENDOCRINE GLANDS

- PINEAL
- HYPOTHALAMUS
- PITUITARY
- THYROID
- PARATHYROID
- THYMUS
- ADRENALS
- PANCREAS
- GONADS

A GLAND ILLUSION

Quick & Dead Summary for the U.S.

102,369 Number of Americans who died from hormone-related causes

52 Percent of those over age 75

71,372 Of all hormonal deaths, the number who died from diabetes

20,686 From other endocrine disorders

4,345 From anemia (for nutritional-deficiency-caused anemia see the "Starvation" chapter)

3,372 From pancreatic gland disorders

1,918 From thyroid gland disorders

338 From adrenal gland disorders

334 From other pituitary gland disorders

Endocrine Times

9 Number of glands, designed to drip hormones into the blood or lymph systems: the adrenals, gonads (testes/ovaries), hypothalamus, pancreas, parathyroid, pineal, pituitary, thymus, and thyroid

1,229,541 Number of people worldwide who died from endocrine malfunctions

80 Percentage of those deaths caused by diabetes

1905 Year the word *hormone* was coined by

Cambridge physiologist William Hardy. The Greek *hormaein* means "set something in motion," which is essentially what hormones do

75 Percentage of all hormonal deaths in people over 60

11 Percentage of all hormonal deaths in people under 44

55 Percentage of annual worldwide endocrine deaths among females

54 The same percentage in the U.S.

AGE	HORMONAL DEATH %
0—4	4
5—44	8
45—59	17
60—69	23
70+	48

Adrenal Rush

2 Number of adrenal glands in your body, each perching on top of a kidney, to produce the steroid and adrenaline hormones that affect stress response, sexual development, metabolism, the immune system, and your body's balance of salt and water

7 Number of U.S. deaths from Addison's disease, a shortage of the adrenal hormone cortisol

22 Number of U.S. deaths from Cushing's syndrome, caused by too much cortisol

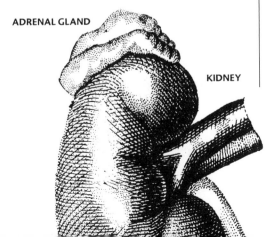

ADRENAL GLAND

KIDNEY

Gonads Over Easy

2 Number of gonads in the human body. Gonads—testes in men, ovaries in women—are simultaneously organs and endocrine glands for sex hormones. Men's testes pump out androgens (chiefly testosterone). Women's ovaries produce estrogen and progesterone. After conception, the same cluster of cells develop into either testes or ovaries as the fetus develops its gender characteristics

3 to 1 Ratio by which women die from ovarian disorders compared to men dying from testicular disorders

17 Age when testosterone levels hit their peak in young men; they slowly start to slide in the 30s and 40s

50 Percentage at age 80 of typical testosterone production compared to age 17

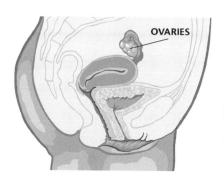

OVARIES

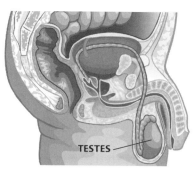

TESTES

AGE GROUP, WORLD MALES	HOMICIDES PER 100,000
0–4	5.8
5–14	2.1
15–29	19.4
30–44	18.7
45–59	14.8
60+	13.0

Hypothalamus

1/4 Diameter in inches of the pea-size hypothalamus, a gland that sits behind the eyes and exerts influence over the pituitary gland, which in turn stimulates the gonads to make sex hormones. The hypothalamus also helps regulate weight and appetite, body temperature, salt in the body, emotions, sleep, growth, childbirth, and milk production

3 Number of U.S. deaths from insomnia. Most major sleep disorders are hormonally based, and the hypothalamus is a key player in regulating sleep

5 Number of U.S. deaths from narcolepsy and cataplexy

474 Number of U.S. deaths from sleep apnea (see "Bad Wiring" for more information on sleep disorders)

Flash in the Pancreas

2 Number of vitally important hormones produced by the pancreas. Insulin and glucagon regulate sugar levels in the blood

171 million Number of people worldwide who have diabetes, caused by too little insulin. This figure is expected to more than double to 366 million by 2030

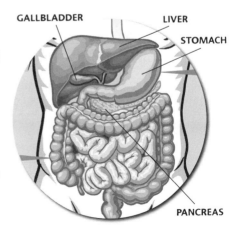

GALLBLADDER
LIVER
STOMACH
PANCREAS

Fats & Fictions

Obesity is a serious health problem for a number of reasons. One of them is the markedly increased chances of getting type 2 diabetes. Once a mostly exclusive malady of fat adults, type 2 has reached down to embrace overweight children as well.

3,139 Number of U.S. deaths directly attributed to obesity. Excessive body fat is also the #1 cause of diabetes, and a contributing factor in heart disease and other grave ills, so the actual number of deaths is almost certainly higher

27 Percentage increase in U.S. meat consumption between 1990 and 2003

31 Percentage of U.S. high school students who did not engage in recommended amounts of physical activity in 2001

138 Percentage increase in obese Americans ages 20–74 from the early 1960s to 2000

31 Percentage of obese Americans at the end of the twentieth century

230 Percentage increase of U.S. per capita consumption of high-fructose corn syrup between 1980 and 2002

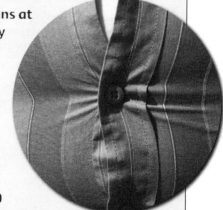

63 Pounds of high-fructose corn syrup consumed per American in 2002

19 Pounds consumed in 1980

Losing Our Cash

Diabetes can be controlled over a lifetime through diet and injected insulin. Johnny Cash, for example, lived 71 years before diabetic complications killed him in 2003.

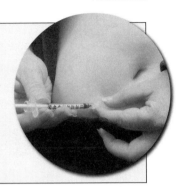

986,837 Number of deaths worldwide from diabetes

74,744 Number of U.S. deaths from pancreatic disorders

71,372 Of these, from diabetes

3 Number of major insulin-based diabetes types. Type 1, usually diagnosed in childhood, is the result of the pancreas making little or no insulin. In type 2, the pancreas stops making enough insulin; it usually appears in adults, though childhood obesity is bringing it on earlier. Type 3, gestational diabetes, can appear during pregnancy

90 Percentage of diabetes cases that are type 2 diabetes. Many of its victims die from it before they discover that they have it

1.7 times Increased odds of diabetes for Hispanic Americans over white Americans

1.8 times For African Americans

2.2 times For Native Americans

226 Average daily U.S. deaths from diabetes during February, the deadliest

82,000 Number of lower-limb amputations performed on American diabetics in 2002

1 Ranking of West Virginia in death rate from diabetes per 100,000, followed by Louisiana, Ohio, and North Dakota

50 Ranking of Alaska in diabetes death rate. The next lowest states are Colorado, Nevada, and Hawaii

single month. Cold weather seems to bring on more diabetes deaths: After February's peak, the figures drop during March and April

180 Average daily U.S. deaths from diabetes during August, the month with the lowest rate. Warm weather seems to decrease the number of diabetes deaths: The next lowest months are July and June

4 times Increased odds of dying from heart disease for an adult diabetic, compared to an adult nondiabetic

1 in 1,000 Proportion of infants, children, and adults afflicted with hypoglycemia, a disease in which blood sugar is abnormally low (the opposite of diabetes). Ironically, most hospital emergency treatment is for diabetics reacting to insulin taken to reduce their blood sugar levels

17 The number of annual U.S. deaths that occur after a nondiabetic hypoglycemic coma

Parathyroid

114 Number of U.S. deaths from malfunctions of the parathyroid gland. Located next to the thyroid in the front and base of the neck, the parathyroid regulates the balance of calcium, magnesium, and phosphorus in blood and bones

14 Of the above deaths, the number caused by hypoparathyroidism, or an underperforming parathyroid

100 The number caused by hyperparathyroidism, or an overachieving parathyroid

Pineal Cone

1 Number of hormones that we definitely know come from the pineal, a cone-shaped gland hiding behind the third ventricle of the brain. It isn't yet understood perfectly, but we do know that the pineal secretes melatonin directly into the spinal fluid, which eventually takes the hormone into the bloodstream to regulate wake/sleep patterns, seasonal adjustment, and parts of the reproductive system

PINEAL GLAND

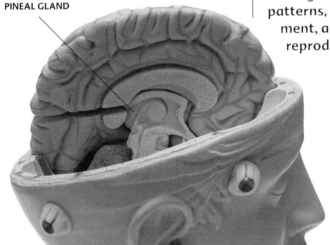

Pituitary the King

3 Functions of the pituitary, a pea-size gland at the base of the brain. The anterior lobe pumps out hormones for growth, giving milk, and stimulating the adrenal, thyroid, ovaries, and/or testes. The intermediate lobe controls skin pigmentation. And the posterior lobe controls the kidneys' absorption of water from the blood and, after childbirth, contracts the uterus and stimulates milk flow

1 in 250,000 Proportion of people who suffer from

The Long and Short of It

The pituitary gland controls growth hormones. Too much of it can cause gigantism; too little, dwarfism.

- The tallest documented human, measuring 8 feet, 11.1 inches, Robert Wadlow of Indiana died at age 28 from complications of his great height. Doctors blamed a tumor on his pituitary gland.
- The shortest documented adult human: at 22.5 inches, Gul Mohammed of India. He died at age 40 in 1997 from smoking-related lung problems.

diabetes insipidus, which has nothing to do with the insulin-related diabetes diseases. It is caused by a lack of the vasopressin hormone from the pituitary gland, preventing the kidneys from retaining enough water, making the victim perpetually thirsty

5 Gallons of urine a DI sufferer may pass in a 24-hour period. Diabetes insipidus is treatable and not usually fatal

Thymus

15 Percentage of its original size the thymus shrinks to by middle age. Located just below the neck, this gland produces hormones that stimulate the protection of infection-fighting cells—the most famous of which are white blood cells known as T cells

3,076 Number of U.S. deaths from white-blood-cell disorders, including 87 people who died from hemophilia type A, the genetic disorder that infected most of the royal families of Europe, thanks to Queen Victoria, who was a carrier

1 in 5,000 Rate of occurrence of hemophilia type A in men. The disorder is caused by an inherited defective gene on the X chromosome, so it occurs primarily in males

538 Number of deaths from immunodeficiency. This number includes cases in which the primary cause is genetic such as severe combined immuno-deficiency

12 Number of years "Bubble Boy" David Vetter lived in a plastic, germ-free bubble—before he died of SCID

Thyroid

2 Number of lobes in the thyroid, a butterfly-shaped organ that cocoons around the neck's trachea. The thyroid's follicles produce thyroxine and tripodothyronine, which help regulate metabolism

1,540 Number of U.S. deaths from hypothyroidism, in which the thyroid doesn't produce enough hormones, slowing energy-burning to dangerously lethargic rates

281 Number of U.S. deaths from hyperthyroidism, in which the thyroid produces too much, burning up energy faster than it should

1 in 3,000 Proportion of babies born with incomplete thyroid development

2 to 1 Proportion of girl babies to boy babies born with the condition. Most afflicted newborns show few or no symptoms because their thyroid hormones are only slightly deficient. Those who are profoundly hypothyroidal, however, often behave sluggishly and develop a distinctive puffy face, dull eyes, and large, protruding tongue

5–8 times Increased odds of thyroid problems among women compared to men

20 million Estimated number of Americans who currently have some sort of thyroid disease

44 Number of annual U.S. deaths from goiters, thyroid glands that have become enlarged in an effort to pump out more hormones. Chances are increased among those with a family history of goiters, an iodine deficiency, and females

85 Percentage of hyperthyroidism patients with Graves' disease

2 Percentage of women who experience Graves' disease, usually between age 20 and 40. It's an autoimmune disease that causes an overactive thyroid, producing symptoms including trouble sleeping, irritability, rapid heartbeat, trembling hands, conception difficulties, and lightened menstrual flow. It can cause bulging eyes, a swelling of the tissue around them, and a lumpy reddening of the shin skin. Extreme cases left untreated can be fatal

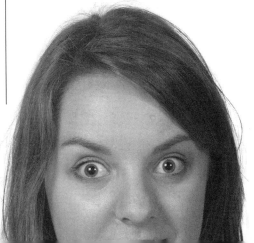

PHOBIAS:

Diabetophobia: *fear of diabetes*
Iatrophobia: *fear of doctors*
Nosemaphobia: *fear of becoming ill*
Nosocomephobia: *fear of hospitals*
Obesophobia: *fear of gaining weight*
Pathophobia: *fear of disease*
Patroiophobia: *fear of heredity*
Tabophobia: *fear of a wasting sickness*

Other Endocrine Ends

242,705 Number of worldwide deaths from other endocrine disorders, including nonnutritional-related anemia deaths. This is in addition to the 474,666 worldwide deaths from nutritional deficiencies (see "Starvation" chapter)

20,686 Number of U.S. deaths that fall into the CDC category "Other Endocrine Disorders"

15,697 Number of U.S. deaths from metabolic disorders. This includes 4,503 deaths from dehydration, 482 deaths from cystic fibrosis, and 1 from lactose intolerance

4,345 Number of U.S. deaths from non-nutritional anemias (see iron-deficiency-anemia deaths in the "Starvation" chapter) that are affected by endocrinal factors. This includes 475 anemia deaths from sickle-cell disorders and 21 from thalassemia, an inherited disorder of the blood

Most at Risk of Premature Death from Hormones

WORLDWIDE DEATH RATES, 2002
(per 100,000 population)

AGE	MALE	FEMALE
0–4	6.9	7.8
5–14	.8	.8
15–29	1.8	1.8
30–44	4.8	4.3
45–59	24.8	23.6
60–69	76.6	84.5
70+	207.4	215.6

Main Cause

Diabetes

Prevention

■ WATCH YOUR DIET

■ GET EXERCISE

■ GET REGULAR MEDICAL EXAMINATIONS

#1 Cause of premature death in the world
2002 (under age 70)

#7 Cause of premature death in the USA
2001 (under age 75)

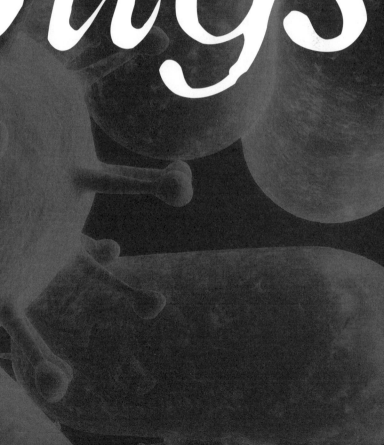

Bugs

QUESTION: How much deadlier is the human penis than the mosquito's beak? **ANSWER: 2 times**

In the world in 2002, 3 million people died from HIV/AIDS and other sexually transmitted diseases versus 1.2 million from malaria and dengue fever.

Are you more likely to die salmon fishing or from salmonella? **A: Fishing**

62 fishermen died in the U.S. in 2001 versus 41 deaths from salmonella.

What kills more, your tabby cat or your tampon? **A: Tampon**

2001 U.S. toxic-shock deaths were 36 male and 39 female, approximately 50% from tampons, versus 16 from toxoplasmosis (8 male/8 female).

What's worse for baby, a runny nose or a running car?

A: Runny nose

In the U.S. in 2001, 299 children under age 1 died from flu and pneumonia while 144 died in motor vehicle accidents.

Are you more likely to die of HIV/AIDS in the world if you're 45–59 or 0–4? **A: 0–4**

Children have a higher death rate from HIV in the world than older people, although the highest rates are ages 30–44.

Which bug kills more people in the U.S., bacterium, virus, fungus, parasite, or prion? **A: Bacterium**

Bacterial blood poisoning kills more than the human immunodeficiency virus (HIV).

Which plant kills more per year, a poisonous mushroom or the common rose? **A: The rose**

Although only 1 death was reported in the U.S. from pulmonary sporotrichosis (otherwise known as rose gardener's disease) in 2001, hundreds die annually versus the 1 death per year on average from eating poisonous mushrooms.

Are you more likely to die in the U.S. of Lyme disease if you live in the East or West? **A: East**

In 2002, there were 6 deaths from Lyme disease: 1 in Indiana, 2 in Minnesota, 2 in Missouri, and 1 in Pennsylvania. Ticks primarily feed off mice (which are Lyme carriers) in the East, versus lizards (which don't get infected) in the West.

Bugs World Death Rates
by WHO Region (per 100,000 population)

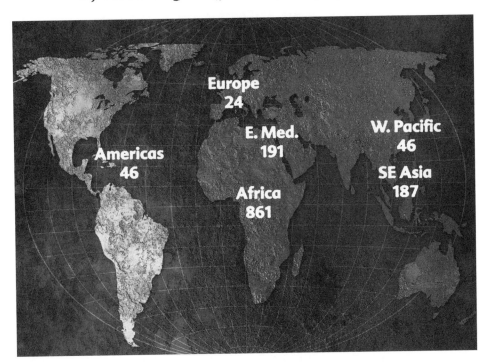

Europe
24

E. Med.
191

W. Pacific
46

Americas
46

SE Asia
187

Africa
861

BUGS DEATHS, 2002—ALL AGES

Americas (incl USA):
394,598

USA: **61,370***

Europe: **211,046**

E. Mediterranean: **959,145**

Africa: **5,786,522**

W. Pacific: **793,528**

Southeast Asia: **2,967,504**

* USA totals are for 2001.

Parasitic and Infectious Disease Deaths Worldwide, 2002

Disease	Deaths
HIV/AIDS	2,821,472
Diarrhea	1,767,326
Tuberculosis	1,604,819
Childhood cluster (measles, tetanus, whooping cough, diptheria, polio)	1,360,278
Malaria	1,222,180
STDs (syphilis, chlamydia, gonorrhea)	179,697
Meningitis	173,152
Hepatitis	156,265
Tropical cluster (leishmaniasis, trypanosomiasis, schistosomiasis, Chagas')	129,503
Dengue fever	18,565
Japanese encephalitis	13,957
Intestinal nematode infections (ascariasis, trichuriasis, hookworm)	11,771
Leprosy	6,168
Other	1,656,978
TOTAL	**11,122,131**

WHEN surgeon Joseph Lister presented his controversial theory in 1877—that deadly infections were caused by microscopic organisms—his colleagues ridiculed him. "Where are these little beasts?" heckled a prominent surgeon. "Show them to us and then we'll believe in them. Has anyone seen them yet?"

Actually, a number of people had, starting with Antoni van Leeuwenhoek in 1642, who saw microbes swimming around under his pioneering microscope and exclaimed, "Hundreds of little beasties!" But as late as the nineteenth century, the best medical minds still believed that sickness came from bad air or an imbalance of the "four humours."

By now, we understand that the "little beasties" kill more people than anything else; we know them as bacteria, viruses, fungi, parasites, protozoa, prions, and worms. But good health requires us to embrace them, at least in small quantities: that is the theory behind vaccination. For a healthy immune system that's ready to spring into action and repel sickness, you can't live in a clean and sterile atmosphere. We can't always live with these little beasties, but we can't live without 'em, either.

LITTLE BEASTIES

Note: All deaths cited are for 2001 in the U.S. and 2002 in the world, unless otherwise noted

Quick & Dead Summary for the U.S.

61,370 Number of U.S. deaths from "bugs"—not insects, but microscopic beasties; 39% or 24,260 are over age 75. This is not a complete count of all bug-related deaths. For example, the figure for annual flu deaths is included in the "Bad Breath" chapter

37,231 Number of U.S. deaths from diseases and infections caused by bacteria

21,895 Number who died from viruses

1,389 From fungi

635 From parasites

220 From prions

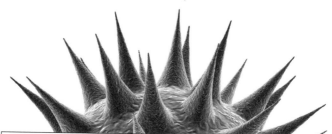

TOP 5 MOST LETHAL BUGS IN THE U.S., 2001

RANK	TYPE OF DISEASE	DEATHS
1	Blood poisoning (septicemia)	32,238
2	HIV/AIDS	14,175
3	Hepatitis	6,105
4	Tuberculosis	764
5	Meningitis	727

BACTERIA

1,000 Number of bacteria in a single line that could fit across the top of a pencil eraser. Most bacteria are harmless, and many are beneficial (for example, the ones that change milk to yogurt, make soil fertile, or live in your intestines and help you digest food)

3/4 Percentage of earth's total history in which bacteria have been present. These single-celled creatures have adapted to every natural environment, making them by far the most populous species on earth

Reality Bites

Forget the myth about how clean a pet's mouth is: dog and cat bites contain more than a hundred kinds of bacteria that can make you sick, including the most common bacteria that cause meningitis and blood infections.

Anthrax

1 Number of U.S. anthrax deaths among humans. It is much more common among sheep, cattle, goats, and other wild and domesticated animals and can infect humans exposed to sick animals

Blood Poisoning

32,238 Number of U.S. deaths from bacterial blood poisoning. Called septicemia, this poisoning can quickly spread from bacterial infections anywhere in the body

88 Percentage of those deaths in people 55 or older

60 Percentage of those deaths that occur in a hospital or medical center

Bubonic Plague

1,000 BC Estimated date of first account of the bubonic plague, found in the Hebrew scriptures' book of Samuel. The villain is the *Yersinia pestis* bacterium

1 in 3 Proportion of Athenians, including the famous statesman and general Pericles, who were killed by what is believed to be the bubonic plague in 430 BC

60 Number of years that an epidemic of bubonic plague reigned during the sixth century AD, killing millions of people in the lands around the Mediterranean Sea

25 Estimated percentage of Europe's 80 million

Epidemic or Pandemic: What's the Diff?

It's essentially a matter of scale. *Epidemic*, from the Greek *epi* and *demos* or "upon people," means an unexpected level of illness among a specific population, as small as a tribe or as large as the earth. *Pandemic*, from the Greek for "all" and "people," denotes an epidemic that covers an extensive geographical area.

population wiped out by another major bubonic pandemic during the fourteenth century. This "Black Death" was part of a 400-year plague that ebbed and flowed through Africa, Asia, and Europe from the mid-1300s until the mid-1700s

6 Number of reported bubonic plague deaths worldwide from 1998 to 2000. This is, we hope, the tail end of a pandemic that first struck in Hong Kong in 1894 and then spread to all continents, killing millions. Today, the disease can be treated with antibiotics (see "Rats" in the "Accidents—Flora & Fauna" chapter for more information)

Sometimes Fiction Is Stranger Than Truth

Pyotr Tchaikovsky, composer of the holiday standard ballet *The Nutcracker*, died of cholera when he accidentally drank contaminated water. Or, at least, that's the official story. In recent decades, however, rumors have abounded that Tchaikovsky actually took his own life with arsenic and covered up the evidence by drinking tainted water. As the story goes, Tchaikovsky was caught in a relationship with the tsar of Russia's nephew. When his peers discovered letters between the two, they confronted Tchaikovsky and determined he must kill himself to keep this secret. It's a dramatic story, and certainly true that Tchaikovsky struggled with his homosexuality, but unlikely. Drinking contaminated water was not uncommon in that day, particularly during cholera outbreaks. And homosexual acts in the upper classes weren't so uncommon either. Most likely the official story is, indeed, official.

Cholera

100 times Factor by which cholera becomes more infectious after passing through the human body, according to experiments with mice. The theory is that a genetic "switch" may be activated when the bacteria detach from intestinal walls

5 Number of hours that human-activated cholera can remain infectious in a pond. After that time, the bacteria wait in a less infectious state until someone drinks the water and begins the process over again

1 Amount of liquid in liters that the body can lose per hour from diarrhea caused by cholera. Losing 5–10 liters can be fatal if the water, salts, and sugars are not replaced fast enough. Of untreated cases, 50% can be fatal, but that rate falls below 1% if a cocktail of water and electrolytes are provided. Children are especially prone to cholera death

2,728 Number of cholera deaths reported worldwide from 184,311 cases, a survival rate of 98.52%

Diarrhea–Antibiotic

1,332 Number of U.S. deaths from antibiotic-associated diarrhea because hospitals began routinely giving antibiotics before medical operations. Our natural intestinal bacteria are in balance; antibiotics kill off most of them but not *Clostridium difficile,* which creates a substance that can inflame and infect the intestinal walls. Three million cases of diarrhea occur from this annually in the U.S., making it the most common cause of serious diarrhea in hospitals

Diphtheria

5,440 Number of world deaths from diphtheria, a bacterium that easily spreads by respiratory droplets as well as contaminated food. Once inside the body, the bacteria's toxin can spread to the heart and nervous system with lethal results

0 Number of U.S. diphtheria fatalities in a typical year. Thanks to the DTP (diphtheria, tetanus, and pertussis) vaccine regularly given to young children, the last U.S. fatality was in 1999

E. coli

6 Number of U.S. deaths from *Escherichia coli*. Although hundreds of strains of *E. coli* are in the healthy human body's intestines, the one called enterotoxic *E. coli* produces a powerful toxin that can cause severe illness. It can come from contaminated ground beef, raw milk, or contaminated water

Legionnaires' Disease

70 Number of U.S. deaths from *Legionella pneumophila*, a bacterium that can survive in warm, moist air-conditioning systems of large buildings and infect the lungs

1976 Year of the first known outbreak of Legionnaires' disease. It occurred during an American Legion convention in Philadelphia. Of the 221 victims, 34 died

Leprosy

6,168 Number of worldwide leprosy deaths, from 763,917 new cases reported. The slow-acting bacteria that cause the disease can take as long as 20 years to appear

1 Number of U.S. leprosy deaths. If diagnosed early, the disease can be treated with antibiotics. Otherwise, patients can be plagued with skin lesions, plaques and overgrowths, nerve damage, and even death

2 Number of nonhuman animals that scientists know can harbor the leprosy bacterium: armadillos and mice

600 BC Date of the first written documentation of leprosy, which has been around from ancient times in China, Egypt, and India. Biblical references to "lepers" are believed to be mistranslations of terms that refer to any disfiguring skin diseases

Lyme Disease

2 Number of U.S. deaths from Lyme disease, caused by bacteria transmitted by infected deer ticks (for more information, see "Ticks" in the "Accidents— Flora & Fauna" chapter)

Meningitis

762 Number of U.S. deaths from meningitis, an infection of the spinal cord and brain fluid. It can be contracted from several bacteria or viruses, but the bacterial form is more dangerous. Some are contagious by way of coughs, kisses, and pet bites

173,152 Number of meningitis deaths worldwide. Meningitis can also cause

brain and nerve damage and hearing loss. If caught in time, the bacteria can be killed with antibiotics

The Infectious Charms of Mary Mallon

Mary Mallon, a New York City cook, was a typhus carrier. Although she herself never exhibited symptoms, she spread typhoid disease to the affluent families she cooked for between 1900 and 1906—when, after noticing the pattern of sickness, health authorities quarantined her. Released in 1910 with the understanding that she was not to go back to food handling, she was again discovered working as a cook in 1915. She was arrested and quarantined until her death in 1938. "Typhoid Mary" had been responsible for infecting 47 people, 3 of whom died.

Salmonella

580 Estimated number of U.S. deaths from the Salmonella bacteria, including deaths categorized as "other"

41 Number of reported U.S. salmonella deaths. The diarrhea-causing bacterium

comes from the feces of people and other animals, so you can catch it from baby-occupied swimming pools, people, bathrooms, pets, chickens, reptiles, and uncomposted natural fertilizer. Most often it is spread through contaminated foods (for more information see "Chickens" in the "Accidents—Flora & Fauna" chapter)

0 What salmonella has to do with salmon. Fish don't carry salmonella bacteria in their intestines. The name honors American pathologist Daniel Elmer Salmon (1850–1914)

1,767,326 Number of worldwide diarrheal deaths, mostly children.

Besides salmonella, this includes other bacterial diseases such as cholera, botulism, *E. coli,* and campylobacter enteritis, as well as viruses and parasites

2,119 Number of known worldwide typhoid deaths. The disease is highly contagious and caused by *Salmonella typhi*

A Bacterium Is What Got Him

You'd think big-time gangster Al Capone would've gone down in a shoot-out with the Feds, guns blazing. Not such a glorious ending as all that for Scarface. It was syphilis—contracted from his girlfriend and former prostitute in one of Capone's brothels—that finally did him in.

Sex, Lives, and Bacteria

36 Number of U.S. deaths from syphilis. It can easily be cured by antibiotics if caught within the first year. Still, there were 156,927 worldwide deaths

9.1 Rate of death from syphilis in 1935 per 100,000 U.S. population

0.0 Rate of death from syphilis in 2001

9,415 Number of deaths from chlamydia worldwide. U.S. deaths are nearly nil. Untreated, the bacteria can lead to infertility, premature delivery, and infant blindness or pneumonia

7 Number of U.S. deaths from gonorrhea. Worldwide, there were 959 deaths

500 Percentage increase in cases of children born with syphilis in Baltimore from 1995 to 1996 due to a crack cocaine epidemic that caused a dramatic increase in risky sexual behavior. Still, in all of the U.S. in 1996 there were only 73 deaths attributed to syphilis, 18 of which were congenital

Strep

80 Minimum number of different types of streptococcal bacteria just waiting to invade nearly every part of the body

3 Number of U.S. deaths from scarlet fever, a streptococcal disease related to strep throat. Other strep bacteria can cause kidney disease, infections in the urinary tract, heart, spine, lungs, blood, and skin (impetigo and "flesh-eating disease"). One strain of strep also causes tooth decay

Emerging Bugs

When a scary bug arrives on the horizon, it's hard to know if it is fated to become a worldwide menace (such as HIV) or fizzle out without much impact (such as swine flu in the 1970s, in which the mass inoculation killed more people than the disease). Here are some of our newly emerging or reemerging bugs:

WEST NILE VIRUS Long common in Africa, West Asia, and the Middle East, this mosquito-borne disease arrived in New York City in 1999.

HEPATITIS C VIRUS First identified in 1989, hepatitis C now causes about 20% of all acute viral liver disease in the U.S., leading to 8,000–10,000 deaths and 1,000 liver transplants a year.

THE O157:H7 STRAIN OF E. COLI BACTERIA First recognized in 1982, about 10–15% of infected people—particularly children and the elderly—come down with hemolytic uremic syndrome, a serious complication that can lead to kidney failure and death.

HANTAVIRUS pulmonary syndrome is an often-fatal lung disease that first appeared in 1993 in the southwest U.S. with the rise of the rodent population attributed to climatic changes.

LYME DISEASE emerged in the northeast U.S. in 1975, spread by deer ticks.

As this is written, a BIRD FLU from Asia is spreading around the world, with scientists publicly warning about a pandemic that could spread like wildfire if the virus mutates into a form that can travel from human to human.

Tetanus

292,478 Number of worldwide tetanus deaths. Spores of the *Clostridium tetani* bacteria can live in the soil and enter the human body through punctures and wounds. The bacteria's waste products are toxic to the nervous system

1 in 3 Odds of dying if a tetanus infection is untreated

5 Number of U.S. tetanus deaths. With modern medicine, tetanus is rarely fatal. However, in much of Africa it remains a deadly public health problem that is responsible for 10–30% of all infant deaths

Toxic Shock

75 Number of U.S. deaths from toxic shock syndrome, a multiple-organ dysfunction caused by toxin from the *Staphylococcus aureus* bacteria

45 Percentage of toxic shock cases not associated with menstruation, even though the syndrome is associated in the public mind with highly absorbent tampons

Tuberculosis

764 Number of U.S. deaths from tuberculosis. TB was once the leading cause of death in the U.S.

55 Rate of death per 100,000 population in the U.S. in 1935 from tuberculosis

0.3 Rate of death from TB in 2001

14,000 Estimated number of people in the U.S. with active tuberculosis. The disease is spread through the air when a person with active TB of the throat or lungs coughs or sneezes

2 billion Estimated number with latent TB—approximately $1/3$ of the world's population. Although they don't feel symptoms and aren't contagious, the tuberculosis bacterium lives in their bodies. In many cases, people with latent TB never develop the disease unless their immune system is impaired through HIV or other causes

1,604,819 Number of worldwide TB deaths. The fatality rate is creeping upward again as tuberculosis microbes have become drug-resistant

Whooping Cough

17 Number of U.S. deaths from pertussis, also known as whooping cough

301,412 Number of whooping cough deaths worldwide. Spread by the *Bordetella pertussis* bacteria, the disease mostly kills children and is spread by droplets launched by the coughing of an infected person

Viruses

21,895
Number of U.S. deaths from viruses of all sorts: Even smaller than bacteria, they can't live for long outside a living host (whether plant or animal)

Chicken Pox/Shingles

26 Number of U.S. deaths from chicken pox, so highly contagious that if you haven't had it yet, you can get it just from being in the same room with somebody who has it. It is caused by 1 of the 8 varieties of the herpes viruses, and—despite its name— has nothing to do with chickens

55 Percentage of chicken pox deaths in the over-20 age group. It's best to get it when you're young

123 Number of U.S. deaths from shingles, a painful localized skin blistering. After a patient recovers from chicken pox, the virus lays dormant in the nervous system, kept in check by the immune system. Later in life, aging, stress, or immunity-related diseases can allow the chicken pox virus to reemerge and attack

Dengue Fever

18,565 Number of world-wide deaths from dengue fever. Caused by any of four viruses in the genus *Flavivirus*, dengue is spread by a mosquito that bites in the daytime

5 Percentage of fatality rate for dengue, usually

among children and young adults. You can contract it more than once because antibodies for 1 of the 4 viruses don't give immunity for the other three

2 Number of U.S. deaths from all four types of dengue

Ebola

1,200 Number of deaths worldwide from the Ebola virus from when it was first identified in 1976 through 2004. Only 1,850 cases were reported during the same time, representing a 65% fatality rate, making Ebola one of the most virulent viruses known to humankind

2–21 Incubation period in days after contact with the blood, secretions, organs, or corpses of Ebola-infected people or animals. The onset of the disease is sudden, characterized by fever, weakness, muscle pain, sore throat, and headache. This can quickly be followed by vomiting, diarrhea, and internal and external bleeding, then death

Encephalitis

318 Number of U.S. deaths from encephalitis, an inflammation of the brain usually caused by any of a variety of viral infections, which can come from food, drink, insect bites, airborne droplets, skin contact, or (extremely rarely) vaccinations

13,957 Number of worldwide deaths from Japanese encephalitis. Standing water from increased rice production in Asia over the past 2 decades has led to more mosquitoes, which spread the virus from birds and pigs to humans

Flu

25 Estimated percentage of Americans who come down with flu every year, resulting in 20,000 to 40,000 deaths (for more information on influenza, see "Bad Breath")

20–40 million Number killed worldwide in 1918–19 by the "Spanish flu." Despite its name, the disease seems to have made the jump from fowls to humans in a Kansas army camp and spread quickly because of soldiers traveling worldwide during World War I

28 Percentage of Americans who came down with the Spanish flu. Unlike most flu viruses, which tend to kill the very old and young, this one most affected adults between 20 and 40. As many as 675,000 Americans died, out of a population of 104 million

10 Number of years cut off from the average life span during the Spanish flu pandemic

German Measles

760,090 Number of worldwide deaths from rubella, also known as the German measles and the 3-day measles, of the 30 million who contract it each year. The measles come from a contagious virus spread through close contact or airborne particles

85 Percentage reduction of worldwide annual rubella deaths since 1989, when 5.3 million deaths were attributed to this virus. Today, immunizations are widespread; the biggest danger is from birth defects if a woman has rubella during early pregnancy

3 Number of rubella deaths in the U.S. in 2002. Compare this with a horrible U.S. outbreak in 1964—65: 12.5 million cases resulted in 13,350 miscarriages, stillbirths, and newborn deaths, 11,600 cases of deafness, 3,580 cases of blindness, 1,800 cases of mental retardation, and 5,000 preventative abortions, although abortion was widely illegal at the time

0 Target number of cases of rubella in the U.S. this year. Since the development of the MMR (measles, mumps, rubella) vaccination, developed countries have been approaching that number. In 2005, with 95% of all new school kids vaccinated, the CDC announced that rubella had been eliminated in the U.S.

Hepatitis

6,105 Number of U.S. deaths from hepatitis, a viral liver disease that can also cause liver cancer and cirrhosis (for more information see chapters "Cancer" and "Bad Plumbing")

156,265 Number of worldwide deaths from hepatitis. Types B and C are generally transmitted via blood, shared needles, and sexual contact

6 Number of viruses that infect the liver and cause inflammation (or hepatitis). Other viruses, such as Epstein-Barr and cytomegalovirus, may cause hepatitis, but the liver is not the primary targeted organ

#2 The most common way to get hepatitis A—in other words, it's spread by getting something in your mouth that's been contaminated by the stool of somebody else with hepatitis A. Hep A isn't in the same league as its more malicious siblings, usually caus-

The Six Hepatitis Viruses

A Found throughout the world. The most common cause of hepatitis cases in the U.S.

B Highest in Asia, sub-Saharan Africa, the South Pacific, South America, and the Mideast. Discovered in 1963

C Discovered in 1989 as the major cause of acute hepatitis from blood transfusions

D Found worldwide with a high prevalence in South America. Requires hepatitis B to replicate

E&G Largely waterborne, they are rare in the U.S.

ing something between no symptoms whatsoever to flulike symptoms that can last as long as six months

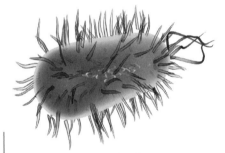

Herpes

183 Number of U.S. deaths caused by 1 of the 2 herpes simplex viruses that are commonly spread by kissing and/or sexual contact. Type 1 traditionally appears on the lips, mouth, and face, and type 2, on the genitals

1 in 5 Ratio of adults and teens over 12 who have experienced genital herpes in the U.S.—45 million Americans, according to the CDC. There was an increase of 30% of cases between the sexually liberated late 1970s and the media-driven herpes scare of the early 1990s

HIV/AIDS

36.1 million Estimated number of worldwide victims of the HIV/AIDS virus from 1984 to 2000

2,821,472 Number of HIV/AIDS deaths worldwide. Caused by the human immunodeficiency virus, AIDS is spread by the exchange of blood, semen, and other bodily fluids through sex, blood transfusions, use of injected drugs, and to babies from their moms. There is no known cure, although certain drugs can slow the progression of the disease

10 Number of years HIV can incubate inside the body without showing AIDS symptoms. Victims can infect others without knowing it

HIV DEATH RATES, WORLD 2002

(per 100,000 population)

AGE	MALE	FEMALE	TOTAL
0–4	59.7	60.3	60.0
5–14	8.8	9.0	8.9
15–29	34.9	54.0	44.2
30–44	107.7	72.0	90.1
45–59	58.5	33.0	45.7
60–69	19.6	11.8	15.5
70–79	5.1	4.0	4.5
80+	0.7	0.3	0.4

TRENDS IN U.S. DEATH RATES FROM HIV/AIDS

(per 100,000 population)

DEADLIEST COUNTRIES IN THE WORLD FOR HIV/AIDS
(per 100,000 adults)

RANK	COUNTRY	DEATHS	DEATH RATE	% OF ADULTS INFECTED
1	Botswana	26,000	1,664.5	39
2	Zimbabwe	200,000	1,578.3	34
3	Lesotho	25,000	1,340.4	31
4	Zambia	120,000	1,146.9	22
5	Swaziland	12,000	1,026.3	33
6	South Africa	360,000	842.7	20
7	Namibia	13,000	665.2	23
8	Burundi	40,000	641.9	8
9	Rwanda	49,000	616.0	9
10	Kenya	190,000	593.3	15

14,175 Number of U.S. deaths from HIV/AIDS

5,553 Number of HIV/AIDS deaths from bacterial and viral infections

962 Number from cancer

102 Number of HIV/AIDS cancer deaths from Kaposi's sarcoma

7,660 Number of HIV/AIDS deaths from other causes

1 Ranking of Washington, D.C., in American AIDS, syphilis, and TB death rates, with 164.6 cases per 100,000 population. Last is North Dakota, with 0.4 cases per 100,000

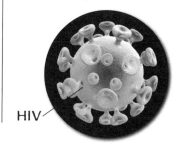

HIV

Mononucleosis

16 Number of U.S. deaths caused by infectious mono-nucleosis, commonly known as mono, or the kissing disease. Mono is usually spread by the Epstein-Barr virus, causing swollen tonsils, sore throat, high fever, and lethargy

Poliomyelitis

858 Number of worldwide deaths attributed to polio, a viral infection of the central nervous system

338 Number of polio deaths in the U.S.

3,000 Estimated number of deaths from polio in 1952 before a vaccine, created by Jonas Salk, was widely available. With more parents refusing to vaccinate their children these days, however, poliomyelitis may one day become a threat again in the U.S.

Rabies

43 Average annual number of rabies deaths in Thailand, the country reporting the most deaths from the rabies virus to the WHO from 1994 through 2002

3 Number of U.S. deaths from rabies in 2004. No deaths were recorded in 2001, 3 in 2002, and 2 in 2003

Smallpox

0 Number of worldwide smallpox deaths per year. A scourge of humanity for some 3,000 to 12,000 years, smallpox once routinely killed, disfigured, and blinded large numbers of children

90 Percentage of reduction in the native populations in Mexico and Central America in the 1520s thought to have been wiped out from smallpox brought to the New World unintentionally by European explorers. The

Dr. Edward Jenner was a country doctor in Gloucestershire, England, who noticed that people who worked near cows seemed to be immune to the plague of smallpox that was causing widespread death in Europe. That knowledge was actually well-known among the country folk he worked with, and a milkmaid clued him in. The good doctor took the knowledge one step further, during a time when research standards weren't strict. To test his theory, in 1796 Dr. Jenner took pus from a milkmaid's cowpox pustule and inoculated an 8-year-old boy with it. Six weeks later, he inoculated the boy with deadly smallpox, but the pint-size research subject didn't get sick. Jenner coined the term vaccination for his procedure, from the Latin *vacca* meaning "cow." The smallpox vaccine quickly spread around the world. The empress of Russia was so pleased by Jenner's breakthrough that by her decree the first child who got the injection took the name Vaccinov and was educated at the expense of the nation.

intentional use of the small-pox virus as a weapon of war against Native Americans in the New World first occurred during the French and Indian War in 1763.

300 to 500 million

Estimated number of worldwide deaths from the *Variola virus* (smallpox) since its first appearance until well into the twentieth century. The disease has been traced back to agricultural settlements in Africa around 10,000 BC and is thought to have killed more people than the bubonic plague.

1977 Latest year in which smallpox was recorded. A concerted worldwide effort wiped the disease out, although the continued existence of the virus in lab samples is still a concern, since children are no longer routinely inoculated against it

West Nile Fever

500 Estimated number of U.S. deaths through late 2005 from the West Nile virus since it first appeared in North America in 1999

15,000 Estimated number of Americans who tested positive for the disease, spread by mosquitoes

1 Percentage of people who develop serious symptoms when exposed to the West Nile virus

Fungi

1,389 Number of deaths from all fungi causes in the U.S. Fungi are actually primitive vegetables, some of which can live in the human body, but only about half of those can cause illness

359 Number of U.S. deaths from mycoses, which are diseases caused by fungi that affect skin, nails, body hair, internal organs, and the nervous system

319 Number of U.S. deaths from candida, a yeast infection found within a healthy person's skin. When the fungus gets out of balance, it can infest the esophagus, vagina, gastrointestinal tract, mucous membranes, lungs, or skin wounds

245 Number of U.S. deaths from pneumocystis, a once rare disease that most often affects AIDS patients. Cryptococcosis similarly attacks people with weakened immune systems and killed 126 people in the U.S.

192 Number of U.S. deaths from aspergillosis, a fungus that lives in a healthy person's outer ear and can also cause serious respiratory system infection

1 Number of U.S. deaths from rose gardener's disease, caused by the fungus *Sporothrix schenckii,* which grows on rose thorns and lodges under the skin when pricked

Parasites

635

Number of U.S. deaths from all parasites. Of the 50,000 species of protozoa, about 10,000 are parasitic and live in animals or plants

The Worm Turns

90 Percentage reduction in U.S. trichinosis deaths since a peak of 500 in 1947 to fewer than 50 annually now. The *Trichinella* worm lives in undercooked pork or game meats

3,403 Number of worldwide deaths from the parasitic roundworm *Ascaris lumbricoides*, which commonly makes its way into humans in areas where human feces is used as fertilizer

Trichinella

3,017 Number of worldwide deaths from trichuriasis. Not to be confused with trichinosis, trichuriasis is a common whipworm that lives in the soil in humid, warm areas. Kids are most likely to eat dirt and so are most likely to ingest the worm, which then lodges on the inner walls of their intestines. If they are ingested in large quantities, chronic, bloody diarrhea can lead to dangerous anemia and dehydration

2,943 Number of worldwide deaths from hookworm, caught by walking barefoot on, or eating, contaminated soil. After penetrating the skin, the tiny worms travel through the bloodstream to the lungs, then to the throat, where they are swallowed into the small intestine

1 Amount of time in weeks that the hookworm takes to make the circuitous trip from foot to intestine

Malaria

4 Number of different protozoa that can infect humans and cause malaria. They are transmitted to people via mosquito, not by foul-smelling swamps as originally believed (*mal aria* means "bad air" in Latin)

1,222,180 Number of annual worldwide malaria deaths

90 Percentage of worldwide malaria cases that occur in Africa

75 million Number of cases of malaria in India in 1951 versus 50,000 in 1961, due to the extensive spraying of DDT, which was later banned. Six years after Sri Lanka banned DDT, its number of malaria cases

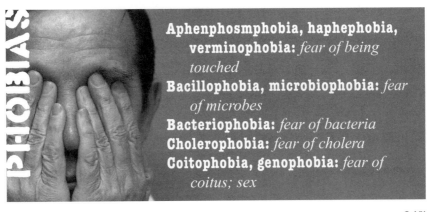

PHOBIAS

Aphenphosmphobia, haphephobia, verminophobia: *fear of being touched*
Bacillophobia, microbiophobia: *fear of microbes*
Bacteriophobia: *fear of bacteria*
Cholerophobia: *fear of cholera*
Coitophobia, genophobia: *fear of coitus; sex*

rose from 17 to more than 500,000

50 Number of years it took the former Soviet Union to eradicate malaria

5 Number of years it took the parasite that causes malaria to return in force to Russia after it had been eradicated

9 Number of malaria deaths in the U.S.

Toxoplasmosis

16 Number of U.S. deaths from the "kitty litter disease," toxoplasmosis. Spread by the protozoan parasite *Toxoplasma gondii,* it can be caught eating contaminated food or through contact with animal feces, including cat litter boxes. A small number of infants born from infected mothers have serious eye or brain damage

A Tropical 1-2 Punch

129,503 Number of worldwide deaths from what the World Health Organization calls tropical-cluster diseases, based on where the diseases usually occur (for more information on the insects and bugs that spread these diseases, see "Accidents—Flora & Fauna")

51,134 Number of worldwide tropical-cluster deaths

from leishmaniasis, caused by parasites that live in the gut of the sand fly. Of the 15–16 subspecies, some attack the mucous membranes, others internal organs such as the spleen and liver

48,080 Number of deaths from sleeping sickness. Spread by tsetse flies, the parasites travel under the skin and into the nervous system

15,387 From schistosomiasis, caused by blood flukes that enter the body through infected surface water

14,483 Number of worldwide deaths from Chagas' disease, caused by protozoa that live in the saliva of "assassin bugs," which emerge in the night to suck your blood. Only 3 people died in the U.S. from this parasite that attacks muscles and nerves

418 Number of worldwide deaths from lymphatic filariasis, caused by a nematode worm that is transferred to humans by the bite of the female culex mosquito

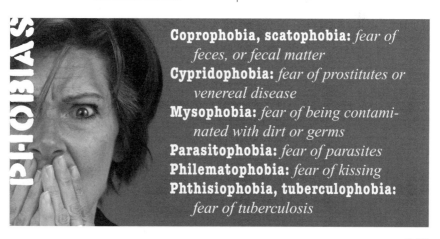

PHOBIAS

Coprophobia, scatophobia: *fear of feces, or fecal matter*
Cypridophobia: *fear of prostitutes or venereal disease*
Mysophobia: *fear of being contaminated with dirt or germs*
Parasitophobia: *fear of parasites*
Philematophobia: *fear of kissing*
Phthisiophobia, tuberculophobia: *fear of tuberculosis*

Prions

2,500 Estimated number of kuru deaths recorded in New Guinea in the 1940s and 1950s. Most were females who apparently got the prion-caused disease from funeral rituals in which women eat the brains of deceased relatives

Creutzfeldt-Jakob

220 Number of U.S. deaths from the Creutzfeldt-Jakob prion. Prions are protein particles that cause infections or diseases; unlike viruses they do not contain DNA or other genetic material—they are abnormal proteins that somehow encourage the proteins in your brain to malfunction.

The most notorious variant is vCJD, the human form of mad cow disease

139 Number of worldwide deaths reported from vCJD, caused by eating contaminated beef, between 1996 and 2000. Most of these deaths—130 of the 139—were in the UK, Scotland, Wales, and Ireland

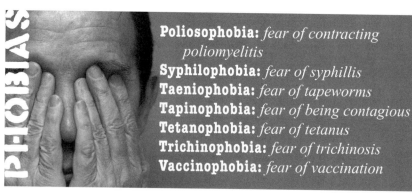

PHOBIAS

Poliosophobia: *fear of contracting poliomyelitis*
Syphilophobia: *fear of syphillis*
Taeniophobia: *fear of tapeworms*
Tapinophobia: *fear of being contagious*
Tetanophobia: *fear of tetanus*
Trichinophobia: *fear of trichinosis*
Vaccinophobia: *fear of vaccination*

Most at Risk of Premature Death from Bugs

WORLDWIDE DEATH RATES, 2002
(per 100,000 population)

AGE	MALE	FEMALE
0–4	748.3	803.1
5–14	47.8	59.1
15–29	69.7	85.4
30–44	175.8	110.0
45–59	184.0	99.1
60–69	220.8	120.2
70+	349.9	221.9

Avoid Being a Premature Death Statistic from Bugs

BE CAREFUL
BE SMART

- WASH YOUR HANDS
- WASH YOUR FOOD
- ENGAGE IN SAFE SEX
- BE CAREFUL WHEN TRAVELING
- BE CAREFUL WHEN ENTERING THE HOSPITAL

Suic...

#8 Cause of premature death in the world
2002 (under age 70)

#8 Cause of premature death in the USA
2001 (under age 75)

QUESTION: Are you more likely to kill yourself quickly with alcohol or your toaster? **ANSWER: Toaster**

47 people accidentally died in the U.S. from small electrical appliances such as their toaster in 2001 versus 26 who committed suicide by alcohol.

Q If you're older, are you more likely to kill yourself in the USA or rural China? **A: China**

In 1999, the rate of 75–84-year-old Chinese suicides was 102.2 per 100,000 people versus 18.4 in the U.S.

Q What are the worst days of the week for someone who's suicidal? **A: Mondays and Tuesdays**

Q How many times more likely are you to kill yourself if you're a male? **A: Six**

Of the 3,963 suicides in the U.S. in 2001 between ages 15-24, 3,401 were males versus 562 females

Q If you were in the U.S. military in 2002, were you more likely to die in combat or kill yourself?

A: Kill yourself

2 people died from operations of war versus 130 who committed suicide.

Q If guns are the weapon of choice for suicides in the U.S., is it the same in Finland? **A: No**

Finns are more likely to kill themselves by hanging (366 deaths out of 1,204 suicides in 2001) and poison (359 deaths) before they shoot themselves (225 by gun).

Q If you're a woman, should you worry more about yourself or the man you love? **A: Yourself**

In 2001, 5,950 women killed themselves in the U.S. versus 4,753 who were murdered (usually by a loved one).

Q What percent of mass murderers commit suicide? **A: 50%**

In a *New York Times* study of 102 mass murderers, 50% committed suicide, 37% more stayed at the scene of the crime, and only 13% fled the scene

Q What percent of suicides are related to mood disorders? **A: 90%**

Per the CDC, of the 29,350 people who died by suicide in the U.S. in 2000, more than 90% had a diagnosable mental disorder, most often depression or substance abuse disorder.

Q Who has a higher suicide rate, black Americans or Native Americans? **A: Native Americans**

In the U.S., in 2000, whites killed themselves at a rate of 11.3 per 100,000 versus 9.8 for Native Americans and 5.9 for Hispanics. Blacks and Asians tied for last place at 5.5 each.

Suicide World Death Rates
by WHO Region (per 100,000 population)

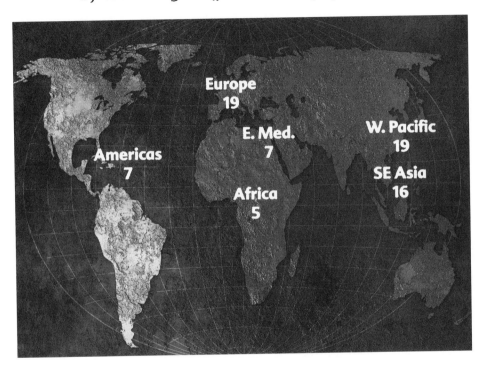

SUICIDE DEATHS, 2002—ALL AGES

Americas (incl USA): **63,592**

USA: **30,622***

Europe: **164,150**

E. Mediterranean: **33,922**

Africa: **34,568**

W. Pacific: **332,938**

Southeast Asia: **246,656**

* USA totals are for 2001.

Intentional Injury Deaths Worldwide, 2002

Cause	Deaths
Self-inflicted (suicide)	876,524
Violent (murder)	558,566
War (incl genocide)	178,170
Law (legal intervention)	12,832
Total	**1,626,092**

BE ALL, AND END ALL

"**NINE** men in ten are suicides," wrote Benjamin Franklin in 1749. His point is not that most of us deliberately end our lives, but that we nearly always bring on premature death by our own actions. At what point does a risky behavior become suicide? For example, shooting yourself with a gun is proof that death was your intention. But is it still suicide if you die while playing Russian roulette? Brandishing a toy pistol in a standoff with police? Ignoring gun safety rules? Walking fur-clad in the woods during bear season?

What about more common occurrences: premature death from smoking? From speeding and talking on a cell phone while drunk? From eating junk food and not exercising? Old Ben judges all of these suicide, but most of us find the absolute line harder to draw.

This chapter's suicide statistics are much more conservative. We've ruled out everything but the most blatant cases of suicide, but we acknowledge that the truth may really lie somewhere between our stats and Ben Franklin's estimate.

Note: All deaths cited are for 2001 in the U.S. and 2002 in the world, unless otherwise noted

Quick & Dead Summary for the U.S.

30,622 Number of deaths attributed to suicide

9 Percentage of those suicides among people 75 or older

24,672 Number of suicides each year by men

4 Factor by which men are more likely
to kill themselves than women

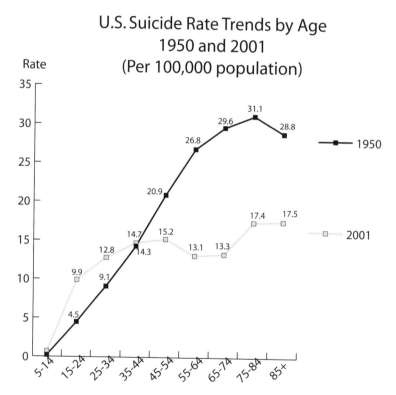

U.S. Suicide Rate Trends by Age
1950 and 2001
(Per 100,000 population)

Stop the World . . .

55 Percentage of worldwide suicides by people 15–44 years old in 2002

40 Percentage of worldwide suicides by people 15–44 years old in 1950

47 times Factor of difference between the highest reported national suicide rate (Lithuania, 51.6 suicides per 100,000 people) and the lowest (Azerbaijan, 1.1 per 100,000). Reported suicide rates are not always accurate for a number of reasons, including a disincentive to be honest about the cause of death in places where suicide violates deep cultural and religious taboos

483,352 Number of worldwide suicides between ages 15 and 44

3 to 2 Worldwide ratio of male-to-female suicides

13 times Increased likelihood of suicide among Canadian Inuits between 15

Till Death Does Its Part

A thousand-year tradition of suicide continues to kill women in some rural areas of India. Although outlawed in 1829, the practice of suttee—in which a widow was expected to throw herself onto her husband's burning funeral pyre—still occasionally surfaces. Such a devoted woman would attain divine status. Although the practice was supposedly voluntary, some women were dragged to the fire, drugged, or coerced with a mix of social pressure and grief.

and 25, compared to that of the average Canadian. A similar, less extreme, difference has been observed in other indigenous groups, such as the aboriginals of Australia

195 Number of Inuit suicides per 100,000 persons

15 The same ratio for the general Canadian population

THE WORLD'S "SUICIDE BELT"
(per 100,000 population)

COUNTRY	DEATH RATE
Lithuania	51.6
Russia	43.1
Belarus	41.5
Estonia	37.9
Kazakhstan	37.4
Latvia	36.5
Hungary	36.1
Ukraine	33.8
Slovenia	33.0
Finland	28.4
Croatia	24.8
Belgium	24.0

11 Percentage of worldwide suicides by people 70 and older

75 Of the 12 countries with the lowest rate of reported suicide, the percentage that are overwhelmingly Christian Catholic, a religion that considers suicide a mortal sin that can prevent you from getting into heaven. The countries are the Philippines (2.1 suicides reported per 100,000 people), Armenia (2.3), Paraguay (4.2), Greece (4.2), Colombia (4.5), Mexico (5.1), Georgia (5.3), Portugal (5.4), and Brazil (6.3)

2 Number of the lowest 12 that are predominantly Muslim, a religion that also considers suicide a deep affront to God: Azerbaijan (1.1) and Kuwait (2.0)

1 Number that are predominantly Buddhist, a philosophy that has a more tolerant view of suicide: Thailand (5.6)

1 Number of geographic regions in which female suicides between ages 15 and 54 outnumber those of men. In rural China, 53% of its suicide victims are women

12 Number of World Health Organization (WHO) designated European region countries that report the highest suicide rates in the world: 3 from high-income countries (Slovenia, Finland, and Belgium) and 9 from low-income countries.

Where in the U.S.

TOP 10 BEST STATES FOR SUICIDE, 2001			TOP 10 WORST STATES FOR SUICIDE, 2001		
RANK	STATE	DEATH RATE	RANK	STATE	DEATH RATE
1	New York	7	1	New Mexico	20
2	Massachusetts	7	2	Montana	19
3	New Jersey	7	3	Nevada	18
4	Connecticut	8	4	Wyoming	17
5	California	8	5	Colorado	16
6	Rhode Island	8	6	Alaska	16
7	Maryland	8	7	Idaho	16
8	Illinois	9	8	West Virginia	16
9	Minnesota	10	9	Oklahoma	15
10	Pennsylvania	10	10	Oregon	15

Per 100,000 population.

100 Percentage of American states with the 10 lowest suicide rates that voted Democratic in the 2004 presidential election

90 Percentage of American states with the 10 highest suicide rates that voted Republican

When

12 Rank of December in suicide rates by month. The notion that "holiday suicides" are unusually frequent is a misconception

4 Rank of winter in suicide rates by season. The greatest number of suicides occur in spring, followed by autumn, summer, and finally winter

95 Average number of suicide deaths in the U.S. on a Monday or Tuesday in 2002, the days with the highest rates

78 Average number on Saturdays in 2002, the day with the lowest rate of suicide

17.2 Average number of minutes that will pass before another person commits suicide somewhere in America

Crazy Writers

The suicides of writers such as Sylvia Plath (stuck her head in a gas oven), Ernest Hemingway (shot himself in the head), and Virginia Woolf (walked into the river Ouse with heavy stones in her pockets) are tragic losses to the arts, but much more common than we'd like. *Scientific American* reports that writers and artists are 10 times more likely to suffer from clinical depression than members of the general population. Writers' incidence of suicide may be as much as 18 times higher than that of the general population.

SUICIDE BY METHOD & SEASON OF YEAR, 2003

METHOD	SPRING	SUMMER	FALL	WINTER
Gun	4,064	4,434	4,401	4,008
Strangulation	1,511	1,695	1,752	1,677
Drugs (incl painkillers & sedatives)	773	883	928	760
Gases	313	369	317	357
Jump from high place	152	194	189	188
Sharp object	127	122	158	164
Jump in front of moving object	70	72	72	73
Drown	55	103	87	94
Fire & explosives	28	44	44	36
Crash car	27	26	28	23
Solvents	23	14	19	16
Other chemicals	23	24	25	19
Alcohol	9	8	11	6
Pesticides	2	5	9	3
Blunt object	0	1	0	2
Death following suicide attempt	25	15	7	15
Other	60	53	74	52
Total Number of Deaths	**7,262**	**8,062**	**8,121**	**7,493**

It's (Mostly) a Guy Thing

80 Percentage of American suicide victims who are male. While females statistically make more suicide attempts, they tend to use methods that allow for rescue or a change of heart

20.9 Rate of suicide per 100,000 American males ages 25–34

15.1 Rate of suicide per 100,000 inmates in U.S. prisons and jails, 1999–2000

9 Rate of suicide per 100,000 U.S. military personnel on active duty in 2001

11 Rate of suicide per 100,000 active-duty military in 2004 (down from a peak between 1980 and 2006 of 15 in 1995)

29 Percentage of suicide victims who had alcohol in their system, according to a 20-year coroners' study in Memphis, Tennessee

Busy Hands Are Happy Hands

6 Position of suicide in top 9 causes of fatal work injuries in the U.S. (after transportation, contact, fall, murder, and harmful exposure but before fire and animal assaults)

4 Percentage of all 5,915 workplace deaths resulting from suicide

0.8 Percentage of all U.S. suicides taking place at work

Suicide by Murder

1 Suicide by firing squad in 1997 of Gary Gilmore, who fought to be executed after murdering 2 people

2 Number of teenagers who committed suicide after they went on a shooting rampage at Columbine High School in Colorado in 1999, killing 12 fellow students and a teacher and wounding 24 others

4 Number of suicides attributed to 9/11 terrorists in 2001. All other deaths, including World Trade Center jumpers, were categorized as homicide deaths (for more information see the "Murder" chapter)

11 Percentage of Los Angeles police killings from 1987 to 1997 that were "suicide by cop," or people forcing the issue as a way of intentionally committing suicide

136 Number of suicide bombing missions by Palestinians in Israel between 1993 and 2002

3,912 Number of Japanese military personnel who died in kamikaze missions during the closing months of World War II. The suicide bombers sank 34 ships, damaged 288 more, and killed thousands of American sailors and airmen

TOP 10 METHODS OF SUICIDE IN THE U.S. IN 2001

RANK	METHOD	DEATHS
1	Guns	16,869
2	Hanging, strangulation, suffocation	6,198
3	Poison	5,191
4	Jump	926
5	Sharp object, cut, pierce	458
6	Drown	339
7	Fire	147
8	Motor vehicle crash	91
9	Terrorism	4
10	Explosive	4

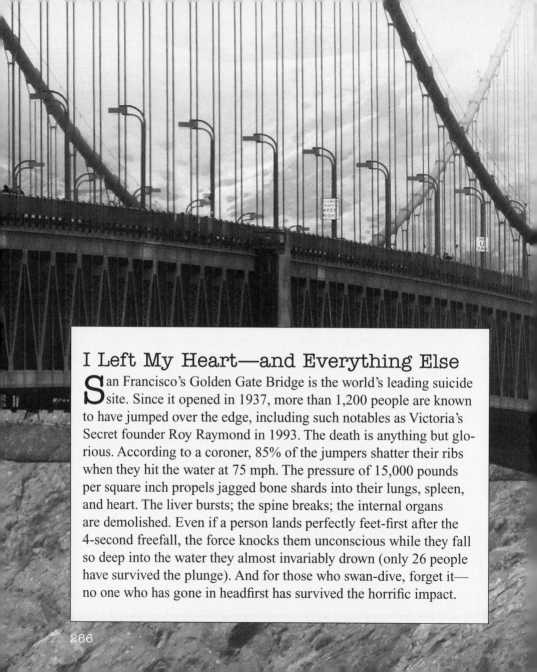

I Left My Heart—and Everything Else

San Francisco's Golden Gate Bridge is the world's leading suicide site. Since it opened in 1937, more than 1,200 people are known to have jumped over the edge, including such notables as Victoria's Secret founder Roy Raymond in 1993. The death is anything but glorious. According to a coroner, 85% of the jumpers shatter their ribs when they hit the water at 75 mph. The pressure of 15,000 pounds per square inch propels jagged bone shards into their lungs, spleen, and heart. The liver bursts; the spine breaks; the internal organs are demolished. Even if a person lands perfectly feet-first after the 4-second freefall, the force knocks them unconscious while they fall so deep into the water they almost invariably drown (only 26 people have survived the plunge). And for those who swan-dive, forget it— no one who has gone in headfirst has survived the horrific impact.

Suicide is a crisis of the moment: If the suicidal person is deterred, the chances of long-term survival are quite high, particularly with medical intervention. In 1978, the University of California's Dr. Richard Seiden studied a group of 515 people who, between the years of 1937 and 1971, had been prevented from jumping from the bridge. He found that 94% of the would-be suicides were either still alive at the time of his study or had died of natural causes.

The Empire State Building, the Eiffel Tower, and the Sydney Harbor Bridge have all put up safety barriers, bringing their suicide rates down close to zero. However, the city of San Francisco has been reluctant to put up a barrier on the Golden Gate Bridge. Currently, hidden cameras and regular patrols are the only line of defense for despondent jumpers. These methods prevent an estimated 50 to 80 people from going over the edge each year; about 30, or 1 every 12 days, goes into the water.

Aw, Shoot!

55 Percentage of self-inflicted deaths committed with a gun

92 Percentage of gun-related suicide attempts that are fatal

2/3 Proportion of teen suicides committed with a family-owned firearm

3 to 2 Ratio of suicides by firearms to homicides by firearms

11 to 1 Odds that a gun in your home will be fired to attempt suicide, rather than in self-defense

Did Nobody Lend the Guy an Ear?

On July 27, 1890, Vincent van Gogh took a gun and an easel, walked out into the cornfields he so often painted, and shot himself in the abdomen. When the doctor told him he might survive, Vincent said, "Then I will have to do it all over again." He died soon after. Van Gogh did not shoot himself in a fit of madness. He suffered from guilt about living off money from his brother, Theo. Vincent also feared his periodic bouts of insanity, writing that "a more violent attack may destroy forever my ability to paint."

How's It Hanging?

84 Percentage of hanging, strangulation, and suffocation deaths among males

59 Of these, the percentage among males between 20 and 44

1 in 5 Proportion of autoerotic asphyxia deaths among all U.S. strangulation deaths. Some men have succumbed to the folk legend that cutting off circulation to the brain will enhance the intensity of orgasm

Name Your Poison

69 Of the 5,191 Americans who killed themselves with poison in 2001, the percentage who chose legal or illegal drugs

28 Percentage of Americans who used "gases or vapors," most notably carbon monoxide

1 in 200 Proportion of self-poisoning Americans who use alcohol (for slower deaths from alcohol, see "Bad Plumbing")

1 in 288 Proportion who kill themselves with pesticides

Death by Cigarette

Arsenic and other chemicals found in cigarettes enable 440,000 people, out of 2.4 million annually in the U.S., to kill themselves slowly with tobacco every year.

Chemicals found in cigarettes: acetone, ammonia, arsenic, butane, cadmium, carbon monoxide, cyanide, DDT, formaldehyde, Freon, geranic acid, hydrogen cyanide, maltitol, methoprene, nicotine, sulfuric acid, and tar.

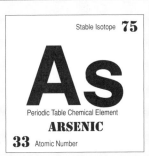

Stable Isotope **75**

As

Periodic Table Chemical Element
ARSENIC
33 Atomic Number

Letting Work Get to You

TOP 5 U.S. OCCUPATIONS FOR WORKPLACE SUICIDES, 1992–2001

RANK	OCCUPATION	# OF DEATHS	RELATIVE RISK*
1	Public service, police, and detectives	53	7.0
2	Military personnel	92	5.4
3	Farmers	53	4.7
4	Auto mechanics	44	3.2
5	Private guards and police	52	2.4

Number of times more likely worker will commit suicide over general U.S. population

Dying for a Cause

914 Number of people who died in Jonestown, Guyana, in 1978 after their leader, the Reverend Jim Jones, ordered them to drink poisoned grape punch. Jones then shot himself in the head

241 Number of Americans who died in a suicide bombing against a marine barracks in Beirut in 1983.

Suicide bombings for political and military reasons have occurred in more than 20 countries for a variety of causes

7 Number of Buddhist monks who died in 1966 by setting themselves on fire while protesting against the South Vietnamese government

Most at Risk of Premature Death from Suicide

WORLDWIDE DEATH RATES, 2002
(per 100,000 population)

AGE	MALE	FEMALE
0–4		
5–14	1.4	1.1
15–29	18.6	12.8
30–44	22.3	12.8
45–59	28.7	15.6
60–69	35.2	16.3
70+	50.1	25.4

Main Cause

Depression

Prevention

▪ BE HAPPY

▪ GET EXERCISE

▪ TALK TO FRIENDS

Bad Wir

#13 Cause of premature death in the world
2002 (under age 70)

#9 Cause of premature death in the USA
2001 (under age 75)

Q UESTION: What's worse, not sleeping or having a headache?

ANSWER: Migraine

5 people died of migraine in the U.S. in 2002 while only 2 died from insomnia.

Q Who's more likely to be anorexic—an American or a Japanese? **A: Japanese**

The death rate from eating disorders in Japan is .15 per 100,000 versus .08 in the U.S.

Q If you're mentally ill, how much more likely are you to commit suicide? **A: 9 times**

About 1 in 7,000 people will kill themselves in the world at a rate of 14 per 100,000; 90%, or 12.6 per 100,000 of the suicides, suffer from mental illness, versus 1.4 who do not.

Q What was the age of the youngest Alzheimer's victim in the U.S. in 2001? **A: 25**

The youngest recorded deaths from Alzheimer's were 2 deaths between ages 25–34.

Q What's worse, the obsession to wash your hands or coming into contact with hot water?

A: Hot water

In the U.S. in 2001, 3 people died of obsessive-compulsive disorder versus 50 who died from contact with hot tap water.

Q If you're over 75, are you more likely to die because of a heart attack or from the disease that makes you forget you have a heart?

A: Heart attack

In the U.S. in 2001, 334,211 Americans aged 75+ died of heart attack versus 110,805 who died from Alzheimer's.

Q How much more likely are women to die from Alzheimer's disease in the U.S. than men?

A: 2.3 times

In the U.S. in 2003, females died at a rate of 30.5 per 100,000 versus 12.8 for males. Although the rate of death was higher than in 1999, the variance with male deaths is approximately the same.

Q How many more years are American women expected to live than men? **A: 5.4 years**

In the U.S. in 2003, females lived to age 79.9 versus 74.5 for men. The variance of 5+ years has not changed since 1999.

Bad Wiring World Death Rates
by WHO Region (per 100,000 population)

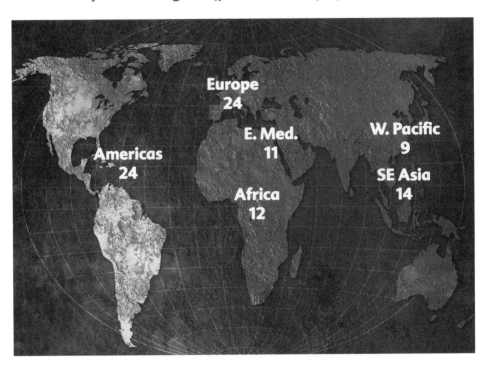

Europe 24

E. Med. 11

W. Pacific 9

Americas 24

SE Asia 14

Africa 12

BAD WIRING DEATHS, 2002—ALL AGES

Americas (incl USA): **208,530**

USA: **137,743***

Europe: **206,575**

E. Mediterranean: **53,398**

Africa: **80,942**

W. Pacific: **150,031**

Southeast Asia: **228,846**

* USA totals are for 2001.

Neuropsychiatric Condition Deaths Worldwide, 2002

Cause	Deaths
Alzheimer's and other dementias	395,288
Epilepsy	124,775
Parkinson's disease	98,262
Schizophrenia	22,928
Multiple sclerosis	15,952
Unipolar depressive disorders	13,339
Mental retardation, lead-caused	5,519
Bipolar disorder	728
Post-traumatic stress disorder	56
Other	254,004
Total	**930,851**

OUR nervous system streams information from the sense organs to the brain, then to the muscles. Electricity fires through brain synapses, filing and accessing memory and managing the human systems that keep us thinking, moving, living. When everything works right, we can do exquisitely complicated things, such as walk, eat, sing, balance, catch, dance, drive, breathe, and talk. (Even several at the same time.) But what happens when circuits shut down or get misrouted or blow a fuse? When we can no longer guide our muscles, perceive through our sense organs, maintain consciousness, or use our memories?

A breakdown in human wiring can mean death, and something every bit as fearful: losing control over the mind. Many suicides—and

GOING HAYWIRE

homicides—are attributed to people who just haven't been able to adapt to the misfirings in their minds and bodies. For those of us still sitting in the glow of full consciousness, it's hard to not have a deep compassion for those whose lights are dimmed.

This chapter's statistics generally exclude suicides, accidents, homicides, etc., all of which are covered in other chapters and some of which may be motivated by bad wiring.

Note: All deaths cited are for 2001 in the U.S. and for 2002
in the world, unless otherwise noted

Quick & Dead Summary for the U.S.

2 in 9 Proportion of American adults who suffer from an identifiable mental disorder in any given year

137,743 Number of U.S. deaths from bad wiring

80 Percentage of those deaths among people 75 or older

92,514 Number of U.S. deaths from Alzheimer's disease and other forms of dementia

16,544 Number from Parkinson's disease

3,053 From multiple sclerosis

1,292 From epilepsy

869 From depressive and bipolar disorders

221 From eating disorders

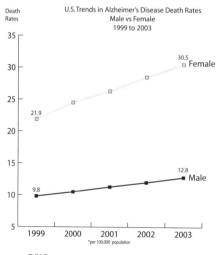

Death Rates

U.S. Trends in Alzheimer's Disease Death Rates
Male vs Female
1999 to 2003

35 — 30.5 Female — 21.9 — 12.8 Male — 9.8

1999 2000 2001 2002 2003
*per 100,000 population

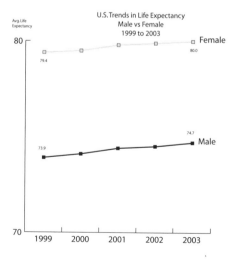

Avg. Life Expectancy

U.S. Trends in Life Expectancy
Male vs Female
1999 to 2003

80 — Female 80.0 — 79.4 — 74.7 Male — 73.9

1999 2000 2001 2002 2003

Forget Me Not

4 million Estimated number of Americans affected by Alzheimer's disease

395,288 Number of worldwide deaths from Alzheimer's and other dementias

92,514 Number of U.S. deaths

8–10 Average duration in years from the onset of Alzheimer's symptoms until death

1 Rank of India in list of countries with the least incidence of Alzheimer's. Turmeric, a common curry ingredient, is thought to protect against the disease

0 Knowledge actually contributed by Dr. Alois Alzheimer toward better understanding the disease that bears his name. His colleague Dr. Emil Kraepelin—who had first defined schizophrenia and manic-depressive disorder—generously named the disease after Alzheimer after his paper brought the symptoms to Kraepelin's attention

Hollywood superstar Rita Hayworth was considered unusually kind and professional, so it was a surprise when in her early 40s, she became difficult to work with: sloppy about her lines and belligerent. At the time, this behavior was attributed to excess alcohol consumption. When Hayworth was finally diagnosed with Alzheimer's disease in 1980, she became the poster girl for bringing much needed information about this illness into the mainstream.

RANK	STATE	DEATH RATE
TOP 10 STATES FOR ALZHEIMER'S DEATHS *(per 100,000 population)*		
1	North Dakota	46.4
2	Maine	39.6
3	Washington	36.2
4	Oregon	31.9
5	Montana	31.3
6	Iowa	30.6
7	Kansas	27.8
8	Nebraska	26.6
9	Alabama	26.5
10	Vermont	26.4

RANK	STATE	DEATH RATE
BOTTOM 10 STATES FOR ALZHEIMER'S DEATHS *(per 100,000 population)*		
1	New York	9.4
2	Alaska	9.5
3	Hawaii	11.3
4	Nevada	11.6
5	Utah	13.1
6	California	15.4
7	Maryland	15.9
8	Delaware	15.9
9	Connecticut	16.5
10	Texas	17.4

Strange Appetites

218 Number of U.S. deaths from eating disorders. Of these, 42 were from anorexia (drastically restricted eating), 7 from bulimia (binge eating followed by regurgitation or laxative-induced diarrhea), and 169 from "other" (including compulsive overeating)

Karen Carpenter, lead singer and drummer of the 1970s group the Carpenters, was anorexic at a time when the condition wasn't yet well-known. She died at 33 from a heart attack caused by abusing her body with laxatives, vomiting, malnutrition, and thyroid pills. Her death brought eating disorders to the forefront of public consciousness.

1–2 Percentage of U.S. women who suffer from an eating disorder, according to the National Institutes of Health

10 to 1 Ratio of female to male sufferers. Societal pressure on women to be ultrathin seems to be a large component in eating disorders. Other Western cultures share the affliction, but eating disorders are rare in non-Western societies, with one notable exception. . . .

190 Percentage increase in eating-disorder fatalities if the U.S. death rate were as high as Japan's

Mood Indigo

5 Minimum number of depression symptoms (see chart on next page) lasting 2 weeks or more that indicate a major depressive disorder

18 million Estimated number of Americans—representing all ages, races, and income levels—who suffer from depression. Women are diagnosed nearly twice as often as men

783 Number of U.S. fatalities directly attributed to depression, excluding accidents, suicides, etc.

90 Percentage of suicides that are related to mood disorders and other psychiatric illness (see "Suicide" chapter for more information)

17 Minimum estimated percentage of returning Iraq War veterans with symptoms of major depression, anxiety, or post-traumatic stress disorder

11 The similar percentage for returning Afghanistan veterans

Symptoms of Major Depression

1. Trouble sleeping or excessive sleeping
2. Dramatic change in appetite, often with weight gain or loss
3. Fatigue and lack of energy
4. Feelings of worthlessness, self-hate, and inappropriate guilt
5. Extreme difficulty concentrating
6. Agitation, restlessness, and irritability
7. Withdrawal from usual activities, loss of interest in activities once enjoyed
8. Feelings of hopelessness and helplessness
9. Thoughts of death or suicide

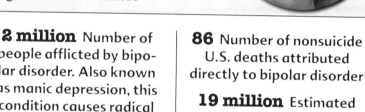

2 million Number of people afflicted by bipolar disorder. Also known as manic depression, this condition causes radical swings from frenzied highs to inconsolable lows

10 Minimum number of years required for a physician to correctly diagnose bipolar disorder in more than $1/3$ of victims surveyed. More than half said they visited at least 3 doctors before this happened

86 Number of nonsuicide U.S. deaths attributed directly to bipolar disorder

19 million Estimated number of Americans age 18–54 who suffer from an anxiety disorder, including obsessive-compulsiveness, post-traumatic stress, or phobias

56 Number of worldwide deaths attributed to post-traumatic stress syndrome

31 Number of U.S. deaths attributed to panic disorder

3 To obsessive-compulsive disorder

1 in 3 Proportion of Americans ages 18–54 who develop agoraphobia, a fear of leaving familiar surroundings

Schizophrenia

456 Number of U.S. deaths attributed to schizophrenia

22,928 Number of schizophrenia deaths worldwide

5 Number of recognized types of schizophrenia

1 Percentage of worldwide population believed to be schizophrenic

1 to 1 Approximate ratio of women to men with schizophrenia, although men tend to exhibit symptoms at an earlier age (late teens to early 20s) than women (20s to early 30s)

The Five Types of Schizophrenia

CATATONIC: Stupor, rigidity, lethargy, agitation, echolalia, decreased sensitivity to pain

PARANOID: Delusions of persecution and plots, guardedness, tenseness, suspicion, visual and auditory hallucinations

DISORGANIZED: Delusions, disorganized speech patterns, inappropriate emotional reactions, unpredictable grinning or grimacing, hallucinations, silliness, eccentricity

RESIDUAL: Reduction in the most prominent symptoms, but some effects remain

UNDIFFERENTIATED: Symptoms are mixed or unclear enough that the patient cannot be placed into one of the above categories

Multiple Sclerosis

3,053 Number of U.S. deaths from multiple sclerosis, the result of damage to myelin, a fatty tissue that surrounds nerve fibers and helps them conduct electrical impulses. The catalyst seems to be the autoimmune system; symptoms include reduced use of muscles, bladder control, balance, and cognitive function. MS isn't necessarily fatal and doesn't necessarily interfere with a long and happy life

Epilepsy

19 Maximum age when most incidences of epilepsy begin

5 Minimum age for the first recognized seizure in most patients

1,292 Number of U.S. deaths from epilepsy

2 Number times more frequently black American males died from epilepsy (1.0 per 100,000) than white males (0.5) in 2003

1 Rank of Chile in world epilepsy death rates, followed by Mexico, Portugal, and Colombia. The countries with the lowest rates are Denmark and Iceland

Parkinson's Disease

16,544 Number of U.S. deaths from Parkinson's disease, first described by English physician James Parkinson in 1817. The disease can cause difficulty with walking and other coordinated movement

1 in 500 Odds of contracting Parkinson's disease if you're American. It most often develops after age 50

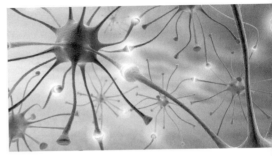

Other Wiring Issues

5,547 Number of U.S. deaths from spinal muscular atrophy (SMA) and related syndromes

5,398 Number of those deaths from motor neuron disease, which includes Lou Gehrig's disease

36 Number of SMA deaths from infantile spinal muscular atrophy. SMA is a genetic disease that is incurable, untreatable, and fatal, killing babies more than those of any other age. The mind stays sharp, but the ability to use muscles—including sometimes the ones that allow swallowing and breathing—fades away

1,155 Number of U.S. deaths from infantile cerebral palsy, a birth condition that disrupts the formation of motor skills, resulting at times in paralysis, spasticity, or seizures. Unlike muscular dystrophy or atrophy, the condition does not progressively worsen. Fatalities from CP are often the result of choking or drowning

693 Number of U.S. fatalities from Huntington's disease, an incurable genetic illness causing stumbling, mental confusion, aggression, mood swings, and uncontrollable muscle movements. Symptoms usually appear between ages 30 and 50, and the patient becomes completely incapacitated over time

50/50 Odds of contracting Huntington's disease if one of your parents has it

529 Number of U.S. deaths from tobacco-related mental and behavioral disorders

423 Number of U.S. deaths from lead-induced mental retardation. Lead has been used with reckless abandon in gasoline, paints, craft hobbies, art supplies, pewter, batteries, water-pipe solders, bullets and shot, fishing supplies, curtain weights, etc., and is still poisoning kids

9 Number of U.S. deaths attributed to hypochondria and other disorders in which the patient feels symptoms that may have a psychological cause instead of a physical one

5 Number of U.S. deaths attributed to migraine headaches

679 Number of U.S. fatalities from hydrocephalus (excessive fluid in the brain)

447 Number of annual U.S. deaths from sleep disorders

12 million Estimated number of Americans with sleep apnea. Untreated, apnea's snoring and chronically interrupted breathing seriously interrupt sleep and can cause cardiovascular disease, memory problems, motor impairment, headaches, impotence, and weight gain

Dust Bowl–era folksinger and activist Woody Guthrie was deeply affected when his mother was placed in a mental hospital during his teen years. Unfortunately, he wound up inheriting the same mind-wasting condition years later: Huntington's disease. Two of Guthrie's daughters have also died from this genetic disease.

Most at Risk of Premature Death from Bad Wiring

WORLDWIDE DEATH RATES, 2002
(per 100,000 population)

AGE	MALE	FEMALE
0–4	7.9	6.5
5–14	2.6	2.6
15–29	3.6	2.9
30–44	5.4	3.4
45–59	9.5	8.2
60–69	23.2	18.5
70+	50.1	216.4

Main Cause

Alzheimer's

Prevention

- BE HAPPY
- GET EXERCISE
- USE YOUR MIND

Bad Bir

#6 Cause of premature death in the world
2002 (under age 70)

#10 Cause of premature death in the USA
2001 (under age 75)

QUESTION: Are you more likely to die of sudden infant death syndrome (SIDS) or an accident before age 1? **ANSWER: SIDS**

In the U.S. more than twice the number of babies die of SIDS than from accidents.

Q Which is the worst country to be born into in Africa: Angola or Rwanda? **A: Angola**

In 2004, the rate of infant mortality was 192.5 deaths per 1,000 live births in Angola versus 101.68 in Rwanda.

Q Are you more likely to die as an infant in the U.S. or Cuba?

A: U.S.

In 2004 the rate of infant mortality per 1000 live births was 6.63 in the U.S. versus 6.45 in Cuba.

Q Are you more likely to die of a heart attack under age 1 if you're male or female? **A: Male**

In 2001, 2 times more boy babies (10) died of heart problems than girls (5).

Q Are you more likely to die young if your parents are less educated? **A: Yes**

Of the 7 U.S. states with death rates in 2002 greater than 1,000 per 100,000 population, 5 were also in the lowest rank of public elementary and secondary expenditures per pupil: Arkansas (#3 in death rates, ranked #47 in education), Alabama (#4 in death rates, ranked #48), Oklahoma (#5 in death rates, ranked #44), Mississippi (#6 in death rates, ranked #46), Florida (#7 in death rates, ranked #42).

Q If every pregnancy resulted in a live, healthy baby, how much faster would the U.S. population grow? **A: 40%**

Approximately 40% of pregnancies in the U.S. don't result in live births.

Q What's worse, a mother who is not healthy while pregnant or not careful during baby's bath time?

A: Not healthy while pregnant

Although drowning in the bathtub is a top 5 cause of death to infants in the U.S. (44 deaths to babies under age 1), it pales in comparison to the number of babies who die from low birth weight (4,482).

Bad Birth World Death Rates
by WHO Region (per 100,000 population)

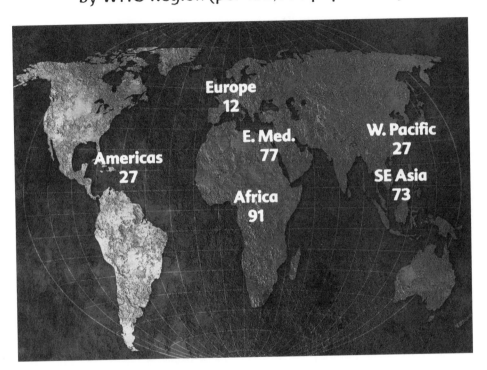

Europe 12

E. Med. 77

W. Pacific 27

Americas 27

SE Asia 73

Africa 91

BAD BIRTH DEATHS, 2002—ALL AGES

Americas (incl USA): **232,853**

USA: **24,329***

Europe: **104,858**

E. Mediterranean: **385,518**

Africa: **609.646**

W. Pacific: **458,127**

Southeast Asia: **1,161,475**

* USA totals are for 2001.

Perinatal Conditions and Birth-Defect Deaths Worldwide, 2002

Disease	Deaths
Low birth weight	1,270,449
Birth trauma	724,128
Congenital abnormalities	493,409
Other perinatal conditions	469,290
(between 28th week of pregnancy and 28th day after birth)	
TOTAL	**2,957,276**

LITTLE
ANGELS

A late-term miscarriage or the death of a new baby can be the worst kind of horror for the grieving parents. But the cause is most often the result of defective fetal development; the tragic ending of life is nevertheless nature's way of saving the parents and child from even more sadness in the future.

As with maternal deaths, one of the few cold comforts is that things were much worse in the past. A century ago, 10% of U.S. babies perished before reaching their first birthdays. Only a few places on earth are left with such a high infant mortality rate today.

We can be thankful for everything that has contributed to this reduction. Not just better medical treatment, but also more effective prenatal advice, better-educated parents, a higher standard of living, pasteurized milk, more effective contraception, a horseless transportation system, and effective sewage disposal.

Note: All deaths cited are for 2001 in the U.S. and 2002 in the world, unless otherwise noted

Quick & Dead Summary for the U.S.

27,568 Number of babies who died before age 1 from all causes

24,329 Number who died from birth problems and birth defects (19,247 before age 1)

13,887 Number that were the result of conditions occurring during pregnancy or birth

10,442 Number that were the result of birth defects

5,513 Number of birth-defect deaths that occurred before age 1

784 Number of birth-defect deaths that occurred age 75+

8,321 Number of babies who died before age 1 from other than birth problems or birth defects

CAUSE	# DEATHS AGE 0–1
Sudden infant death syndrome (SIDS)	2,234
Accidents	1,085
Bad breath	699
Bugs	648
Bad plumbing	634
Broken heart	622
Hormones	395
Murder	332
Bad wiring	239
Other	1,433
Total	**8,321**

Birth & Death: A World of Progress

100 Number of infant deaths from all causes out of every 1,000 who were born at the turn of the century. These grim odds, combined with a lack of effective birth control, made it likely that families would lose at least 1 child early in life

3 in 10 Odds of dying from all causes before age 1 in certain U.S. cities a century ago

402,800 Number of infants who would die each year from all causes if we still had the same infant death rate

65 Worldwide infant mortality rate per 100,000 people in 1990

54 The same rate in 2004

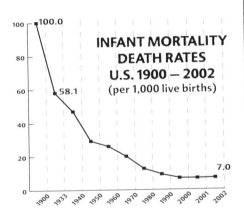

INFANT MORTALITY DEATH RATES U.S. 1900 – 2002 (per 1,000 live births)

"We accept her, we accept her. One of us, one of us!" In the 1932 film *Freaks,* director Tod Browning paired genuine actors with circus "oddities" to make the point that beauty on the outside doesn't necessarily reflect the heart on the inside. Some of the freaks in the film were what the circus biz called pinheads, small-headed people who suffer from the congenital birth defect microcephaly. Two of these pinheads were Zip and Pip (Elvira and Jenny Lee Snow), fairly well-known sideshow twins at the time. They later were the inspiration for Bill Griffith's comic character Zippy the Pinhead.

Not All Born Equal

2 to 1 Odds of infant death among black Americans compared to whites. This gap has actually increased since the early 1900s

868.9 Infant mortality rate per 100,000 total population in Angola

406.8 In Rwanda

132.1 In India

52.9 In Brazil

40.7 In Saudi Arabia

16.3 In Russia

9.4 In the U.S.

7.9 In Cuba or Estonia

5.3 In France

3.5 In Germany

3.1 In Japan

2.2 In Singapore, the world's lowest

23 Rank of the U.S. in lowest infant mortality rate—above most of the Third World, but below most of the industrialized nations

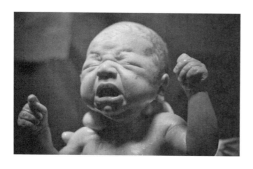

U.S. CHILDHOOD DEATH RATES
(per 100,000 population by race & sex)

CAUSE	BLACK MALES	LATINO MALES	WHITE MALES	BLACK FEMALES	LATINO FEMALES	WHITE FEMALES
Birth problem	15.8	6.7	3.7	10.9	5.3	2.7
Birth defects	5.1	4.7	3.6	4.4	4.1	3.2

Low Birth Weight

1,270,449 Number of babies worldwide who died from low birth weight. Causes can include maternal smoking, drinking, malnutrition, stress, drug use, genetic factors, and poor placental development

4,482 Number of American babies who die from low birth weight

1 in 13 Number of U.S. babies whose birth weight is judged to be low

5.5 Minimum in pounds of normal birth weight

3.3 Minimum in pounds to escape "very low birth weight"

38 Percentage decline in pregnant mothers who smoked from 1990 to 2002 (18.4% in 1990; 11.4% in 2002)

23 Percentage decline in infant deaths per 1,000 live births (9.2 in 1990 to 7.0 in 2002)

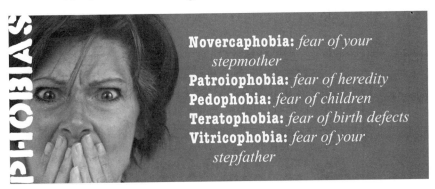

PHOBAS

Novercaphobia: *fear of your stepmother*
Patroiophobia: *fear of heredity*
Pedophobia: *fear of children*
Teratophobia: *fear of birth defects*
Vitricophobia: *fear of your stepfather*

Birth Asphyxia and Trauma

724,128 Number of babies worldwide who died from complications arising during labor and birth, including asphyxia (lack of sufficient oxygen)

4,385 The same number for the U.S. Asphyxia can also result in permanent brain and organ damage and is a factor in some cerebral palsy cases

Defective Parts

262,092 Number of worldwide fatalities from congenital heart defects

4,109 Number for the U.S.

23,432 Number of worldwide fatalities from congenital spine defects

138 Number for the U.S.

18,022 Number of worldwide fatalities from congenital brain defects

275 Number for the U.S.

3,761 Number of worldwide fatalities from congenital defects of the abdominal wall

341 Number for the U.S.

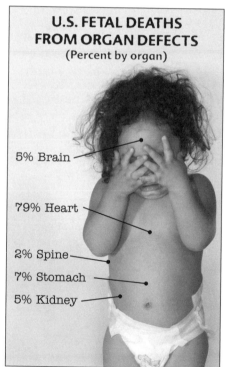

U.S. FETAL DEATHS FROM ORGAN DEFECTS
(Percent by organ)

5% Brain
79% Heart
2% Spine
7% Stomach
5% Kidney

2,240 Number of world-wide fatalities from congenital kidney defects

273 Number for the U.S.

1,549 Number of worldwide fatalities from congenital cleft lip and palate

2 Number for the U.S.

1,105 Number of worldwide fatalities from congenital stomach defects

38 Number for the U.S.

Down Syndrome

23,692 Number of worldwide deaths from Down syndrome

828 Number for the U.S. The condition is now recognized as genetically caused by the presence of an extra #21 chromosome

250 Highest estimate of the number of genes on #21, the smallest chromosome of the human body. As a

Who Says a Congenital Disability Has to Keep You from Achieving Your Dreams?

Not actor Chris Burke, who wanted to work in Hollywood since he was a child. Burke has Down syndrome, but that hasn't stopped him from appearing in several made-for-TV films and starring in his own TV series for four years, *Life Goes On,* as Corky Thatcher. He's won numerous awards and honors for his roles and is a spokesperson for the National Down Syndrome Society.

result, people with Down syndrome may have a varying set of attributes beyond mental retardation (for example, half suffer from hearing or vision impairment)

10 Percentage of babies born with Down syndrome that include intestinal malformations that may require surgery

What's in a Name?

Dr. John Langdon Down, an English doctor, first identified the characteristics of Down syndrome in 1866. He called sufferers Mongoloids, thinking they resembled people from Mongolia. By the 1960s, ethnic sensitivities revised the condition's name to Down's syndrome. A 1970s American revision of scientific terms inexplicably dropped the possessive, and now it's commonly called Down syndrome.

Abortion

800,000 Estimated number of illegal U.S. abortions per year before the *Roe v. Wade* court case made the procedure legal nationwide in 1973

200,000–1,200,000 Estimated number of annual illegal U.S. abortions, according to researchers, in 1955.

6,401,000 Number of U.S. pregnancies in 2000

4,060,000 Number of those pregnancies that resulted in live births

63 Percentage of live births to total pregnancies

1,310,000 Number of pregnancies that resulted in induced abortions

1,031,000 Number that resulted in other fetal losses (miscarriages, stillborn babies)

404 Number that resulted in maternal death (see "Childbearing" chapter)

13.2 Rate per 1,000 American women ages 15–44

who had an abortion in the U.S. in 1972

29.3 Rate in 1980, the highest abortion rate between 1972 and 2000

21.4 Rate in 1999

21.3 Rate in 2000

U.S. NUMBER OF ABORTIONS AND RATES PER 1,000 WOMEN, 1972–2000

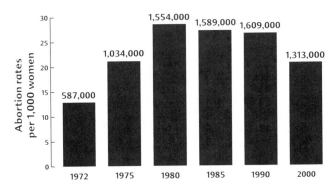

Poor Catharine of Aragon. When she bore King Henry VIII a son, there was much celebrating. Things got ugly when the boy died 7 weeks later. Catharine kept trying, though, only to have one stillbirth follow another. She did give birth to a daughter, Mary, but it wasn't enough to satisfy Henry. He soon banished her from court, broke with the Catholic Church, and made way for a new bride, his second of six: Anne Boleyn.

TOP 10 COUNTRIES WITH HIGHEST NUMBER OF REPORTED LEGAL ABORTIONS, 1999		
(per 1,000 Women Age 15—44)		
RANK	COUNTRY	ABORTIONS
1	Vietnam	63
2	Russia	62
3	Belarus	58
4	Romania	52
5	Estonia	48
6	Ukraine	45
7	Bulgaria	43
8	Kazakhstan	35
9	Latvia	34
10	Ukraine	32

TOP 10 COUNTRIES WITH LOWEST NUMBER OF REPORTED LEGAL ABORTIONS, 1999		
(per 1,000 Women Age 15—44)		
RANK	COUNTRY	ABORTIONS
1	Spain	6
2	Belgium	6
3	Netherlands	7
4	Germany	8
5	Uzbekistan	10
6	Italy	11
7	Finland	11
8	Azerbaijan	11
9	Japan	13
10	France	13

Most at Risk of Premature Death from Bad Birth

WORLDWIDE DEATH RATES, 2002
(per 100,000 population)

AGE	MALE	FEMALE
0−4	500.8	432.4
5−14	1.7	1.8
15−29	1.6	1.3
30−44	0.6	0.6
45−59	0.7	0.8
60−69	1.0	0.8
70+	1.0	1.8

Main Cause

Low birth rate

Prevention

■ DON'T SMOKE WHEN PREGNANT
■ WATCH WHAT YOU PUT IN YOUR MOUTH
■ GET EDUCATED

Mur...

#10 Cause of premature death in the world
2002 (under age 70)

#11 Cause of premature death in the USA
2001 (under age 75)

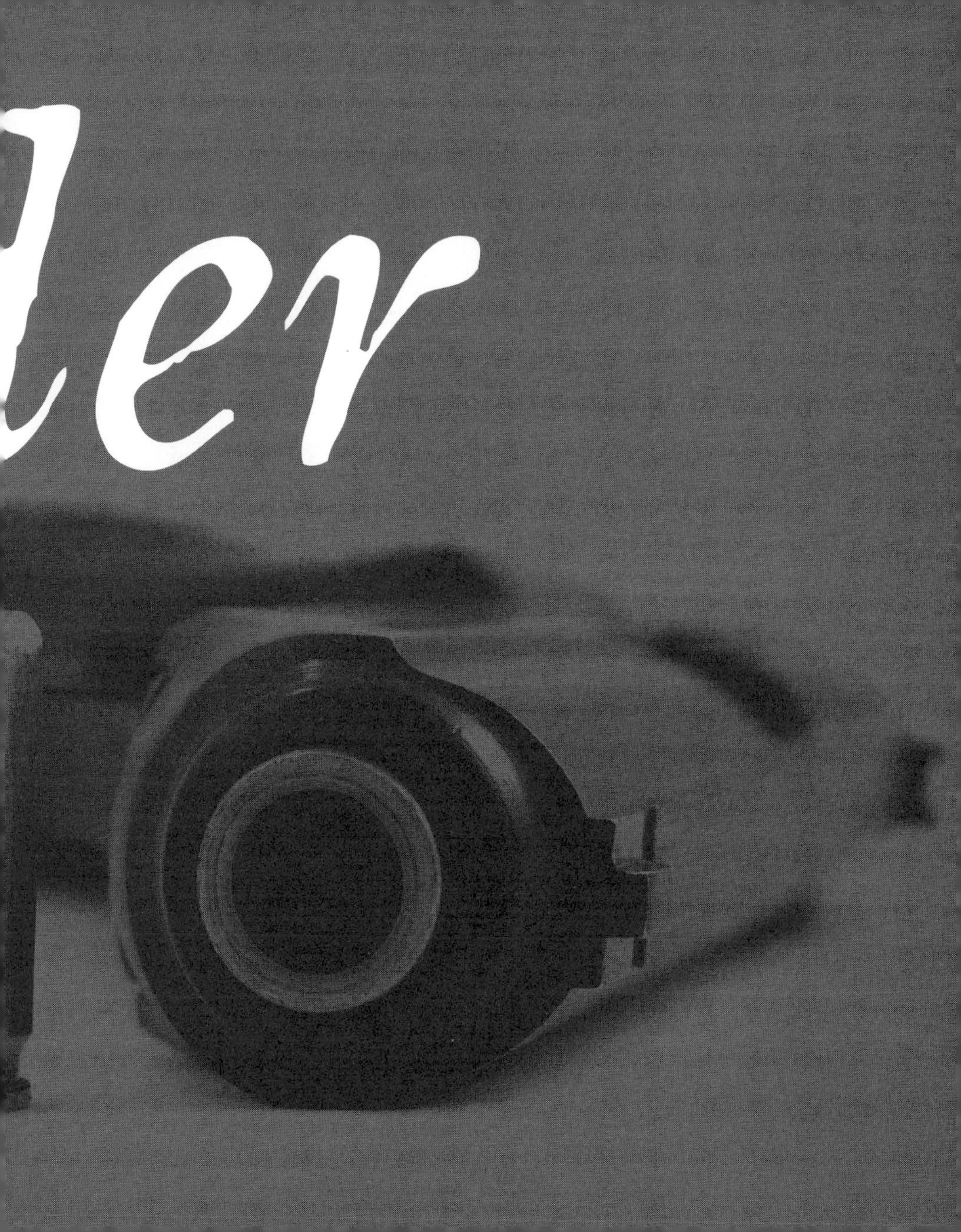

QUESTION: What happened to homicide rates in the U.S. for the generation affected by the passage of Roe v. Wade in 1973?

ANSWER: They went down

Murder rates for high-risk males ages 20–24 (born 1973 to 1975, Per 100,000): 1993, 42; 1999, 26.

What day of the week are you more likely to be murdered in the U.S.? **A: Saturday**

The average number of homicides from 2002 through 2004 was 57 on Saturday, 56 on Sunday, 46 on Friday, 45 on Tuesday and 44 on Monday, Wednesday, and Thursday.

In 2002 in the U.S., were you more likely to kill yourself or be murdered between the ages of 25–34? **A: Kill yourself**

The death rate for suicide was 13 versus 11 for murder (per 100,000 population in that age range).

How much more does California spend per prisoner than student? **A: 3-1/2 times**

In 2001, California spent $25,053 per prisoner and only $6,987 per student.

What percentage of U.S. murderers experienced child abuse?

A: 94%

In a study of 150 murderers 94% had experienced severe physical and sexual abuse as children.

Does Texas, the state with the highest number of executions, also have the highest murder rates?

A: No

Texas doesn't even make the top 10. Top 10 U.S. murder states, 2003, and death rates (per 100,000 population): **1**-Louisiana,13; **2**-Maryland, 10; **3**-Mississippi, 9; **4**-Nevada, 9; **5**-Arizona, 8; **6**-Georgia, 8; **7**-South Carolina, 7; **8**-Illinois, 7; **9**-California, 7; **10**-Tennessee, 7

In the U.S. are you more likely to die from HIV/AIDS or murder?

A: Murder

In 2001, 20,308 Americans were murdered at a rate of 7.1 per 100,000, while 14,175 died from HIV/AIDS at a rate of 5.0. If the 2,926 9/11 terrorism murders in 2001 are excluded, murder is still higher at 6.1 per 100,000.

What are the five most dangerous cities in the U.S.?

A: Highest U.S. City Murder Rates, 2002 (per 100,000 population): **1**-New Orleans, LA, 53.1; **2**-Washington, DC, 45.9; **3**-Detroit, MI, 41.8; **4**-Baltimore, MD, 37.7; **5**-Atlanta, GA, 34.9

What civilian occupation is just as statistically dangerous as being a policeman? **A: Clergy**

In the U.S. in 2003, both died at a rate of 8 per 100,000.

Murder World Death Rates
by WHO Region (per 100,000 population)

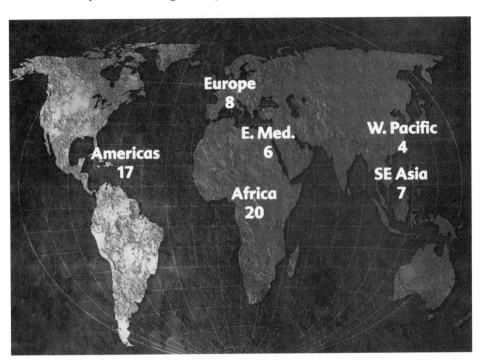

Europe
8

E. Med.
6

W. Pacific
4

Americas
17

SE Asia
7

Africa
20

MURDER DEATHS, 2002—ALL AGES

Americas (incl USA):
145,801

USA: **20,308***

Europe: **71,822**

E. Mediterranean: **26,400**

Africa: **134,115**

W. Pacific: **66,577**

Southeast Asia: **112,396**

* USA totals are for 2001.

Intentional-injury Deaths Worldwide, 2002

Cause	Deaths
Self-inflicted (suicide)	876,524
Violent (murder)	558,566
War (incl genocide)	178,170
Law (legal intervention)	12,832
Total	**1,626,092**

MURDER AMONG FRIENDS

IN 3 out of every 4 murders, the victim is a friend, a loved one, or an acquaintance of the killer. Comforting or distressing? At least the victim may understand the motivation: jealousy, for example, or unrequited love. But there's little comfort in knowing that your chances of being killed by a family member are just about the same as being killed by a non-relative. Within these statistics are other disquieting discrepancies. For example, what are we to make of the fact that girlfriends/wives are more than twice as likely to be killed as boyfriends/husbands? That women are more likely to be killed by men they know, and that men are more likely to be killed by strangers? That you're 36 times more likely to be killed because of an argument than a love triangle? Whatever the case, most murderers are amateurs, which means there's no guarantee they'll even perform the task competently.

Note: All deaths cited are for 2001 in the U.S. and for 2002 in the world, unless otherwise noted

Quick & Dead Summary for the U.S.

20,308 Number of murders recorded in the U.S. (including 2,927 9/11 terrorism murder deaths)

60,548 Number of murder mysteries listed on Amazon.com in Summer 2006. Being a fictional person may be more dangerous than being a real one

11 to 3 Proportion of U.S. male murder victims to female

5.3 times Increased odds of being murdered if you're a black man instead of a white one

2.8 times Increased odds of being murdered if you're a black woman instead of a white one

2.6 times Increased odds of being murdered if you're a Hispanic male instead of a white male

2 Percent of U.S. murders occurring to Americans over age 75

WORLDWIDE MURDER CAPITALS*

CATEGORY	#1 IN THIS CATEGORY	DEATHS PER 100,000
Highest UN reporting country	Swaziland, 2000	88.61
Highest U.S. region	The South, 2001	6.7
Highest U.S. state	Louisiana, 2001	11.2
Highest U.S. city	New Orleans, 2001	44.0

*U.S. murder rates in 2001, as reported by the FBI, exclude the events of 9/11.

Deadly Differences

95 Percentage of the 571,399 worldwide murder victims under 70

80 Percentage who are male

57 Among males, percentage between 15 and 44

15,555 Number of U.S. men murdered per year

44 Among males, percentage who are black

39.3 Rate of black male deaths per 100,000 American black men

14.5 Rate of Hispanic male deaths per 100,000 American Hispanic men

5.6 Rate of white male deaths per 100,000 white males

4,753 Number of women murdered in the U.S.

98 Number of pregnant women murdered on average

annually in the U.S. (out of 6 million annual pregnancies, a rate of 1.6 per 100,000 pregnant women)

416 Number of U.S. women who died as a result of their pregnancy

3 to 2 Ratio of murdered women of childbearing age to those murdered who are pregnant

65 Percentage of murdered U.S. women who are white

7.6 Rate of black female murder deaths per 100,000 black females

3.2 Rate of Hispanic female murder deaths per 100,000 Hispanic females

2.4 Rate of white, non-Hispanic female murder deaths per 100,000 white females

Murder Over Time

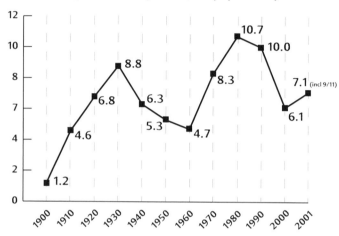

U.S. HOMICIDE RATE TRENDS
(Death rates per 100,000 population)

Dying to Go Abroad

6 Of the 10 countries reporting the highest murder rates in 2000, number located in the Americas. These include #2 Colombia (63 murders per 100,000 population), #4 Jamaica (34), #5 Venezuela (33), #6 Guatemala (25), #9 Mexico (14), and #10 Panama (14)

2 Number located in Africa: #1 Swaziland (89) and #3 South Africa (51)

2 Number located in the former USSR: #7 Russian Federation (20) and #8 Kazakhstan (16)

14.8 times Increased odds of being murdered in Swaziland versus the U.S. (6)

12 times Increased odds of being murdered in the U.S. versus Japan (0.5). The U.S. has the highest murder rate of the world's economic powers

521 times Magnitude of difference between the nation with the highest reported murder rate (Swaziland 88.61) versus the lowest (Qatar .17)

1 Number of murders reported in Qatar in 2000

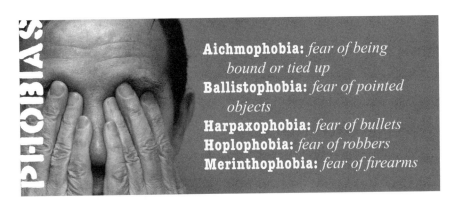

PHOBIAS

Aichmophobia: *fear of being bound or tied up*
Ballistophobia: *fear of pointed objects*
Harpaxophobia: *fear of bullets*
Hoplophobia: *fear of robbers*
Merinthophobia: *fear of firearms*

Worked to Death

11 Percentage of workplace deaths in the U.S. that are homicides

643 Number of U.S. homicides that took place at work (excluding the events of 9/11)

3 Ranking of homicide in causes of U.S. workplace deaths, after motor vehicles and falls

42 Number of U.S. taxi drivers murdered in 2000

56 Number of U.S. prisoners murdered in 2000

7 to 1 Increased odds of being a U.S. homicide victim among taxi drivers (32.2 per 100,000) versus prisoners (4.4)

2 Ranking of homicide as the cause of workplace deaths among post office employees from 1980 to 1989, after motor vehicles

40 Number of postal workers who were victims of on-the-job homicides during that time

20 Number of these postal workers killed by a coworker or former coworker. Of these deaths, 14 were the result of a single incident

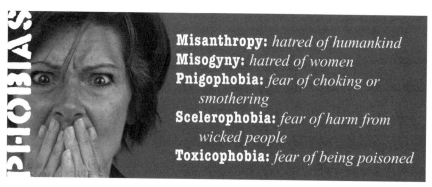

PHOBIAS

Misanthropy: *hatred of humankind*
Misogyny: *hatred of women*
Pnigophobia: *fear of choking or smothering*
Scelerophobia: *fear of harm from wicked people*
Toxicophobia: *fear of being poisoned*

Where and When

80 Percentage of U.S. murders that take place in metropolitan areas

1 Ranking of the South as the U.S. region with the highest murder rate

43 Percentage of all homicides occurring in the South

14 Percentage of all homicides occurring in the Northeast, the region with the lowest murder rate

32 Average number of minutes between 2002 homicides in the USA (16,204 recorded intentional homicides completed)

24 Average number of minutes between homicides in South Africa that same year (21,553 homicides)

MURDER BY MONTH IN THE U.S.
(excluding events of 9/11)

MONTH	% OF ALL U.S. MURDERS
July	9.5
October	9.3
December	9.2
August	9.1
September	8.7
June	8.4
November	8.4
May	8.2
January	8.0
April	8.0
March	7.2
February	6.1

TOP OCCUPATIONS IN WORKPLACE HOMICIDES, 2003

NUMBER OF WORKERS	OCCUPATION	NUMBER OF HOMICIDES IN WORKPLACE	HOMICIDE RATE PER 100,000 WORKERS
18,730	Door-to-door sales, news deliverer, street vendor	10	53.39
131,880	Taxi drivers and chauffeurs	46	34.88
17,680	Barbers	5	28.28
37,630	Clergy	3	7.97
612,420	Police	46	7.51
53,410	Physicians	3	5.62
123,680	Real estate agents	6	4.85
961,660	Security guards	37	3.85

Why

40 Of known murder circumstances in the U.S., percentage of murders that occurred during an argument, in 2001

12 Percentage that occurred during a robbery, burglary, or carjacking

9 Percentage that were the result of a juvenile-gang killing

6 Percentage that resulted from drug trafficking

3 Percentage resulting from fights under the influence of drugs or alcohol

1 Percentage resulting from a romantic triangle

.4 Percentage of homicide victims killed by their babysitter (37 deaths)

Who

1 Ranking of a man, with a gun, killing his wife/girlfriend, as a murder perpetrator

76 Percentage of known murder circumstances in which the victim knew the killer

61 Percentage of homicide victims under 5 (747 in 2001) killed by their parents or stepparents

ALL IN THE FAMILY: KILLING KINFOLK IS A RELATIVE THING

RELATIONSHIP TO MURDERER	% DISTRIBUTION
Wife	34
Son	14
Daughter	12
Husband	8
Father	6
Mother	5
Brother	4
Sister	1
Other family member	16

32.3 Percentage of female victims murdered by their husband or boyfriend

24 Percentage of all U.S. homicides committed by a family member

6 Percentage of girlfriends killed by their lovers

1.9 Percentage of husbands killed by their spouses

How

MURDER BY METHOD IN THE U.S., 2001

METHOD	# MEN KILLED	# WOMEN KILLED
Guns	9,532	1,816
Terrorism—9/11	2,220	702
Sharp objects	1,375	596
Hanging, strangulation, and suffocation	244	446
Blunt objects	131	68
Bodily force	106	36
Fire, steam, and other hot items	89	59
Crashing motor vehicle	56	30
Pushed in front of a moving object or off a high place	57	16
Drowning	44	24
Drugs	27	15
Neglect and abandonment	23	20
Pushed off a high place	12	5
Corrosives, gas, and other noxious substances	10	12
Explosives	4	2
Other	1,625	906
Total	**15,555**	**4,753**

Shooting Pains

48 Percentage of U.S. households with at least one gun. This compares to 29% in Canada, 27% in Switzerland, 20% in Australia, and 5% in England and Wales

1 Estimated number of guns each American man, woman, and child would own if they were distributed equally, based on manufacture and legal import rates. Statistics are not precise because, unlike cars and other lethal objects, guns are not registered

95 to 1 Ratio of firearms deaths between the Americas and Asia

8 to 1 Ratio of firearms deaths between the U.S. and other comparably developed countries

28,217 Number of U.S. deaths by firearms (16,869 used to commit suicide and 11,358 to commit murder at a combined rate of 9.9 per 100,000)

12,700 Number of firearms fatalities Japan would have experienced in 2002 if it had the same rate as the U.S.

23 Actual number of Japan's gun deaths in 2002

1 Rank of Alaska in state death rates by firearms in 2002 (19.7 deaths per 100,000 inhabitants), followed closely by Louisiana (19.5), Wyoming (19.0), Arizona (17.7), Mississippi (17.1), Nevada (17.0), New Mexico (16.4), Arkansas (16.3), Alabama (16.1), and Tennessee (15.6)

50 Rank of Hawaii in firearms death rates (2.9). At the bottom of the list, it's joined by Massachusetts (3.2), Connecticut (4.2), New Jersey (4.8), Rhode Island (5.1), New York (5.2), New Hampshire (6.0), Minnesota (6.1), Iowa (6.8), and Maine (6.8)

When 1 Isn't Enough

7,096 Of the 7,812 murder incidents in 2002 for which pertinent information is available, number in which one person died

476 In which two people died

162 Three people

60 Four

15 Five

1 Six

2 Seven

Killing by the Numbers

Murdering more than 1 person puts you in one of at least 5 special categories:

A MASS MURDERER kills multiple people at one time and in one location. Many kill themselves as well. Those who have been captured alive have claimed that they can't clearly remember their actions.

A SERIAL MURDERER kills one person at a time with a cooling-off period of days, weeks, or months between victims in which the killer often appears to be a normal person living a normal life. A sexual element is often involved.

A SPREE KILLER is most like a traveling mass murderer, killing people in different locations over hours or days. Unlike serial killers, spree killers don't return to their normal life between murders.

A SOLDIER murders multiple people because a person in authority told him or her to.

Someone who orders soldiers to commit murders is called either a BOLD LEADER or a WAR CRIMINAL, depending on who wins the war.

87 Percentage of 102 mass murderers studied by the *New York Times* who remained at the scene of the crime. Not all were still alive

50 Percentage of those mass murderers who committed or attempted suicide after their crime

Notorious Murderers

CAIN According to Genesis, the son of Adam and Eve killed only 1 person, his brother, Abel. But his notoriety was assured by being the first murderer in history, for killing $1/4$ of the entire known human population of the time, and for being featured prominently in the bestselling book of all time.

GILLES DE RAIS This fifteenth-century French aristocrat kidnapped, raped, and murdered up to 200 children, mostly boys.

ELIZABETH BÁTHORY "The Bloody Lady of Cachtice" was a Hungarian countess who from 1585 to 1610 tortured and killed up to 2,000 young women. Legend has it that she believed bathing in their blood would give her eternal youth, but there is no corroborating evidence.

THUG BEHRAM Leader of India's Thuggee cult in the early 1800s, he admitted to single-handedly strangling 150 people and may have ordered thousands more murders. The Thuggees, who gave us the word *thug*, killed travelers to take their money and to placate Kali, the Hindu goddess of destruction.

"JACK THE RIPPER" Jack's identity may never be known, or even whether he was 1 man or more. But he's responsible for killing at least 5 of the 18 prostitutes discovered dead in London in the second half of 1888.

DR. H. H. HOLMES Holmes (real name Herman Mudgett) trapped, tortured, and killed possibly hundreds of guests, mostly women, at his Chicago hotel during the 1839 World's Fair. He took out insurance policies on his victims before killing them and sold their bodies to medical schools.

DR. HAROLD SHIPMAN An English family doctor, Shipman killed as many as 400 elderly patients from 1971 to 1998.

ED GEIN The inspiration for the killer in *Psycho,* Gein killed at least 2 middle-aged women and dug up many more recently buried ones to decorate his house with their mummified remains. He made a suit of female skin so he could wear it and "talk" to himself in falsetto as his deceased mother.

ROBERT PICKTON Arrested in 2002 after the remains of dozens of missing women were found on his Vancouver-area pig farm, Pickton was charged in 2005 with 27 murders and may be responsible for the deaths of as many as 61 Vancouver prostitutes who disappeared mysteriously over 2 decades. According to the police, some of the bodies may have been ground up with pork.

JOSEPH KIBWETERE In 2000, cult leader Kibwetere nailed his church shut with its members inside and blew it up. Police found another 153 bodies in the cult's house. Days earlier, he had directed them to sell their belongings. He is believed to have taken their money and run.

TED BUNDY A drop-dead-handsome charmer, Bundy admitted to at least 30 murders in which he kidnapped, raped, bludgeoned, strangled, and mutilated his victims during the late 1970s.

ANDREW KEHOE The Columbine high school murders were horrific, but nowhere near the worst school massacre in American history. That was perpetrated by Kehoe in Bath Township,

Notorious Murderers

Michigan, on May 18, 1927. A school board member upset over property taxes, Kehoe killed his wife, set fire to his farm buildings, and drove to an elementary school where he had secretly been stashing dynamite over many months. He detonated it at the school and used it on himself, his car, and the school superintendent—killing 45 people, mostly children, and injuring 58 more.

Epilogue

1 in 8 Proportion of state prisoners in 2001 who committed homicide, a total of 156,300 incarcerated murderers

1 in 50 The same proportion for federal prisoners

14 to 1 Ratio between male and female murderers in prison

10 Percentage of all U.S. black males age 25–29 who were in prison that year

2.9 The same percentage of all Hispanic males of that age

1.2 The same percentage of all white males of that age

1.2 Percentage of murderers released from prison who were rearrested for murder within 3 years, according to a 1994 study

5 Average number of years served by murderers released from federal prison in 2000

41,260 Number of U.S. murders reported in 1995 and 1996

17,488 Number of suspects convicted in those murders. Some were accused of killing more than 1 person

Most at Risk of Premature Death from Murder

WORLDWIDE DEATH RATES, 2002
(per 100,000 population)

AGE	MALE	FEMALE
0–4	2.1	2.0
5–14	1.6	1.5
15–29	22.8	3.8
30–44	20.5	4.6
45–59	16.4	5.0
60–69	11.9	5.2
70+	13.5	5.6

Main Cause

Arguments

Prevention

- BE HAPPY
- GET EDUCATED
- BE COMPASSIONATE

Dru

#15 Cause of premature death in the world,
2002 (under age 70)

#12 Cause of premature death in the USA
2001 (under age 75)

gs

QUESTION: Are you more likely to crash and die in a car from speeding or booze?

ANSWER: Speeding

Speeding causes accidents twice as often as driving under the influence of drugs or alcohol.

Q If you die of a drug OD, how much more likely is it to be accidental than intentional?

A: 4 times

You are 4 times more likely to die from accidentally poisoning yourself. In 2001, 15,793 died from accidental drug use versus 3,559 from drug-related suicides.

Q In 2001, 22.4% of U.S. high school seniors reported using marijuana. How many deaths were attributed to marijuana that year?

A: 3

Two deaths from mental and behavioral disorders due to cannabinoids were reported by the U.S. Centers for Disease Control for ages 25–29. One death was reported from this cause in the 50–54 age group.

Q Are the number of prisoners incarcerated for drugs versus homicide proportional to the number of deaths caused by each? **A: No**

In 2001 there were 251,100 drug offenders and 156,300 murderers in U.S. state prisons. That same year, 21,683 died from all types of drug abuse (including accidents, suicides, homicides, and ODs) versus 20,704 who were murdered.

Q 2.1% of U.S. high school seniors used cocaine in 2001. How many died? **A: 3**

The deaths reported were 3 (age 15–19), 33 (20–29), 113 (30–39), 188 (40–49), and 64 (50+).

Q Is it more dangerous to be a jock or a pothead in high school? **A: Jock**

High school football deaths average 11 per year versus 0 from marijuana. Although the CDC reported 3 deaths from cannabis in 2001, according to drug experts, only 1 known death has ever directly resulted from marijuana use; in the UK, not understanding that active cannabinoids are not water-soluble, 1 fool tried to boil marijuana and inject it—which resulted in his dying from the resulting embolism.

Q If you're an American male, how much more likely are you to die from a weakened heart muscle caused by excess alcohol consumption than a female? **A: 8 times**

Alcoholic cardiomyopathy deaths reported were 499 (out of 26,863 total weak-heart-muscle deaths), 89% of which were male.

Drug World Death Rates
by WHO Region (per 100,000 population)

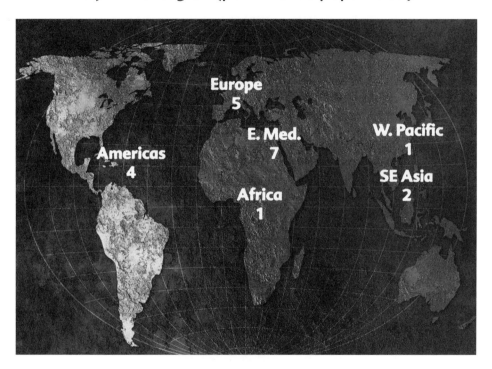

DRUGS DEATHS, 2002 — ALL AGES

Americas (incl USA): **31,886**

USA: **8,558***

Europe: **43,345**

E. Mediterranean: **35,713**

Africa: **9,332**

W. Pacific: **15,498**

Southeast Asia: **37,725**

* USA totals are for 2001.

Alcohol and Drug Abuse Disorder Deaths Worldwide, 2002

Cause	Deaths
Alcohol use disorders	85,992
Drug use disorders	88,020
TOTAL	**174,012**

MOST drug abusers begin with the hope of escaping their normal lives. Over time, however, any sense of transcendence fades away, and soon the goal of the addicted person is to use the drug simply to feel normal again.

Fatalities from drugs, of which alcohol is the deadliest, are not credited by the governmental health agencies in the same way that you'd guess, so to avoid confusion, we follow their lead in this book.

For example, deaths by drunk drivers are not included in this statistic (they fall under "Accidents"). Suicides

TAKE ME AWAY

by drugs show up under "Suicides." Drug-induced liver, nerve, brain, and heart diseases are not counted in the official U.S. drug death tally. Neither are deaths from cigarettes or accidental overdose.

What's left is "drug use disorder." The short description of this syndrome is "addiction." The World Health Organization provides this helpful diagnostic checklist:

- A strong desire to take the substance
- Difficulties in controlling use
- Withdrawal symptoms
- Needing more for the same effect because of tolerance
- Neglect of other interests
- Continued use despite evidence of harm

If you are described by 3 or more of the above symptoms, you have drug use disorder and you need to shake free. If you fail, you'll become one of the following statistics.

Note: All deaths cited are for 2001 in the U.S. and for
2002 in the world, unless otherwise noted

Quick & Dead Summary for the U.S.

8,558 Number of U.S. drug deaths, not including drug and/or alcohol-caused accidental poisoning (16,124), alcoholic liver disease (12,207), or suicide (3,585)

526 Number of drug deaths to Americans age 75+

U.S. DEATHS FROM DRUG USE DISORDERS

TYPE OF DISORDER	# OF DEATHS	TYPE OF DISORDER	# OF DEATHS
Alcohol	6,627	Sedatives/hypnotics	5
Cocaine	401	Cannabis	3
Opiates	211	Hallucinogens	2
Stimulants besides cocaine	35	More than 1 of the listed	1,265
Inhaled solvents	9	**Total**	**8,558**

Dying for a High

72 Percentage of worldwide drug use disorder (DUD) deaths among adults 30 to 59. The vast majority are people whose youthful drug abuse has finally caught up with them

83 Percentage of these middle-aged fatalities who are male

6 Percentage of DUD casualties who live to age 70

1 Rank of the Eastern Mediterranean region in DUD death rate per 100,000 people (7.1). As the premiere producer of opium poppies, it is also the region with the highest ratio of deaths from drugs other than alcohol

1 Rank of Thailand in drug offense convictions per 100,000 (329)

10 Rank of Morocco in drug offense convictions (68). It is the only Eastern Mediterranean country to make the top 10 in drug law enforcement

50 Percentage of DUD death rate of the Americas (3.7) compared to the Eastern Mediterranean

13 Percentage of DUD death rate of the West Pacific region (.9) compared to the Eastern Mediterranean

Booze or Dope?

49.4 Percentage of worldwide drug use deaths that are the result of alcohol. Regional variations are wide

76 Percentage in the Americas

76 Percentage in the West Pacific region (Australia, China, Japan, etc.)

73 Percentage in Africa

54 Percentage in Europe (including Russia)

40 Percentage in Southeast Asia (India, Thailand, etc.)

12 Percentage in the Eastern Mediterranean region, where alcohol is banned by Muslim-based law, but where opium poppies are a major cash crop

O Demon Alcohol!

4 to 1 Ratio between Denmark's death rate due to alcohol-related disorders and that of the U.S.

19,815 Number of U.S. deaths directly attributed to alcohol abuse

12,207 Of these, number killed by alcoholic liver disease

6,627 By alcohol use disorder

499 By alcoholic heart difficulties

303 By accidental alcohol poisoning

114 By an alcohol-degenerated nervous system

26 By deliberate overdose to commit suicide

3,529 Number of the deaths blamed on alcohol use disorder attributed to "dependence syndrome"

1,718 On "harmful use"

633 On "acute intoxication"

163 On "psychotic disorders"

27 On "amnesiac syndrome," an extreme version of amnesia in which the sufferer is unable to store new information in long-term memory

Alcohol and Drunk Driving

3 times Increased chance of a fatal car crash among male drunk drivers age 16–20 compared to male drunk drivers 25 and older

17,419 Estimated number of U.S. alcohol-related traffic fatalities in 2002, an average of 1 every 30 minutes

RANK	TYPE OF ARREST	NUMBER OF ARRESTS
\multicolumn{3}{c}{**TOP 7 ARREST TYPES FOR ALL OFFENSES (EXCEPT TRAFFIC VIOLATIONS) IN THE U.S., 2003**}		
1	Drug abuse violations	1,678,200
2	Driving under the influence	1,448,100
3	Simple assaults	1,246,700
4	Larceny/theft	1,145,100
5	Disorderly conduct	639,400
6	Liquor laws	612,100
7	Drunkenness	548,600

Alcohol and Crime/Murder

1 million Estimated number of U.S. violent crimes in 2002 in which victims were certain the offender had been drinking

31 Percentage of violent-crime victims who reported the attacker was under the influence of alcohol and was a stranger

67 Percentage of domestic violence victims (from a current or former spouse, boyfriend, or girlfriend) who reported alcohol was a factor

The Other Drugs

21,683 Number of U.S. deaths directly attributed to drug abuse

15,793 Number of U.S. deaths from accidental

poisoning by nonalcohol drugs, both legal and illegal. This includes unintentional ingestion by children and accidental overdose by intentional users

3,559 Number of U.S. suicides using drugs

1,931 Number of non-alcohol DUD deaths, the result of hard-core habitual use and addiction

42 Number of U.S. drug deaths that are determined to be homicides

Heroin

1 Rank of Afghanistan in world production of heroin. During the Taliban's strict rule, heroin production was nearly wiped out, but since the U.S. invasion, the country's opium farmers have surpassed pre-Taliban crop yields, reclaiming the #1 position and pushing Burma to #2

92 Percentage of the world's heroin in 2004 that came from Afghanistan— U.S. government estimate (582 of a total 628 metric tons)

2,205 Number of pounds in a metric ton

300–500 Estimated dose in micrograms that Swiss studies determined heroin addicts would typically use per day if given unlimited access. New users typically start at 5–20 mcg.

1 million Estimated number of addicts that a single pound of heroin could keep maintained for a day

211 Number of U.S. deaths attributed to mental and behavioral disorders from using opium derivatives of all kinds, including heroin. The drug itself doesn't kill nearly as many people as the laws against it do—by keeping the price artificially high, they force addicts to engage in prostitution, robbery, and other crimes. Unavailability of clean needles spreads diseases such as hepatitis and HIV/AIDS

36 Estimated percentage of U.S. AIDS cases attributed to use of injection drugs

6–20 times Range of likelihood that a needle-using heroin addict will prematurely die compared with a nonaddict of the same age, in separate studies

Heroin and Afghanistan—a Brief History

1971 Opium production in Eastern Mediterranean (Iran, Afghanistan, Pakistan): 504 tons

1972 Afghan farmers make $300–$360 per hectare from opium, twice the average of $175 for fruit

1978 Opium production in Eastern Mediterranean (Iran, Afghanistan, Pakistan): 1,400 tons

1979 Afghanistan invaded by the Soviet Union. U.S. heroin addicts: 200,000. Pakistan heroin addicts: 0

1981 Afghanistan opium production: 100 tons

1982 Afghanistan opium production: 300 tons. U.S. heroin addicts: 450,000. Pakistan heroin addicts: 5,000

1983 Afghanistan opium production: 575 tons

1985 Pakistan heroin addicts: 1.2 million

1989 Soviet Union withdraws from Afghanistan

Heroin and Afghanistan—a Brief History

1993 Western covert aid to the mujahideen guerrillas expands opium output in Afghanistan and links Pakistan's nearby heroin labs to the world. Burma and Afghanistan rank first and second in supply of heroin. Pakistan heroin addicts: 1.7 million

1996–2001 Taliban in power. They ban poppy cultivation and set fire to heroin labs

2001 U.S. forces topple the Taliban government. Bumper opium crop of 4,600 tons in Afghanistan. UN Drug Control Program estimates around 75% of world's heroin production is of Afghan origin

2002 UN Drug Control and Crime Prevention Agency announces Afghanistan has regained its position as the world's largest opium producer. Supplies 80–90% of heroin in Europe. Approximate opium production of 1,278 metric tons

2004 Expanding poppy cultivation and a growing opium trade accounts for about $7.2 billion, representing $1/3$ of Afghanistan's GDP and 60% of the total U.S. "War on Drugs" budget. U.S. government estimates Afghanistan now accounts for 92% of the world's supply of heroin

Bayer Works Wonders

Like aspirin, heroin was originally marketed by the Bayer pharmaceutical company. In fact, both aspirin and heroin were once brand names that went generic after World War I. Heroin derived its name from heroic; Bayer believed it to be a safe, nonaddictive substitute for morphine. From 1898 through 1910, the Heroin brand was marketed as a benign ingredient in pain medications, patent medicines, and children's cough syrups.

Stimulants

401 Number of U.S. deaths attributed to cocaine use

1 Rank of Colombia in world production of cocaine

90 Percentage of the U.S. cocaine market supplied by Colombia

35 Number of U.S. deaths attributed to other stimulants, from methamphetamines to caffeine

1 Rank of caffeine as the world's most widely used psychoactive drug

80 Minimum estimated percentage of adults in Western countries who regularly ingest enough caffeine to affect the same part of the brain stimulated by cocaine

5 Maximum dosage in grams of caffeine that is regularly nonfatal. A typical cup of coffee ranges from 80 to 120 milligrams

42 to 62 Number of cups of coffee, consumed in less than 10 hours by a healthy, nonpregnant adult, that raise caffeine use to the 5 gram level. Deaths from caffeine overdose are rare and most often related to intentional overdose of caffeine pills (typically 100–200 milligrams each)

4–5 Estimated maximum number of daily cups of coffee to avoid risking miscarriage

High and Getting Higher

34 Percentage increase in U.S. alcohol-related fatalities from 1999 to 2002

36 Percentage increase

in U.S. fatalities directly attributed to legal and illegal drug abuse during the same period

48 Percentage increase in the number of prescriptions filled in the U.S. from

1995 (2.125 billion) to 2002 (3.139 billion)

Turn On, Tune In ... Die!

5 Number of U.S. deaths attributed to cannabis products

2 Number attributed to hallucinogens

U.S. DRUG CRIMINALIZATION DEATHS FROM ILLEGAL DRUG USE VS. DRUG-RELATED MURDERS, 2001–2

YEAR	ILLEGAL-DRUG-USE DEATHS	DRUG-RELATED MURDERS (ASSUMES 100% OF GANG & MAFIA KILLINGS RELATE TO ILLEGAL DRUG ACTIVITY)
2001	211 opioids 401 cocaine 3 cannabinoids 2 hallucinogens	862 juvenile-gang killings 575 illegal-narcotic drug trafficking 118 brawl due to influence of narcotics 76 organized crime killings
	Total illegal-drug OD deaths 617	Maximum murders due to criminalization of drugs: 1,735
2002	281 opioids 437 cocaine 1 cannabinoids 5 hallucinogens	911 juvenile-gang killings 664 illegal-narcotic drug trafficking 85 brawl due to influence of narcotics 75 organized crime killings
	Total illegal-drug OD deaths 724	Maximum murders due to criminalization of drugs: 1,735

Most at Risk of Premature Death from Drugs

WORLDWIDE DEATH RATES, 2002
(per 100,000 population)

AGE	MALE	FEMALE
0−4		
5−14		
15−29	2.2	0.4
30−44	8.0	1.6
45−59	11.8	2.4
60−69	9.0	1.6
70+	7.2	1.5

Main Cause

Too much alcohol
Too many legal and illegal drugs

Prevention

■ WATCH WHAT YOU PUT IN YOUR MOUTH
■ WATCH WHAT YOU INJECT INTO YOUR BODY

Bad
Fran

#16 Cause of premature death in the World
2002 (under age 70)

#13 Cause of premature death in the USA
2001 (under age 75)

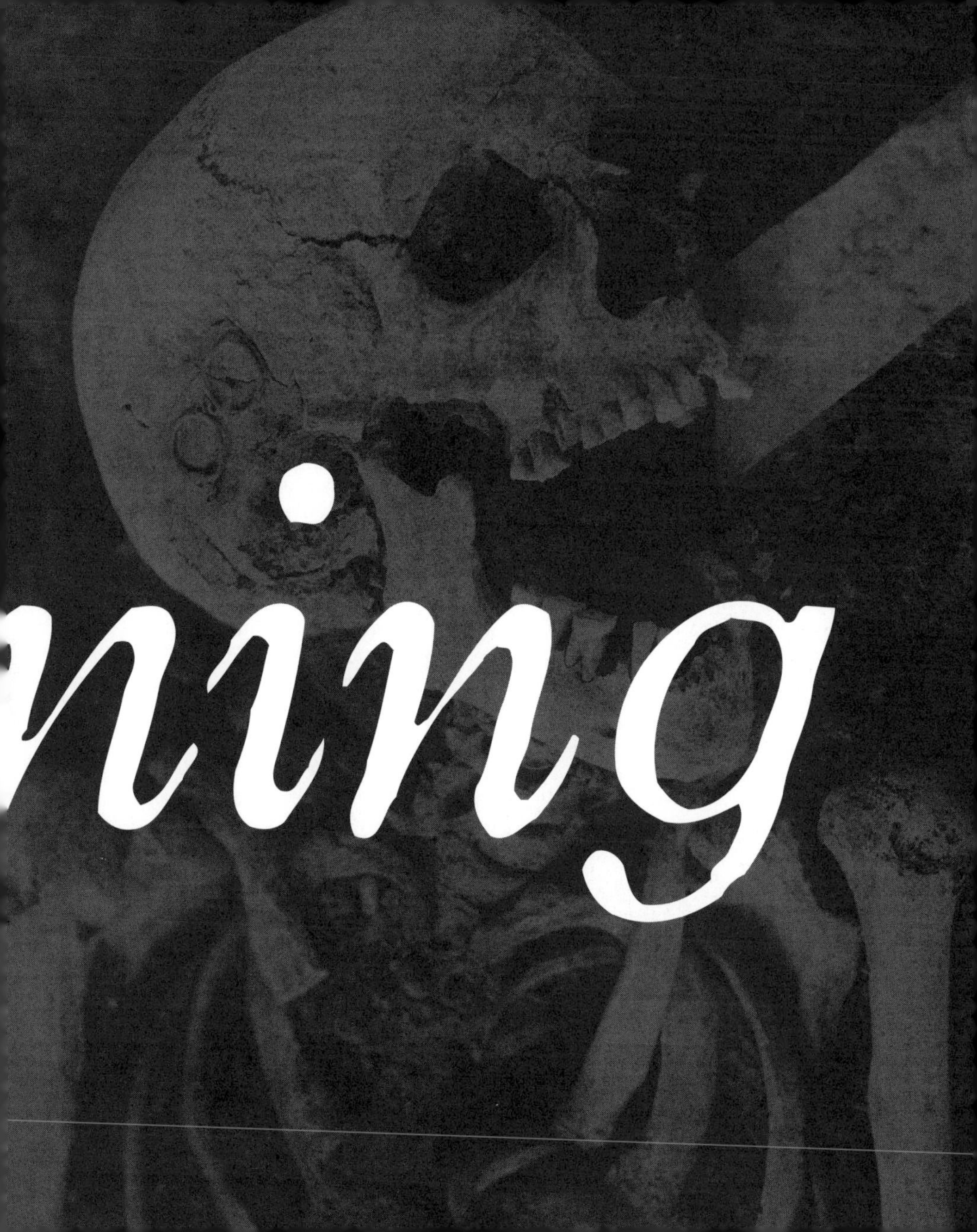
ning

QUESTION: Are you more likely to die of gum disease in sweet margarita-drinking Mexico or in dry sake-drinking Japan?

ANSWER: Mexico

Mexico reported 16 deaths from gum disease (mostly resulting from diabetes) in 1999 versus 1 in Japan.

Q Are you more likely to die of gout in the U.S. or the UK?

A: UK

UK residents died at a rate of .05 per 100,000 (28 deaths total) while U.S. residents died at a lesser rate of .03 (85 total) in 2000.

Q What gets implanted more, knee replacements or breasts?

A: Knee

In 2003 in the U.S. there were 418,000 total knee replacements, primarily for arthritis, versus 323,000 breast-enhancement and reconstruction implants.

Q Are you more likely to die from lack of calcium or contaminated calcium? **A: Lack of calcium**

500 cases of food-borne illness in the U.S. in 2001 were caused by dairy products— none of which resulted in death—versus 1,684 deaths that year from osteoporosis.

Q If you're old in America, which form of neglect is more likely to kill you, starvation or bedsores?

A: Starvation

Of the 1,638 who died from decubitus ulcers in 2001, 1,304 were 75+ versus 2,989 that age who died of starvation.

Q If you were a female age 55–64 in 2004, how much more likely were you to die of a musculoskeletal disease if you had dark skin?

A: 2 times

Black female Americans died at a rate of 12.6 from diseases of the muscles, skin, and bones versus 6.0 for white females ages 55–64 in 2004. Once older women are factored in, white females have the highest overall rate of death.

Q How much more likely were you die of rheumatoid arthritis in 2004 if you were female versus male? **A: 3 times**

1,971 American females died in 2004 versus 600 males.

Bad Framing World Death Rates
by WHO Region (per 100,000 population)

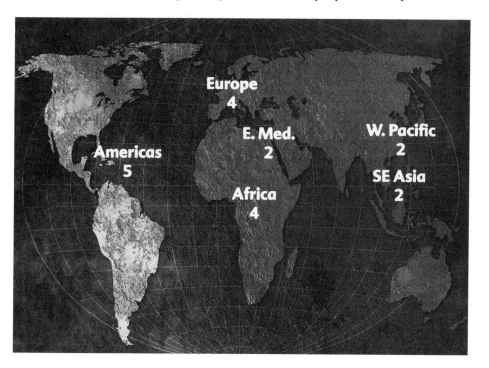

BAD FRAMING DEATHS, 2002 — ALL AGES

Americas (incl USA):
41,708

USA: **18,014***

Europe: **37,945**

E. Mediterranean: **9,492**

Africa: **26,489**

W. Pacific: **30,394**

Southeast Asia: **33,380**

* USA totals are for 2001.

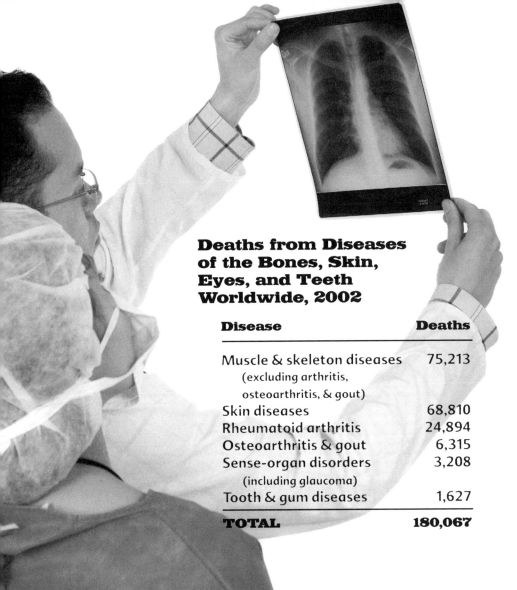

Deaths from Diseases of the Bones, Skin, Eyes, and Teeth Worldwide, 2002

Disease	Deaths
Muscle & skeleton diseases (excluding arthritis, osteoarthritis, & gout)	75,213
Skin diseases	68,810
Rheumatoid arthritis	24,894
Osteoarthritis & gout	6,315
Sense-organ disorders (including glaucoma)	3,208
Tooth & gum diseases	1,627
TOTAL	**180,067**

OUR

bones are analogous to a building's internal support structure. Our skin functions like its walls. Our mouths and sense organs are doors and windows to the outside world. When a building's framing fails, it can droop, shed pieces of its outer skin, or even collapse into itself.

So it is with humans. We may sag, suffer disfigurement and blemishes, or fully collapse into ourselves. Our joints

THE FRAME GAME

may swell and lose their flexibility and strength. Thankfully, "bad framing" doesn't kill as many people as our other major categories. And even if we contract framing diseases, our structures may stand tall and strong for many decades.

Note: All deaths cited are for 2001 in the U.S. and 2002 in the world, unless otherwise noted

Quick & Dead Summary for the U.S.

18,014 Number of deaths from "bad framing"— bad bones, muscles, eyes, ears, skin, and teeth

60 Percentage of those deaths in people over 75

14,057 Of those, the number who died from musculoskeletal disease

3,749 From skin-related diseases

134 From teeth- and gum-related diseases

74 From eye or ear diseases

TOP 5 MOST LETHAL
FRAMING DISEASES IN THE U.S.

RANK	TYPE OF DISEASE	NUMBER OF DEATHS
1	Rheumatoid arthritis	2,643
2	Osteoporosis	1,684
3	Bedsores	1,638
4	Scleroderma	1,378
5	Systemic lupus erythematosus	1,359

Meat and Bones

106,423 Number of worldwide deaths from musculoskeletal diseases (that is, diseases of the muscles and bones) each year. They are responsible for 3 out of 5 bad-framing deaths, more than all other bad-framing categories combined

25–55 Age range when most cases of rheumatoid arthritis first appear. This disease usually affects joints and surrounding tissues, but can also attack other organs

1–2 Percentage of the U.S. population affected by rheumatoid arthritis

DEATH FROM DISEASES OF THE MUSCLES, SKIN, AND BONES
U.S. by race and sex 1999–2004
(Death rate per 100,000 population)

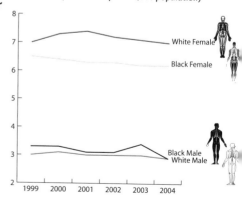

White Female
Black Female
Black Male
White Male

Martian Ending

Ray Walston, whose most famous role was the title character in the TV comedy *My Favorite Martian*, died from lupus in 2001. Another celebrity, beloved journalist Charles Kuralt, known for his folksy reporting about everyday Americans on his CBS series *On the Road*, died of the same disease at the age of 62.

2,643 Number of U.S. deaths from rheumatoid arthritis

1,684 Number of U.S. deaths from osteoporosis, in which calcium leaches from bones. About 10 million Americans suffer from it, and another 18 million have osteopenia, a less severe form

50 Estimated percentage of women over 50 who will suffer a fracture of the hip, wrist, or vertebra. About 20% of women over 50 suffer from osteoporosis; another 30% suffer from osteopenia

1,378 Number of U.S. deaths from scleroderma, in which extra collagen collects in skeletal muscles and skin. Its name means "hard skin" in Greek

1,359 Number of U.S. deaths from systemic lupus erythematosus. Although lupus is an autoimmune disease that can attack organs, blood vessels, and/or the nervous system, we mention it here because nearly all lupus sufferers develop joint pain and arthritis, often the first major symptom that drives many unsuspecting lupus sufferers to the doctor for diagnosis

9 to 1 Ratio of female lupus sufferers to males. Male

lupus patients tend to fare worse due to blood clots, seizures, misdiagnosis, and general misinformation

1,221 Number of U.S. deaths from osteomyelitis, an acute chronic bone infection caused by bacteria or fungi. The infection can produce a pus-filled abscess inside the bone, killing bone

tissue by depriving it of its blood supply

1 in 5,000 Odds of contracting osteomyelitis. Children tend to get it in the long bones, and adults in the vertebrae and pelvis

1 in 233,000 Odds of a U.S. patient dying from osteomyelitis

Swiss-born artist Paul Klee developed scleroderma in 1935 in the middle of a brilliant art career. With his mobility increasingly restricted, his art became more stark and somber. After 5 years of battling the disease, he died at the age of 60.

Give Me Some Skin

1 Rank of bedsores among noncancerous skin diseases as cause of U.S. deaths. Bedsores are ulcers that occur from sitting or lying in one position for too long, cutting off circulation and killing the skin tissue

2 to 1 Ratio of bedsore deaths in women versus men. The bulk of life-threatening bedsores are the result of negligence in nursing homes. Preventing bedsores in people with little or no mobility requires changing their position often

2 Rank of cellulitis as a cause of death among non-cancerous skin diseases in the U.S. Cellulitis is an acute infection of the skin caused by staphylococcus, strepto-coccus, and other bacteria

858 Number of cellulitis deaths in the U.S. We're not talking about cellulite, a common condition of ripply fat on the legs and rears of some women, fatal to nothing but pride

1 in 5,000 Estimated proportion of liposuction patient fatalities, according to a plastic surgeons' task force. Although cellulite is not fatal, trying to fix it definitely can be

705 Total number of U.S. deaths for the 3rd through 8th worst noncancerous skin diseases: #3 discoid lupus erythematosus, an autoimmune disorder that, unlike systemic lupus ery-thematosus (see above), affects the skin only (217 deaths); #4 furuncles and carbuncles, abscess infec-tions around hair follicles (198); #5 pemphigoid and pemphigus, blistering au-toimmune disorders (139); #6 erythema multiforme, a skin allergic reaction (110); #7 psoriasis, a common scaly skin disorder (29); and #8 exfoliative dermatitis, a disease of itching, scaling, and hair loss (12)

1 Number of U.S. deaths from sunburn

Christopher Reeve was known on-screen as Superman, and off-screen as a super man in pushing for stem-cell research. After a paralyzing horse-riding accident, Reeve dedicated his life to finding a cure for paralysis. He succumbed in 2004 to complications from one hazard of being bedridden: a decubitus ulcer, commonly known as a bedsore.

Medical Bloodsuckers

Leeches, rejected in the twentieth century as a hall-mark of discredited medicine, have come back into medical use as an effective way of draining pooled blood around wounds and skin grafts. One of the little suckers' unexpected benefits is in treating arthritis. The painkiller that leeches inject into their victims can reduce arthritic symptoms for up to 6 months per treatment.

Mouthing Off

12 Percentage of heart disease among people missing all of their teeth. According to a study by the Centers for Disease Control, the rate was 11% for those missing 6–31 teeth, 7% for those missing 1–5 teeth, and 5% for those missing no teeth. Researchers theorize that the C-reactive protein coming from gum disease may contribute to problems with arterial plaque

20,000 Number of adult twins participating in a study that found a correlation between chronic gum disease and Alzheimer's disease

67 Number of U.S. deaths from diseases of the saliva

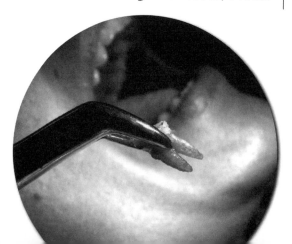

glands. Spit normally flows freely from saliva ducts, but that can change if the salivary glands get infected with viral diseases such as mumps or bacterial infections from poor oral hygiene

25 Number of U.S. deaths from severe mouth ulcers

16 Number of U.S. deaths from severe gum disease or tooth abscesses. It just goes to show that your floss can also be your gain

Now See, Hear!

17 Number of U.S. deaths attributed to blindness and bad vision. Four deaths were specifically related to glaucoma. Other causes include diabetes, macular degeneration, and accidents (injuries from chemicals, racquetballs, bungee cords, fishhooks, fireworks, etc.). Worldwide causes include cataracts, vitamin A deficiency, leprosy, and river blindness, a disease spread by black flies in the Arabian Peninsula and equatorial areas of the Americas

3,208 Number of worldwide deaths attributed to blindness and deafness

3 times Increased chance of developing cataracts among high-altitude airplane pilots. Researchers blame the increased level of cosmic radiation normally

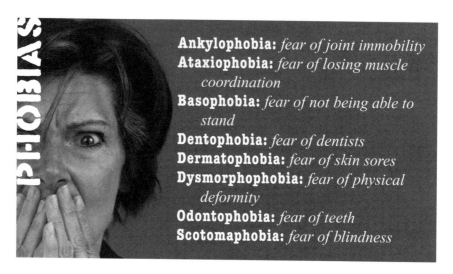

PHOBIAS

Ankylophobia: *fear of joint immobility*
Ataxiophobia: *fear of losing muscle coordination*
Basophobia: *fear of not being able to stand*
Dentophobia: *fear of dentists*
Dermatophobia: *fear of skin sores*
Dysmorphophobia: *fear of physical deformity*
Odontophobia: *fear of teeth*
Scotomaphobia: *fear of blindness*

filtered by the earth's atmosphere. Depletion of the ozone layer will likely increase cataracts in non-pilots for the same reason

25 Percentage of chronic glaucoma cases in which the sufferer has no idea he/she has the disease. 1 to 2% of people over 40 suffer from excess eye pressure, with African Americans 4 times more likely to have it than European Americans

8 Number of U.S. deaths attributed to deafness and hearing loss

22 Number of U.S. deaths attributed to ear infection. The eustachian tubes allow ears to drain liquid and bacteria, and they clog easily in small children, especially when afflicted by colds, allergies, secondhand smoke, adenoid difficulties, or excess mucus and saliva produced during teething

Most at Risk of Premature Death from Bad Framing

WORLDWIDE DEATH RATES, 2002
(per 100,000 population)

AGE	MALE	FEMALE
0–4	0.7	0.8
5–14	0.2	0.3
15–29	0.5	0.7
30–44	0.8	1.3
45–59	2.4	3.4
60–69	6.3	8.5
70+	27.9	39.7

Main Cause

Arthritis

Prevention

- WATCH YOUR DIET
- GET EXERCISE
- GET REGULAR MEDICAL EXAMINATIONS

Starv

#12 Cause of premature death in the world
2002 (under age 70)

#14 Cause of premature death in the USA
2001 (under age 75)

QUESTION: Are you more likely to starve to death in Africa or die of lung cancer in the USA?

ANSWER: Lung cancer

In 2002, per 100,000 people, the rate of U.S. deaths from lung cancer in 2002 was 54.7 versus a rate of 20.3 for starvation in Africa.

Q How much more likely are you to starve to death as an infant in India versus the USA? **A: 3 times**

The rate of death per 100,000 children under age 5 in India is 87 to the U.S.'s 31. Almost 50% of India's children under 3 are malnourished.

Q What's deadlier in the U.S., not eating or eating too much?

A: Eating too much

In 2002 in the U.S., 13 teens between 15 and 19 died from obesity versus 4 from anorexia.

Q What percent of worldwide food crises are the result of war? **A: 35%**

More than 35% of short- and long-term food crises can be attributed to human causes—most by conflict.

Q Are you more likely to die from not eating when you're young or when you're old? **A: Old**

3,986 people age 75+ died of starvation in the U.S. in 2001. Meanwhile, under-30 deaths from all eating disorders (including anorexia) totaled 11. (Eating disorders affect older people, too, killing 210 people over 30.)

Q&A

Starvation World Death Rates
by WHO Region (per 100,000 population)

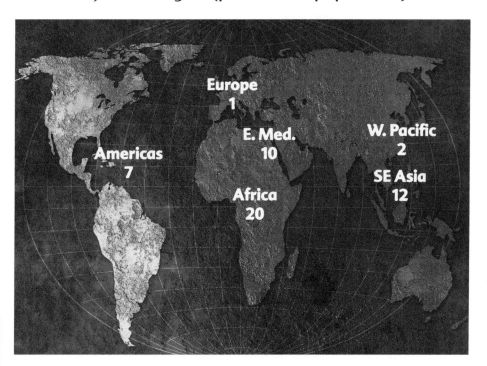

STARVATION DEATHS, 2002—ALL AGES

Americas (incl USA): **60,616**

USA: **3,986***

Europe: **12,008**

E. Mediterranean: **51,295**

Africa: **137,100**

W. Pacific: **26,076**

Southeast Asia: **186,719**

* USA totals are for 2001.

Malnutrition and Vitamin Deficiency Deaths Worldwide, 2002

Cause	Deaths
Protein-energy malnutrition	249,937
Iron-deficiency anemia	136,983
Vitamin A deficiency	22,901
Iodine deficiency	6,533
Other nutritional disorders	58,312
TOTAL	**474,666**

FOOD FOR THOUGHT

WHY DOES

starvation even exist? Yes, there are 6.4 billion people in the world, but we can grow and raise enough food to feed every 1 of them. Why, then, will nearly 1 in 7 people go hungry tonight? Why do some children get diabetes from gorging too much food, while 1 in 3 are malnourished?

One reason is a vastly inequitable distribution of wealth, in which poverty begets further poverty. Acts of nature, sometimes exacerbated by humans, have caused crop-killing droughts, floods, and weather extremes in parts of the world least able to recover from them. War and civil strife disrupt farming and food distribution; sometimes starvation is even deliberately used as a weapon. Transportation, irrigation, and storage infrastructure difficulties can make food difficult to grow and move to market. Overgrazing, deforestation, erosion, and other poor farming methods are depleting soil. And in some areas of Africa, HIV/AIDS has weakened and killed up to a quarter of the 15–49-year-old age group, the ones who normally grow food and provide for families. Whatever the reasons for world hunger, they are all solvable if more fortunate people would only have the will.

Note: All deaths cited are for 2001 in the U.S. and 2002 in the world, unless otherwise noted

Quick & Dead Summary for the U.S.

3,986 Number who officially died of starvation

80 Percentage of those who were over age 75

3,454 Number of all starvations from malnutrition

130 Number from iron-deficiency anemia

79 From other anemias (not including heriditary disorders such as sickle-cell anemia, found in the "Hormones" chapter)

73 From vitamin B12 deficiency anemia

250 Number from other nutritional deficiencies

38.4 Starvation death rate per 100,000 people 85 and older, the age most affected by starvation in the U.S.

1.9 The same rate for Americans 65 to 74 years

U.S. STARVATION DEATH RATES, AGE 85+—1999 TO 2002

(per 100,000)

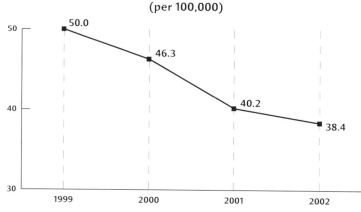

The Skinny on Hunger

815 million Estimated number of people for whom hunger is a common occurrence

474,666 Number of people who starved to death worldwide in 2002

193,515 Number who were infants and toddlers (0–4 years old)

9 Number of 0–4 starvation deaths in the U.S.

21,501 to 1 Increased odds of child starvation outside the U.S.

281,151 Number of world starvation deaths among people 5 years and older

3,977 The same number for Americans

751 Number of American starvation deaths between the ages of 5 to 75

The Elderly

87,090 Number of world starvation deaths among people 70 and older

3,226 Number of

American starvation victims older than 75

81 Of those, the percentage of victims over 85

Regional Cuisine

A COMPARISON OF PER CAPITA FOOD CONSUMPTION U.S. VS. SE ASIA, 1990s

COUNTRY	FOOD ENERGY KCAL/DAY	PROTEIN G/DAY	FAT G/DAY
SE Asian average	2,357	50	39
USA	3,700	107	157

Survival by Gender

9 to 5 Odds that a starved baby 0–4 years old in Southeast Asia (India, Korea, etc.) is a girl. In cultures where boys are more valued than girls, society can allocate scarce resources unevenly

3 to 2 Odds that a starved baby in the Eastern Mediterranean is a girl

11 to 10 Odds in Africa, the Americas, and West Pacific that a starved baby is a boy. More boys than girls are born each year, but statistically baby boys are less resilient

4 to 3 Odds that a starved baby in Europe is a boy

105 Number of American boys born each year per 100 newborn American girls. By the time they reach the 35–39 age group, women have begun outnumbering men, and by 85, the ratio of women to men is 3 to 1

Starvation by War

180,000 Number of Sudanese who died mostly from illness and malnutrition in 18 months of the Darfur genocide as of March 2005. Prior to the 2004 Indian Ocean earthquake and tsunami, the UN called the Darfur conflict the world's worst current humanitarian crisis

20 to 40 million Estimated number of Chinese who starved in the 1950s during Mao Tse-tung's Great Leap Forward—the worst famine in history

1.4 million Estimated number of Jews who died of exposure, beatings, epidemics, and starvation in Nazi death camps during World War II

The Thin and the Fat

170 million Estimated number of malnourished children in the world

3.4 million Number of premature deaths worldwide from complications of malnutrition

1 billion Number of people in high- or middle-income countries who suffer complications from overeating

300 million Of those, number who are clinically obese

500,000 Number of people in North America and Europe who died prematurely from being overweight

7.0 Percentage of U.S. children 5 and under who were overweight in 2005

1.1 Percentage who were underweight

TOP 10 WORST COUNTRIES
FOR UNDERWEIGHT CHILDREN
(under age five, latest year available)

RANK	COUNTRY	% UNDERWEIGHT
1	Afghanistan, 1997	46.2
2	India, 1999	44.4
3	Niger, 2000	43.6
4	Nepal, 2001	43.0
5	Bangladesh, 2004	42.7
6	Yemen, 2003	42.7
7	Timor-Leste, 2002	40.6
8	Cambodia, 2000	39.5
9	Burundi, 2000	38.9
10	Sudan, 2000	38.4

TOP 10 WORST COUNTRIES
FOR OVERWEIGHT CHILDREN
(under age five, latest year available)

RANK	COUNTRY	% OVERWEIGHT
1	Albania, 2000	30.0
2	Ukraine, 2000	26.5
3	Comoros, 2000	21.5
4	Lesotho, 2000	21.0
5	Georgia, 1999	17.7
6	Bosnia and Herzegovina, 2000	16.3
7	Algeria, 2002	15.4
8	Swaziland, 2000	14.9
9	Egypt, 2005	14.1
10	Bulgaria, 2004	13.6

Most at Risk of Premature Death from Starvation

WORLDWIDE DEATH RATES, 2002
U.S. DEATH RATES, 2001
(per 100,000 population)

AGE	WORLD MALE	WORLD FEMALE	U.S.
0–4	29.2	33.5	
5–14	3.5	4.2	
15–29	1.2	1.0	
30–44	1.6	2.6	0.1
45–59	6.3	9.2	0.5
60–69	8.2	12.7	2.0
70+	30.1	31.4	8.7
85+			42.9

Main Cause

War and famine
Neglect

Prevention

■ GET EDUCATED

■ BE COMPASSIONATE

Child
bea

#11 Cause of premature death in the world
2002 (under age 70)

#15 Cause of premature death in the USA
2001 (under age 75)

QUESTION: What's the net increase in world population every second? **ANSWER: 2 persons**

Subtracting new deaths from new births, there's a net increase of 2-1/3 persons every second. That's 73 million new people per year—about the 2003 population of Egypt.

Q If you're pregnant, are you more vulnerable to murder? **A: No**

The murder rate of pregnant women aged 17–44 in 2001 was 1.6 versus 3.2 for those not pregnant.

Q How much more likely were you to die giving birth before the passage of *Roe v. Wade* (January 1973)? **A: 2 times**

If you were a white female, the rate of death was 0.4 in 1972 versus 0.2 in 2002; if you were a black female, the rate of death was 1.7 in 1972 versus 0.8 in 2002.

Q If you are of childbearing age, how much does higher education increase your chance to live?

A: Almost 3 times

Women ages 25–34 die at a rate of 98.6 per 100,000 with 12 years of education versus 36.1 if they have 13 years or more.

Q How much more likely are you to die from a car accident than pregnancy? **A: 15 times**

Between ages 25 and 34 in the U.S. in 2002, 2,934 women died from accidents versus 175 who died from pregnancy. Cancer is the #2 cause with 2,004 deaths.

Q What proportion of pregnant women die in Africa from illegal abortions? **A: 20% to 50%**

In many African countries abortion is illegal and dangerous; 20% of all maternal deaths in east and central Africa and 54% in Ethiopia were due to abortion in 1990.

Q Which country in the world has the highest fertility rate?

A: Somalia

In 2003, Somalian women who gave birth averaged 6.9 births each.

Q Which country in the world has the lowest fertility rate?

A: The Czech Republic

In 2003, Czech women who gave birth averaged 1.2 children each.

Q Which is more dangerous, an illegal abortion or a violent partner? **A: Illegal abortion**

An estimated 20 million unsafe abortions occur in the world of which an estimated 68,000 women die at a rate of 340 per 100,000 abortions. By contrast, approximately 60,000 women of childbearing age 15–44 were murdered in the world in 2002 at a rate of 4.1 per 100,000.

Childbearing World Death Rates
by WHO Region (per 100,000 population)

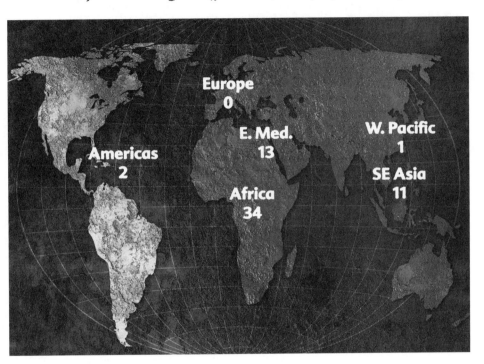

CHILDBEARING DEATHS, 2002—ALL AGES

Americas (incl USA):
16,627

USA: **416***

Europe: **2,776**

E. Mediterranean: **67,148**

Africa: **231,274**

W. Pacific: **20,829**

Southeast Asia: **171,083**

* USA totals are for 2001.

Pregnancy-related Deaths Worldwide, 2002

Cause	Deaths
Bleeding (hemorrhage)	141,751
Infection (sepsis)	75,820
High blood pressure (hypertensive disorder)	71,499
Abortion	65,958
Obstructed labor	43,114
Other	112,051
TOTAL	**510,193**

TO HERE FROM MATERNITY

DEATH is something we all face. Without it, we wouldn't be able to fully appreciate life. (Not to mention the overcrowding caused by all those really, really old people.) But some deaths are particularly tragic. High on our list are those that happen unexpectedly in childhood, take away parents of young children, or come while bringing forth life.

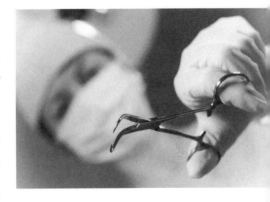

Even the best births are unusually painful compared to those of other species, largely because of the size of the baby's head (evolved to hold our freakishly large brains). Too many human births are life-threateningly complicated—15% of the total, according to pediatric experts—and many expectant mothers don't even make it to the birthing stage. Yes, things were much worse in earlier times, but they remain much worse in many parts of the world—including, to our national shame, poorer sections of the U.S. If we value the continuation of human life, we must take better care of the ones who give it.

Note: All deaths cited are for 2001 in the U.S. and 2002 in the world, unless otherwise noted

Quick & Dead Summary for the U.S.

6,401,000 Pregnancies (in 2000)

4,060,000 Live births (in 2000)

416 Annual deaths from maternity-related problems

Maternity Deaths by Cause:

69 Blood clot (embolism)

53 High blood pressure (hypertension)

42 Delivery

38 Infection

29 Hemorrhage

23 Ectopic pregnancy

19 Miscarriages, abortions, and attempted abortions

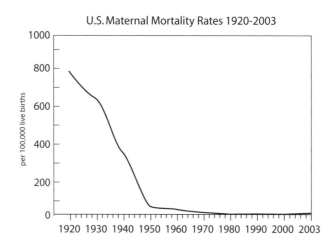

U.S. Maternal Mortality Rates 1920-2003

Century of Progress?

600–900 U.S. women who died from pregnancy-related complications per 100,000 live births at the beginning of the twentieth century

8 The same figure a century later, a 99% improvement

55 Percentage of U.S. hospital births in 1938

Pushing Up the Mums

50 Minimum percentage of annual U.S. pregnancy-difficulty deaths that could be saved by appropriate existing medical procedures

4 to 1 Factor by which a black American mother is more likely to die from maternity than a white one in 2001

2 to 1 The same factor

90 Percentage of U.S. hospital births in 1948

71 Percentage reduction of maternal mortality between 1939 and 1948

200 Years it took the U.S. to elect a president who had been born in a hospital (Jimmy Carter, 1976)

U.S. TEENAGE CHILDBEARING (UNDER AGE 18)	
(% of Live Births by Race, 2001)	
Black	7.3
American Indian or Alaska Native	6.8
Hispanic or Latina	5.8
White	2.3
Asian or Pacific Islander	1.3

for black women at the beginning of the twentieth century

2.5 to 1 Factor by which a

Hispanic American mother is more likely to die from maternity than a white one in 2001

50 Percentage of U.S. pregnancies that are unintended

75 Percentage of unintended pregnancies in mothers under 20

20 Percentage of U.S. women who don't obtain prenatal care during their first trimester

50 Percentage of U.S. unintended pregnancies forgoing first-trimester prenatal care

21 U.S. ranking for maternal mortality among industrialized nations

1 U.S. ranking for per capita cost of medical care

200 Millions of women who become pregnant worldwide annually

510,193 Women who died from pregnancy-related causes worldwide

96 Percentage of maternal deaths for women between 15 and 44

In Agra, India, sits one of the most splendid structures ever built: the Taj Mahal. It was constructed in the seventeenth century by emperor Shah Jahan, in memory of his beloved queen Mumtaz Mahal. She died while giving birth to their fourteenth child.

Problems

Heavy Bleeding

2–4 Percentage of pregnancies complicated by maternal hemorrhage. This can occur as early as 4½ months before delivery or 6 weeks after

141,751 Number of women worldwide who died from maternal hemorrhage

29 Number of annual U.S. maternal deaths from hemorrhage

28 Percentage of worldwide maternal deaths from hemorrhage

1 Ranking of hemorrhage among causes of worldwide maternity deaths

5 Ranking of hemorrhage among causes of U.S. maternity deaths

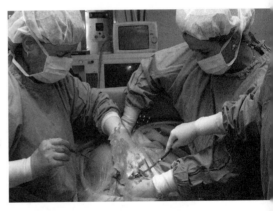

Infection

40 Percentage of 1920s U.S. maternal deaths caused by sepsis, commonly called bloodstream infection. About half of these deaths were from bad medical procedures, including overuse of labor induction, forceps, cesarean deliveries, and episiotomies, usually under less-than-sterile conditions

20 Percentage of 1920s U.S. maternal deaths from infection resulting from illegal abortions

75,820 Number of worldwide maternal infection deaths

15 Percentage of maternal deaths worldwide from infection

38 Number of annual U.S. maternal deaths from infection

9 Percentage of U.S. maternal deaths from infection

High Blood Pressure

71,499 Number of pregnant women worldwide who died from hypertension

5–10 Percentage of women who develop hypertension during their pregnancy. The onset usually comes after the 24th week and is more likely among first pregnancies; women under 15 or over 35; smokers; overweight

mothers; pregnancies with multiple babies; and mothers with a family history of high blood pressure

14 Percentage of worldwide maternal deaths from hypertension

13 Percentage of U.S. maternal deaths from hypertension

Miscarriage and Abortion

65,958 Number of women worldwide who died from miscarriages, abortions, and attempted abortions

13 Percentage of worldwide pregnancy deaths

caused by a prebirth ending the pregnancy

3 Percentage of U.S. pregnancy deaths from prebirth endings

Embolism

69 Number of annual U.S. deaths from pregnancy-related blood clots

1 Ranking of blood clots as the cause of U.S. maternity deaths. Air, bacteria, or amniotic fluid can enter the bloodstream from surgical intervention or birth. The resulting clots can cause sudden, unexpected death if they lodge in the lungs, heart, or brain

Adolescent Mothers

2–4 Number of times more likely a young pregnant woman (under age 20) will die than an older pregnant woman from complications of childbirth or unsafe abortion

70 Percentage of adolescent mothers experiencing obstructed labor in Kenya

45 Percentage of all vesicovaginal fistula cases (tearing of the wall between bladder and vagina during childbirth) occurring in Kenya in 1992 that were to pregnant adolescents

36 Percentage of Saudi Arabian mothers experiencing an infant's death

67 Percentage of mothers in Saudi Arabia under age 19

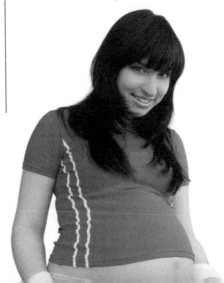

Murder?

514 If murder of pregnant women were classified as a maternity-related problem, the number of childbearing deaths in 2001 (versus 416 not counting murder)

15.3 Percentage of U.S. women with unwanted pregnancies who reported spousal/partner abuse during the pregnancy

5.3 The same percentage for women with wanted pregnancies

12.6 Percentage of women experiencing abuse who are not pregnant

98 Average annual number of pregnant women murdered in the U.S. between 1990 and 2004.

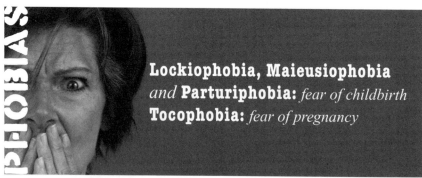

PHOBIAS

Lockiophobia, Maieusiophobia *and* **Parturiphobia:** *fear of childbirth*
Tocophobia: *fear of pregnancy*

Most at **Risk of Premature Death** from **Childbearing**

WORLDWIDE DEATH RATES, 2002
(per 100,000 population)

AGE	FEMALE
15–29	33.0
30–44	36.1

U.S. DEATH RATES, 2001
(per 100,000 population)

AGE	FEMALE
15–24	0.3
25–34	0.5
35–44	0.2

Main Cause

Excessive bleeding

Prevention

- GET EDUCATED
- WATCH YOUR DIET
- GET REGULAR MEDICAL EXAMINATIONS DURING PREGNANCY

Lare

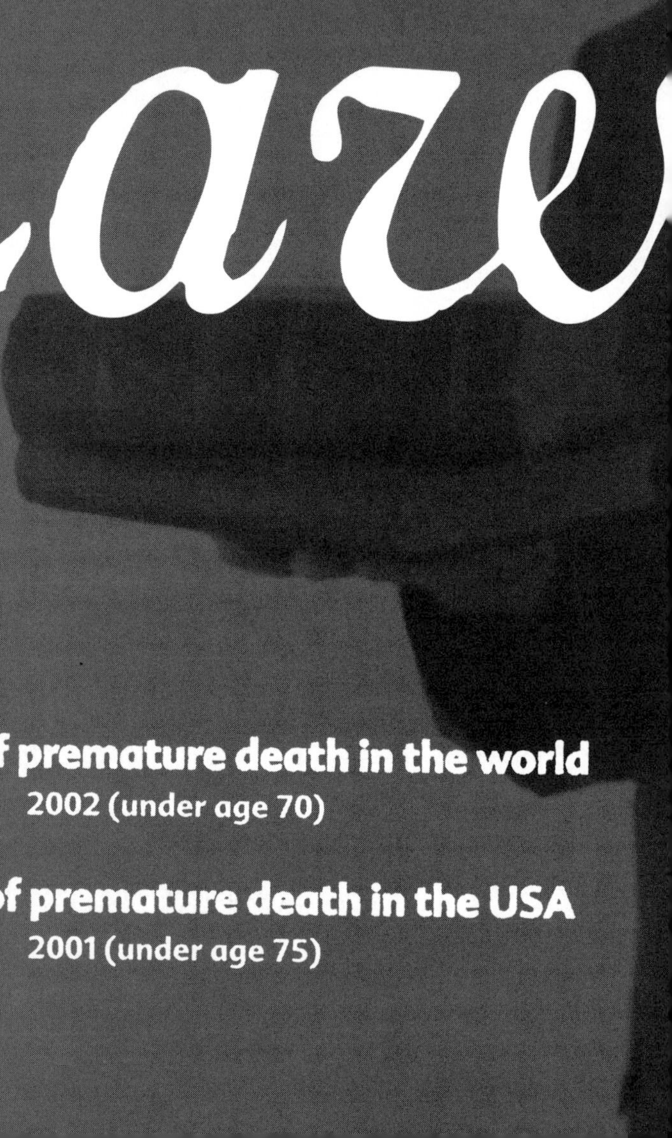

#17 Cause of premature death in the world

2002 (under age 70)

#16 Cause of premature death in the USA

2001 (under age 75)

QUESTION: Were more child offenders executed in Iran or the U.S.? **A: U.S.**

Between 1990 and 2003, 19 child offenders were executed in the U.S., before the Supreme Court changed the law. In the same period, 7 were executed in Iran.

Q How many countries in the world have higher death-penalty conviction rates than the U.S.? **A: 5**

In 2000, only Dominica (6.85), Barbados (1.87), Singapore (.70), Swaziland (.19), and Egypt (.11) had higher rates than the U.S. with 214 new prisoners under sentence of death in 2000 at a rate of .08 per 100,000 U.S. population.

Q Which European country with high drug-conviction rates had the highest number of deaths from drug use in 2001? **A: Finland**

With 22 drug-use-disorder deaths and a 123.65 drug-offense-conviction rate per 100,000 inhabitants.

Q Are some capital punishments actually aided suicides? **A: Yes**

Although Gary Gilmore's execution by firing squad in Utah in 1977 was categorized as a legal intervention, after he attempted suicide twice in prison, his last words before his execution were "Let's do it."

Q Before 1936, how much more likely were you to be lynched than killed by a bear in North America? **A: 86 times**

With 4,648 mostly African Americans killed by lynching (on average, 86/year) between 1882 and 1936, that is 86 times more than the average of 1 person killed annually by a bear.

Q Which is more likely to kill you, overexertion or an armed police officer? **A: Armed officer**

There were 330 deaths from legal intervention in 2001 (not counting 63 executions) versus 8 deaths from overexertion.

Q In the U.S., are you more likely to die from an Africanized-bee sting or be innocently sent to death row? **A: Sent to death row**

Over 120 people have been freed from death row betweeen 1973 and 2007—an average of 3.5 per year. The 7 deaths from Africanized-bee stings between 1985 and 2004 averaged fewer than 1 per year.

Q In the U.S.in 1999, the year with the most executions since the death penalty was reinstated in 1976, were you more likely to die from legal execution or lightning?

A: Execution

88 Americans were executed in 1999 versus 64 who died from lightning. Even though legal executions fell to 60 in 2003, they were still higher than the 47 lightning deaths that year.

Law World Death Rates
by WHO Region (per 100,000 population)

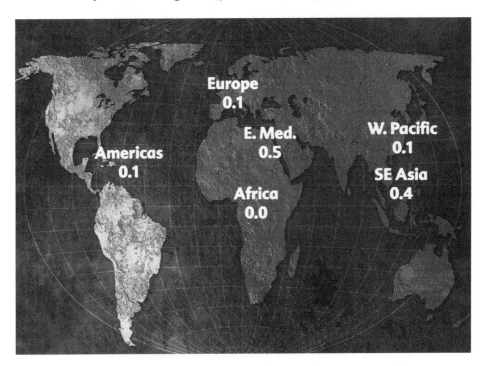

Europe
0.1

E. Med.
0.5

W. Pacific
0.1

Americas
0.1

SE Asia
0.4

Africa
0.0

LAW DEATHS, 2002—ALL AGES

Americas (incl USA): **1,148**

USA: **396***

Europe: **694**

E. Mediterranean: **2,516**

Africa: **1**

W. Pacific: **2,084**

Southeast Asia: **6,331**

* USA totals are for 2001.

Intentional Injury Deaths Worldwide, 2002

Cause	Deaths
Self-inflicted (suicide)	876,524
Violent (murder)	558,566
War (incl genocide)	178,170
Law (legal intervention)	12,832
Total	**1,626,092**

I fought the law, and the law won.

—THE BOBBY FULLER FOUR

A HEAD-ON

collision between government and an individual is like a moth flying at a car's grill. It's that sense of inevitability that has long inspired would-be martyrs and suicides. A significant number of deaths by law have really been a form of suicide, deliberately using the state as an instrument for one's own death: suicidal cases who brandish guns at cops and dare them to shoot, or the Gary Gilmores of the world who refuse appeals, determined to leave this world by execution. But government more often kills people who have no interest in dying.

DEATH BY LAW

Some of them have later been found to have been innocent, which may be one reason most civilized countries have banned the death penalty—it's easier to partially redress injustice to a live victim than a dead one.

Note: All deaths cited are for 2001 in the U.S. and 2002 in the world, unless otherwise noted

Murder and capital punishment are not
opposites that cancel one another, but similars
that breed their kind. It is the deed that
teaches, not the name we give it.

—GEORGE BERNARD SHAW

Quick & Dead Summary for the U.S.

396 Number of civilian deaths from law-related intervention

5 Number of those deaths over age 75

323 Of those deaths, number that were killed by law enforcement officers using guns

63 Number that were killed in governmental execution

10 Number of deaths caused by all other governmental interventions

19 to 1 Proportion of males killed to females

3 to 1 Of the male victims, proportion of whites killed compared to blacks

2 times Likelihood a black male will be killed by law authorities (.4 per 100,000 population) over a white male (.2)

20,704 Number of U.S. homicides

2 Percentage of those homicides that were interventions by law enforcement officers

221 Number of U.S. justifiable homicides by private citizens

378 Number by law enforcement personnel

Executing Justice

12,832 Number of legal-intervention deaths self-reported by governments worldwide. The figure is probably low, because governments that kill many of their own citizens are often secretive about it

3 Percentage of all re-ported intentional killings that were the result of legal interventions, out of a worldwide total of 571,399 violent deaths (not count-ing suicides or war deaths)

80 Of those deaths, the percentage visited upon males

62 Percentage of world executions that were men between 15 and 44

2,756 Number of people worldwide sentenced to death during 2003, accord-ing to 63 countries' official reports to world authorities

1,146 Number of 2003 executions that took place in the 28 countries that officially admitted executing anyone

726 Minimum number of Chinese executions in 2003 estimated by Amnesty International

10,000 Actual estimated number of annual Chinese executions, according to remarks by a senior Chinese legislator in 2004

118 Number of countries that had abolished the death penalty by 2004, by law and/or in practice

Dying for a Little Late-night Revelry

In the eighteenth century BC, the code of King Hammurabi of Babylon listed 25 crimes, none of which was murder, that could bring the death penalty. But the earliest recorded account of a death sentence comes from Egypt in the sixteenth century BC. A member of the nobility, accused of "magic," was ordered to kill himself. By the fifth century BC, the Roman Empire executed people convicted of the murder of a freeman or parent, thievery (among slaves), publication of libels or insulting songs, or creating a disturbance at night. Rome was creative in its methods of execution: crucifixion, live burial, impalement, beating, or drowning, sometimes with bizarre accoutrements—those convicted of killing a parent were immersed with a dog, rooster, viper, and ape.

Britain took Rome's example and extended it considerably. Henry VIII's rule saw an estimated 72,000 executions, including some of his various wives. By the eighteenth century, 222 offenses were punishable by death, including shoplifting, sending threatening letters, sacrilege, pig stealing, damaging London Bridge, counterfeiting, sodomy, highway robbery, or cutting down a tree without authorization. By the 1820s, juries rebelled against the death penalty for minor crimes, and by the early 1860s murder became Britain's only peacetime capital crime. Furthermore, executions moved inside prison walls, eliminating the humiliating public spectacle of dying before a jeering crowd. England saw its last execution in 1964, and its death penalty was officially ended in 1998.

The Death of Sitting Bull

Tantaka-Iyotanka means "buffalo bull obstinately sitting on his haunches." It was the name given to the Lakota Indian chief and holy man we call Sitting Bull. He defeated the U.S. army in many battles and, in 1876, destroyed George Custer's army in a futile attempt to defend the Dakota territories against white seekers of gold. Following years of exile in Canada, Sitting Bull came south to surrender to the U.S. government. He still commanded great respect and authority among his people, which worried American authorities. He was placed under house arrest and was moved from reservation to reservation. In 1890, as one last-ditch Native American rebellion took hold, 43 Lakota policemen were sent by the government to bring Sitting Bull into preventive detention. They burst into his cabin before dawn on December 15, 1890, and dragged him out. When his followers attempted to protect him, one of the policemen put a bullet through the 60-year-old chief's head.

Cashing In Your Chips

1 in 4,508,116 Odds of being legally executed in the U.S. in 2003 (65 executions in a population of 293,027,571)

1 in 1,292,024 The same odds of being executed in Vietnam (64 executions in a nation of 82,689,518)

1 in 555,731 In Iran (108 executions in a nation of 60,018,924 people)

1 in 41,907 In England and Wales in 1801 (219

hangings in a population of 9,177,600)

15 Time in seconds that a head can remain conscious after being guillotined, according to an experiment by scientist Antoine Lavoisier. On his way to the guillotine during the French Revolution, he told a colleague, "Watch my eyes after the blade comes down. I will continue blinking as long as I retain consciousness."

9'4" Proper drop distance for a 140-pound prisoner, according to *The Business of Hanging,* a definitive

Unkindest Cuts of All

Since so many crimes, from pig stealing to sacrilege, carried the death penalty in Olde England, how could a judge make the punishment any worse for more serious crimes such as murder? From the 1500s into the 1800s, a judge's sentence could include not only hanging but also subsequent dissection. Because churches taught that the dead literally rose from their graves into heaven, cutting a body into pieces was considered tantamount to closing heaven's door for eternity. Because of this belief, medical students had a shortage of cadavers to practice on, so they were grateful for the occasional capital criminal thrown their way. One way to end up dissected was to provide fresh corpses at a profit for medical schools. So learned William Burke, a Scot who was convicted in 1829 of murdering 15 people and selling their bodies to medical schools. The day after his hanging, he was publicly dissected and his tanned skin made into leather goods. A genuine Burke-skin wallet is still exhibited in the Anatomy Museum of the Royal College of Surgeons in Edinburgh.

reference book for executioners. Too little rope would risk slow strangulation; too much rope risked lopping off the head

29 Number of years that Sir Walter Raleigh's wife kept his severed head in a red leather bag after his execution. On the morning of his beheading, he wrote a sweet letter to his wife and joked with the executioner about his ax: "Dost thou think that I am afraid of it? This is that that will cure all sorrows."

Scapegoats and Elephants

In centuries past, animals were often put on trial for crimes ranging from witchcraft to theft to murder. The animal that's been prosecuted and executed most is the pig. Other animals that have been condemned to die for murder include moles (Italy, 824), a cow (France, 1546), and a dog (Switzerland in 1906). In America's Salem witch trials, no pigs or cats were sentenced to death, but 2 dogs and 20 innocent people lost their lives. In 1963 in Tripoli, the courts sentenced 75 convicted banknote smugglers to death at one time. They were all pigeons. The only known criminal hanging of an elephant took place in Erwin, Tennessee, on September 13, 1916. The convict's name was Mary (aka Big Mary and Five-Ton Mary), and she had killed her keeper. Mary was hanged by a chain from a railroad crane, to the cheers of 2,500 gawking spectators.

That Witch Haunts Us

Mass fear and hysteria make societies do ugly things. For example, torture and indefinite imprisonment in America's war on "terrorism" after 2001 was foreshadowed by its anticommunist witch hunts of the 1930s to 1950s. The granddaddy of these periodic bouts of xenophobic panic—which gave the witch hunt its name—was the horrifying legal situation in Salem, Massachusetts, in 1692, when the town's most distinguished citizens became convinced that there were hundreds of local witches deserving imprisonment and death. Nobody was immune, not even 4-year-old Dorcas Good, who was jailed for 8 months, during which she watched her mother carried off to the gallows. All told, 19 people, mostly women, were hanged, and an 80-year-old man, slowly crushed to death with boulders. Also, 2 dogs were executed as witches' "familiars." By the end of the year, some colonists had begun a soul-searching self-examination about how they could've succumbed to such insanity, and the prosecutions petered out. The head judge, William Stoughton, complained that he was being forced to stop his work just as he was "clearing the land" of witches. His only consolation was that he became the next governor of Massachusetts.

St. Lawrence Grilled

Saint Lawrence is the Catholic patron saint of cooks and kitchen workers, and here's why. According to the oral history, Saint Lawrence was tied to a barbecue spit and slow-roasted alive by the Roman government in AD 258. During the ordeal, he was quoted as announcing, "Turn me. I am roasted on one side."

Top U.S. Capital Crimes

1600s: Murder, adultery, piracy, witchcraft, and sodomy

1700s: Lose witchcraft, add housebreaking, slave revolt, counterfeiting, and treason

1800s: Piracy goes out of style, and so does its status as a capital crime

1900s: Mainly murder and rape

2000s: So far, mostly murder, although the death penalty is allowed for treason, train-wrecking, drug trafficking, certain types of sexual assault, kidnapping, and aircraft piracy

Justifiable Homicide

5 Number of cases in which homicide can be considered legal: war; defending self or others from grave harm; administration of capital punishment; assisted suicide in some cases; and the rare lethal medical decision in rare cases—for example, when one conjoined twin has to die so the other may live. Most crimes of passion or defense of property fall under manslaughter

29 Percentage decrease in U.S. justifiable homicide between 1992 and 2002

49 Number of U.S. states in which you must attempt to retreat from a confrontation before legally killing someone in self-defense. The single exception is Louisiana

A Dying Punishment

4,646 Number of Americans executed by authorities between 1900 and 1935

2,909 Number from 1936 to 1972

1,077 Number from 1976, when capital punishment was reinstated after being suspended in 1973, through 2005. The millennial milestone was reached on December 2, 2005, in North Carolina

In a Dead State in a Red State

37 Percentage of all U.S. executions in the 29 years after the Supreme Court reinstated the death penalty in 1976 that took place in Texas

1 Rank of Texas in number of executions from 1976 through 2005

394 Number of executions in Texas in that span, beating the total of the next four states combined: #2 Virginia (98), #3 Oklahoma (84), #4 Missouri (66), and #5 Florida (64)

123 Number of death row inmates exonerated and released between 1973 and April 2006

19 Number of Americans executed between 1990 and 2003 for crimes committed before reaching the age of 18

15 Number of under-18 executions in that same period in all other countries where it was legal: Iran (7), Pakistan (3), and China, Congo, Nigeria, Saudi Arabia, and Yemen (1 each)

9 Of the top 10 U.S. states in modern capital-punishment deaths, number that seceded from the Union during the Civil War. Oklahoma didn't yet exist, and Missouri remained in the Union. Along with Texas, Virginia and Florida (mentioned above), North Carolina (#6 with 43), Georgia (#7 with 39), Alabama (#8 with 36), South Carolina (#9 with 36), Arkansas (#10 with 27), and Louisiana (tied at #10 with 27) joined the rebel cause

3 Number of the 749 U.S. executions from 1976 to 2001 carried out by hanging

2 By firing squad

11 By gas chamber

149 By the electric chair

584 By lethal injection

30 Number of states that have banned lethal injection for euthanizing animals. The combination of drugs leaves open a strong possibility that the animal will suffer excruciating pain while kept paralyzed. Yet the method is used routinely on people

Extralegal Murders

3 to 2 Ratio of legal executions to lynchings between 1882 and 1936. Lynchings were a particularly ugly form of racial terrorism, frequently based on trumped-up charges. For many years lynchings were quasi-official functions: the murderers in the lynch mobs were virtually never prosecuted, even when they acted in public, admitted their guilt, and posed for photographs with the body

4,648 Known number of people, mostly African Americans, who were terrorized, tortured, and murdered by mobs in the U.S. between 1882 and 1936. The victims were invariably killed horribly (castrated and dismembered alive, dragged, beaten, set afire, strangled, and/or hanged)

50 Cost in cents of a lynching postcard in 1930

1 Cost in cents to mail the card to a loved one

88 Estimated percentage of lynchings that took place in the South. The Midwest accounted for 7%, the West for 5%, and the Northeast for 0.3%

KKK Postcards?

The battered bodies of Thomas Shipp and Abram Smith hung from a tree in Indiana, surrounded by white men clutching souvenir pieces of cloth and hair, in 1930. The two had been dragged out of a jail cell by a mob shouting, "Get those goddamn niggers!" In the weeks afterward, photographer Lawrence Beitler sold thousands of copies of a commemorative postcard.

The Cost of Justice

$23,600 Cost of keeping an inmate in an American prison for a year

$7,628 Cost of keeping a child in an American public school for a year

43 Percentage of prison inmates without a high school diploma or GED in 1997

1,406,031 Number of inmates in state and federal prisons

3,581 Number of inmates on death row

1 in 12 Proportion of death row inmates who had a prior homicide conviction

1 in 3 Proportion of death row inmates who had no prior felony conviction

1 in 109 Proportion of all U.S. men who are in prison at any given time

1 in 1,613 Proportion of women

1.5 times Increased rate of suicide among prison inmates compared with people on the outside

9 times Increased chance of suicide among newly jailed inmates

65 The number who were executed by the state in 2002 of the 3,562 inmates on death row

4 Number who committed suicide

70 Percentage increase in cost of death-penalty cases over others, including life imprisonment, according to a 2003 Kansas audit

$2.16 million Additional cost per execution incurred by the state compared to the cost of life imprisonment, according to a Duke University study. Most of the costs are associated with additional trial expenses

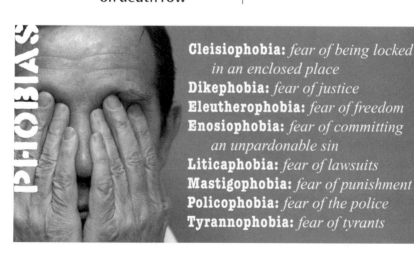

PHOBIAS

Cleisiophobia: *fear of being locked in an enclosed place*
Dikephobia: *fear of justice*
Eleutherophobia: *fear of freedom*
Enosiophobia: *fear of committing an unpardonable sin*
Liticaphobia: *fear of lawsuits*
Mastigophobia: *fear of punishment*
Policophobia: *fear of the police*
Tyrannophobia: *fear of tyrants*

The Execution of Mary, Queen of Scots

Imagine the embarrassment of Queen Mary's executioner. Convicted of plotting against her cousin Elizabeth I, Mary approached the chopping block on February 8, 1587. The nervous executioner wasn't used to chopping the heads off women, especially not in front of all these crowned heads and courtiers. His first ax blow missed the queen's neck completely, cutting into the back of her skull and eliciting a groan and shudder from the queen and onlookers alike. His second and third tries hit the neck, but didn't sever it. Finally, the embarrassed executioner made a grinding motion with his ax and cut through the last sinew. He still had a chance to wow the onlookers by holding the severed head up triumphantly for all to see. He reached down and grabbed the queen's head firmly by her hair . . . but it hadn't occurred to him that she might be wearing a wig. As he raised the bloody artifact, the queen's head—her real hair gray and cut short—slipped out of the wig and bounced and rolled across the floor.

Most at Risk of Premature Death from Law

WORLDWIDE DEATH RATES, 2002
(per 100,000 population)

AGE	WORLD MALE	WORLD FEMALE
0–4	.16	.07
5–14	.07	.04
15–29	.42	.07
30–44	.44	.07
45–59	.32	.13
60–69	.48	.15
70+	.67	.20

Main Cause

Violence

Prevention

■ GET EDUCATED

■ BE COMPASSIONATE

■ BE HAPPY

War

#14 Cause of premature death in the world
2002 (under age 70)

#17 Cause of premature death in the USA

QUESTION: How much more likely are you to die violently if you're in the military? **ANSWER: 1½ times**

In 2004, the U.S. military death rate from hostile action, accident, suicide, and homocide was 92.2 per 100,000 versus 58.2 for civilians ages 15–24.

Q How many countries have 40% or more of their populations under age 15? **A: 34**

Africa (24, including Rwanda); Eastern Mediterranean region (6: Afghanistan, Iraq, Pakistan, Somalia, Sudan, and Yemen); Americas (3: Guatemala , Haiti, and Honduras); and West Pacific (1: Laos). These youth will soon create a bulge in ages 15–24, the age group with the highest death rates for murder and war.

Q Which genocide was deadlier per mile, the Trail of Tears or the Bataan Death March? **A: Bataan**

The 90-mile Bataan Death March in the Philippines in 1942 killed 7,000 to 10,000 POWs—approximately 111 per mile versus the Trail of Tears in the U.S. during the second Seminole Indian war, which killed 4,000 to 15,000 Cherokee Indians in that 1,200-mile forced march with approximately 12½ deaths per mile.

Q Which was deadlier, World War II or the flu? **A: Flu**

The Asian flu took the lives of 50 million people worldwide, including some of the 20.3 million who died in World War I.

Q Which country exploded the most atomic bombs between 1945 and 1992: Russia or the U.S.?

A: U.S.

The Americans exploded 1,039 bombs to the Soviet Union's 718.

Q How many American war deaths were there for every $1 billion spent by the U.S. government on defense in 2003? **A: 1**

The U.S. spent $456.2 billion on national defense in 2003 and reported 344 U.S. military deaths from hostile action—about one death for every $1.3 billion spent by the U.S. government.

Q If you're in the U.S. military, are you more likely to die in battle or kill yourself? **A: It depends**

In 2001, the Department of Defense reported 3 hostile-action deaths and 140 suicides versus 739 hostile-action deaths and 188 suicides in 2004.

Q Which was the first major war where more men died in battle than from disease?

A: World War I (1914–18)

In the Crimean War (1853–56) and others before it, from 3 to 4 times as many people died of disease as directly from warfare.

War World Death Rates
by WHO Region (per 100,000 population)

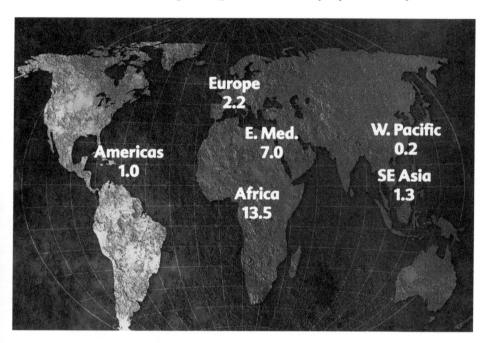

Europe 2.2

E. Med. 7.0

W. Pacific 0.2

Americas 1.0

SE Asia 1.3

Africa 13.5

WAR DEATHS, 2002—ALL AGES*

Americas (incl USA):
8,326

USA: **17**

Europe: **19,286**

E. Mediterranean: **35,137**

Africa: **90,541**

W. Pacific: **3,025**

Southeast Asia: **20,696**

* Cumulative deaths cited are from the Center for Disease Control (CDC) for 2001 in the U.S. and the World Health Organization (WHO) for 2002 in the world. Detailed U.S. war deaths are from the Department of Defense (DoD).

Intentional Injury Deaths Worldwide, 2002

Cause	Deaths
Self-inflicted (suicide)	876,524
Violent (murder)	558,566
War (incl genocide)	178,170
Law (legal intervention)	12,832
Total	**1,626,092**

History is mostly killin' people.

—Theodore "Beaver" Cleaver,
Leave It to Beaver

WAR IS HELLISH

THE tragic flaws of human beings are evident nearly everywhere you look. But the insanities of everyday life pale in comparison with the awful madness of war, still considered a viable response to conflict with other nations after many bloody centuries should long have convinced us otherwise. It's been said that a mob slips down to the level of its worst members, and what are nation-states eager for war but very large mobs? There was a time when kings rode into battle with their hapless minions. Perhaps that should be a prerequisite today: If we required the leaders who ordered the wars to stand in the front ranks, the world might be a much more peaceful place.

Quick & Dead Summary for the U.S.

1 Rank of the Civil War among America's most deadly conflicts

1,268,176 Number of American soldiers known to have died in war (1775–2006)

623,026 Number of American soldiers killed in the Civil War (1861–65)

1,981 Rate per 100,000 U.S. population to die in the Civil War

1942 Most recent year that the U.S. government officially declared war

21 Percentage of its existence through 2006 that the United States has been involved in a major war

739 Number of U.S. active duty military deaths from hostile action reported by the Department of Defense (DoD) in 2004. These are deaths occurring outside of the U.S., which are not tracked by the Center for Disease Control (CDC). In 2003, the DoD reported 344 hostile action deaths and 18 in 2002.

17 Number of Americans who died from operations of war and their sequelae in the U.S. in 2001 as reported by the CDC

3 Number of overseas U.S. active duty military deaths from hostile action reported by the DoD in 2001

The World at War

9 to 1 Ratio of men killed in war to women

74 Percentage of worldwide war deaths in soldiers 15 to 44

20 Percentage of war dead between 45 and 69

3.4 Percentage 70 and older

1.6 Percentage 14 and younger

55 Number of years that the war in Sudan has been going on, as of 2007

1 Rank of Africa in number of war deaths

	A DEADLY TRADITION		
CENTURY	WORLD POPULATION	WAR-RELATED DEATHS	PERCENTAGE OF POPULATION
16th	400 million	1.6 million	0.4
17th	500 million	6.1 million	1.2
18th	800 million	7.0 million	0.9
19th	1.2 billion	19.4 million	1.6

Masters of War

1 Rank of the U.S. as purveyor of military equipment and weapons to world trouble spots

4 Number of the U.S.'s top 10 weapons customers located in the contentious area known as the Middle East. In 2002, these included Egypt (#1), Saudi Arabia (#3), Israel (#4), and Turkey (#9)

2 Rank of China in the top 10 U.S. weapons customers.

Other leading customers include South Korea (#5), Japan (#6), Greece (#7), Singapore (#8), and the United Kingdom (#10)

33.5 Percentage of the $37 billion international weapons market controlled by U.S. arms manufacturers in 2004

16.5 Percentage of world weapons sales by #2 Russia, followed by Great Britain (8.6%), Israel (3.2%), and France (2.7%)

Going Nuclear

2 Number of nuclear bombs exploded in wartime, both by the U.S., against Hiroshima and Nagasaki in World War II

214,000 Number of people killed by those 2 explosions, nearly all civilians

90 Percentage of Hiroshima's buildings destroyed by the bomb

15,000 Estimated number of fatal cancers resulting from nuclear weapons tests in America

2,052 Number of known nuclear test explosions from 1945–2007 as tracked

by the Australian Government

1,039 Number of those explosions conducted by the U.S.

718 By the Soviet Union

198 By France

45 By each of China and Great Britain

3 By India

2 By Pakistan

1 By each of South Africa and North Korea

Land Mines: The Gifts That Keep on Killing

100 million Estimated number of unexploded land mines in 70 countries

1 million Estimated number of people killed or maimed by land mines since 1975

400,000 Number in Afghanistan alone

40 Average daily number of people killed or injured by land mines

23 Percentage of land mine casualties who are children

Chemical and Germ Warfare

1,000,000 Number of recorded cases of venereal disease by the French military during World War I

20 Percentage of those cases from syphilis

20.4 Percentage of U.S. casualties during World War I caused by disease (mostly flu)

16.3 Percentage of U.S. World War I deaths caused by battle

90,000 Number of World War I deaths caused by chemical agents

70 Percentage of those deaths from mustard gas

20 million Amount in gallons of Agent Orange and other herbicides sprayed by U.S. troops over parts of South Vietnam and Cambodia in the 1960s and 1970s

10,000 Estimated number of Vietnam veterans

receiving disability pay as of January 2003 for illnesses related to wartime exposure to Agent Orange and other herbicides

10,000 Projected number of fatal cancers resulting from depleted uranium (DU) weapons dropped by American planes on Kosovo during the war with Serbia

11 Number of diseases related to herbicide exposure recognized by the Veterans Administration

10 times Increased frequency of breast cancer

among Vietnam veterans over the national average

3,000 Estimated number of POWs killed by the Japanese military during World War II as a result of biological warfare experimentation

3,000 Estimated number of Kurds killed by Saddam Hussein with chemical weapons in Iraq

4 times Increased lethality of disease over battle during the Crimean War (1853–56)

3 times Increased lethality of disease over battle during the U.S. Civil War

Death of Innocents

90 Percentage of all worldwide war deaths in the 1990s that were civilians

12 million Estimated number of children left homeless as a result of wars worldwide between 1990 and 2000

4–5 million Estimated number of children handicapped or disabled

2 million Number of children who died

1 million Number of children orphaned or separated from parents

1 million Number of Iraqi children who died as a direct result of sanctions against the country from 1990 to 1996

1 in 10 Proportion of the 100,000–200,000 women kidnapped for use as sex slaves by Japanese soldiers during World War II who survived

110,000 Estimated number of women raped in Berlin by Allied troops (mainly Soviet soldiers) after the end of World War II

250,000 Estimated number of women raped during the 1994 Rwandan genocide

1,000 Percentage increase in Rwanda's HIV rate between 1994 and 1997

17 Percentage of women surviving the Rwandan genocide who were subsequently found to be HIV-positive

More Bang for the Buck

1 Rank of the U.S. in world military spending

143.9 Amount in billions of dollars of the U.S. national defense budget in 1980

460.5 The same figure for 2004

TOP 10 WORLDWIDE MILITARY BUDGETS AND AMOUNTS SPENT PER MALE AGE 15—49 FIT FOR SERVICE

RANK	COUNTRY	MILITARY BUDGET, 2003 (IN BILLIONS OF DOLLARS)	MILITARY MANPOWER FIT FOR MILITARY SERVICE, 2003	BUDGET PER MALE (IN DOLLARS)
1	Israel	9.4	1,279,277	7,348
2	Saudi Arabia	21.3	3,431,281	6,208
3	U.S.	399.1	74,271,000	5,374
4	U.K.	38.4	12,353,942	3,108
5	Russia	65.0	24,000,000	2,708
6	Sweden	4.5	1,800,376	2,499
7	France	29.5	12,079,413	2,442
8	Denmark	2.4	1,094,611	2,193
9	Netherlands	6.6	3,536,586	1,866
10	Australia	7.6	4,339,011	1,752

Strange Wars

THE WAR OF THE WHISKERS (1152–1453). When France's King Louis VII returned from the Crusades clean-shaven, his wife, Eleanor of Aquitane, told him he looked ugly. She divorced him, married King Henry II of England, and demanded Louis cede her dowry, two provinces in what is now southern France. Louis refused, and Henry declared war—a conflict that lasted 301 years.

THE WAR OF THE OAKEN BUCKET (1325–37). This war between the Italian cities of Modena and Bologna was triggered by the theft of a wooden bucket by Modena soldiers. Thousands from both sides died.

THE 100 YEARS' WAR (1337–1453). This struggle between France and England lasted 126 years, with some interruptions, through the reigns of 5 English kings (Edward III to Henry VI) and 5 French kings (Philip VI to Charles VII). The British won most of the battles, but the French won the war, partially thanks to Joan of Arc.

THE WAR OF JENKINS' EAR (1739–43). Naval captain Robert Jenkins was caught smuggling illicit cargo by the Spanish coast guard. Jenkins insulted the customs agent, who in response cut off Jenkins's ear and handed it to him. The British were outraged and kept the ear displayed in Parliament for years as a reminder of how the Spanish could not be trusted. When war between England and Spain was officially declared, it became known as the War of Jenkins' Ear.

TOLEDO WAR (1835–36). Thanks to faulty maps, both Michigan and Ohio claimed the city of Toledo. The issue came to a head

Strange Wars

in September 1835 when both states sent troops to defend their claims. After a standoff through the frigid Midwestern winter, President Andrew Jackson brokered a deal: Ohio would get Toledo and Michigan would get what would become its Upper Peninsula. The only loser wasn't even part of the war: Wisconsin, which had already claimed the territory that Jackson casually handed over to Michigan.

THE HONEY WAR (1838). Militias from Missouri and Iowa squared off over a disputed strip of land after some Missourians felled several trees with beehives inside to take the honey.

THE PIG WARS (1841, 1859, 1906). Three different international military standoffs came to be known as the Pig War. The first was between France and the Republic of Texas over a hotelier's swine that invaded the French ambassador's garden. The second was over a marauding Canadian pig shot by an American farmer on the border of Washington and Canada. The third was a precursor to World War I, in which Serbia stopped trading pork products to the Austria-Hungary and nearly sparked World War I (1914–18) 8 years early.

THE WAR OF THE STRAY DOG (1925). On the tense border between Greece and Bulgarian Macedonia, a dog strayed away from the Greek soldier who'd adopted it and crossed the border. The soldier chased after it and was shot by a Bulgarian guard. Infuriated, Greek soldiers stormed across the border. More than 50 soldiers were killed before the League of Nations intervened and stopped the hostilities.

Democide and Genocide—
Murder by Government

13,000,000 Estimated number of Joseph Stalin's victims during his purges of perceived enemies in Russia, 1934–39

12,000,000 Estimated number of victims of Adolf Hitler's death camps from 1939 to 1945. Of these, about half were Jewish; 4 million were Soviet prisoners of war; 1 million were Gypsies, homosexuals, or handicapped; and another million were considered political opponents

7,700,000 Estimated number of deaths from Mao Tse-tung's Cultural Revolution, 1964–75. Perceived enemies, intellectuals, "counterrevolutionaries," and others deemed insufficiently supportive were humiliated, hounded, imprisoned, sent to work camps, lynched, and executed

5,000,000 Estimated number of civilians and prisoners killed by the Japanese during World War II, 1941–45. These include 2.8 million Chinese and 1.5 million deaths in forced-labor camps, including prisoners of war, some of whom were randomly killed as examples to others or used as living targets for bayonet practice

2,000,000 Estimated number of people slaughtered by the Khmer Rouge in Cambodia, 1975–79. Inspired by China's Cultural Revolution, the regime killed ethnic Vietnamese, rival Communists, college professors, religious workers and monks, intellectuals, and those who looked as if they might become intellectuals (for example, wearers of glasses) in the hope of creating an agrarian utopia

1,600,000 Estimated number of Koreans killed in purges and concentration camps by Kim Il Sung, ruler of North Korea from 1948 to 1987

1,500,000 Estimated number of ethnic Armenians massacred by the Turkish government, 1915–18. Another half million were forcibly deported

500,000 to 1,000,000 Estimated number of Tutsis

killed by Hutu militia groups during 100 days of genocide from April through mid-July 1994 in Rwanda

200,000 to 450,000 Estimated number of Sudanese killed (including disease deaths) by the military and Janjaweed militia group in a conflict begun February 2003 in Darfur and still raging as of July 2007

250,000 Estimated number of Ugandans killed during the bloody reign of Idi Amin, 1972–77

200,000 Estimated number of Yugoslavian victims of Slobodan Milosevic, 1992–96

87,000 Estimated number of Tibetans killed in their revolt against Chinese rule in 1959

50,000 Estimated number of Kurds killed by Iraq's Saddam Hussein during their rebellion, 1960–70

The Only Good Native American?

10–110 million
Estimated range of Native American deaths due to disease pandemics in the century after Europeans first arrived in the Americas

45,000 Number of Native Americans, including women and children, believed killed in more than 40 Indian wars from 1775 to 1890

19,000 Number of European settlers, including women and children, believed killed in the same conflicts

You Say You Want a Revolution?

4,435 Number of American armed forces known to have died from battle during the American Revolution. Some estimates place the battle-death figure as high as 6,800

10,000 Estimated number of American revolutionaries who died of disease. A deadly smallpox epidemic raged; General George Washington's controversial order to inoculate his troops is now seen as one of his most significant strategic decisions

10,000 Estimated number of French who died fighting on the side of the revolutionaries. Deaths of Spanish and Dutch, fighting the British at the same time for their own reasons, are estimated at 5,000 and 500

8,500 Estimated number of British killed from battle or wounds

3,000 Estimated number of American Loyalists and Canadians killed fighting on the British side

3,000 Estimated number

of German mercenaries
hired by the British
who died

500 Estimated number
of Native Americans
killed. Most fought
for the British

America at War

REVOLUTIONARY WAR (1775–83)

Soldiers	Battle Deaths		Non Battle Deaths		
	Killed in Action	Died of Wounds	Died of Disease	Died of Other	Total Deaths
U.S.	6,800		10,000	8,500	25,300
Non U.S.	British army and allies, 30,500 deaths				

WAR OF 1812 (1812–15)

Soldiers	Battle Deaths		Non Battle Deaths		
	Killed in Action	Died of Wounds	Died of Disease	Died of Other	Total Deaths
U.S.	2,300		15,000		17,300
Non U.S.	British Canadians, 3,000 killed in action (KIA)				

MEXICAN AMERICAN WAR (1846–48)

Soldiers	Battle Deaths		Non Battle Deaths		
	Killed in Action	Died of Wounds	Died of Disease	Died of Other	Total Deaths
U.S.	1,700	500	11,000		13,200
Non U.S.	Mexicans, 6,000 to 15,000 KIA				

AMERICAN CIVIL WAR (1861–65)

Soldiers	Battle Deaths		Non Battle Deaths		
	Killed in Action	Died of Wounds	Died of Disease	Died of Other	Total Deaths
U.S.	67,000	43,000	225,000	25,000	360,000
Non U.S.	Confederacy, 290,000 deaths				

SPANISH-AMERICAN WAR (1898)

Soldiers	Battle Deaths		Non Battle Deaths		
	Killed in Action	Died of Wounds	Died of Disease	Died of Other	Total Deaths
U.S.	400		2,000		2,400
Non U.S.	Spanish, 5,000 to 9,000 KIA & wounds + 53,000 deaths from disease				

WORLD WAR I (1914–18)

Soldiers	Battle Deaths		Non Battle Deaths		
	Killed in Action	Died of Wounds	Died of Disease	Died of Other	Total Deaths
U.S.	53,000			63,000	116,000

Allies, 5.1 million dead
Central Powers, 3.5 million dead

WORLD WAR II (1939–45)

Soldiers	Battle Deaths		Non Battle Deaths		Total Deaths
	Killed in Action	Died of Wounds	Died of Disease	Died of Other	
U.S.	292,000			115,000	407,000

Allies, 13.2 million (8.7 Russian, 2.2 Chinese, 2.3 other)
Axis, 7.1 million (3.3 Germans, 2.6 Japanese, 1.2 other)
Total military dead of all causes 20.3 million

KOREAN WAR (1950–53)

Soldiers	Battle Deaths		Non Battle Deaths		Total Deaths
	Killed in Action	Died of Wounds	Died of Disease	Died of Other	
U.S.	33,600			20,600	54,200
Non U.S.	China, North Korea, & the Soviet Union, 617,000 KIA				

+ 1 million from famine & disease
South Korea, 257,000 military deaths from all causes

VIETNAM WAR (1957–75)

Soldiers	Battle Deaths		Non Battle Deaths		Total Deaths
	Killed in Action	Died of Wounds	Died of Disease	Died of Other	
U.S.	47,500	11,000			58,500
Non U.S.	South Vietnamese, 1 million				

North Vietnamese, 821,000

OPERATION IRAQI FREEDOM (2003–?) AS OF 6/2/07

Soldiers	Battle Deaths		Non Battle Deaths		Total Deaths
	Killed in Action	Died of Wounds	Died of Disease	Died of Other	
U.S.	2,193	652		9	2,854
Non U.S.	Iraqi civilians, 50,000–650,000				

World War I, World War II

15.6 million Estimated number of military and civilian deaths from World War I

62.5 million The same estimated number from World War II

43 Percentage of World War I deaths that occurred to civilians

52 Percentage of World War II deaths that occurred to civilians

1/12 Portion of Serbia's population who died in World War I, making it the hardest-hit nation of that war

1/12 Portion of Russia's population who died in World War II, making it the hardest-hit nation of that war

1/2,000 Portion of America's population who died in World War I, making it the least-harmed nation among major combatants

1/375 Portion of America's population who died in World War II

1/7,692 Portion of India's population who died in World War II, the least-affected nation of all

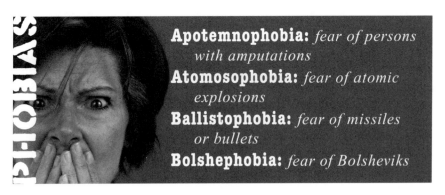

PHOBIAS

Apotemnophobia: *fear of persons with amputations*

Atomosophobia: *fear of atomic explosions*

Ballistophobia: *fear of missiles or bullets*

Bolshephobia: *fear of Bolsheviks*

Vietnam

20 million Estimated number of bomb craters created

3 million Estimated number of people killed in the Vietnam War

2 million Estimated number wounded

1.9 million Estimated number of cattle killed

unexploded ordnance still remaining

150,000–600,000 Estimated number in tons of

58,500 Number of Americans killed

PHOBIAS

Chemophobia: *Fear of chemicals*
Hoplophobia: *Fear of firearms*
Hormephobia: *Fear of shock*
Necrophobia: *Fear of death*
Nostophobia: *Fear of returning home*
Nucleomituphobia: *Fear of nuclear weapons*
Panthophobia: *Fear of suffering*
Traumatophobia: *Fear of injury*

Famous War Casualities

LESLIE HOWARD, the actor who played Ashley Wilkes in *Gone with the Wind*, died when his passenger plane was shot down by World War II German fighter pilots.

Civil war general STONEWALL JACKSON was shot by his own troops. His arm was amputated, but he still died 9 days later. His body and arm are buried in 2 separate spots.

Musician/bandleader GLENN MILLER is still officially considered missing in action. During World War II, as a major in the Army Air Force Band, his plane went down over the English Channel and was never found. Decades later, a British air force officer admitted that his plane may accidentally have downed Miller's craft as it dumped its bombs while approaching England.

The last U.S. execution for desertion was Private EDDIE SLOVIK on January 31, 1945. He was shot in France by his own unit, the 28th Infantry Division, on order of General Dwight D. Eisenhower.

Thirteen-year-old ANNE FRANK's last diary entry was on August 1, 1944. Nazis raided the Franks' Amsterdam hiding place 3 days later. She died at Bergen-Belsen concentration camp the next year.

While settling into formation, Union general JOHN SEDGWICK was playfully mocking his troops for dodging Confederate army bullets: "They couldn't hit an elephant at this distance!" Moments later, he was hit under the eye from enemy fire and died instantly.

DAVY CROCKETT was killed in 1836 as Mexicans took the Alamo. He was bayoneted to death after the official fighting had ended. James Bowie (the bowie knife) also fought at the Alamo. He was spared a gorier death because he succumbed to pneumonia during the battle.

Famous War Casualties

PAT TILLMAN, a heralded pro football player who volunteered for the army in post-9/11 patriotic fervor, was killed accidentally by "friendly fire." The military hid that fact from the public and his family for many months, concocting a story of death by enemy fire.

Before effective antiaircraft guns made camouflage a necessity, World War I pilots tended to paint their planes bright colors as a way of identifying each other. MANFRED VON RICHTHOFEN (known as the Red Baron, though he was not titled) favored red. He was credited with shooting down 80 aircraft during World War I. In 1918, while dogfighting with a Canadian pilot over Allied territory, the Red Baron was fatally hit by Australian ground gunners, who then respectfully buried his body with full military honors.

Iraq and Ruin

655,000 Estimated Iraqi war casualties from March 2003 through October 11, 2006, by the Lancet medical journal, based on interviews with a sampling of Iraqi households

47,781 to 53,014 Estimated range of Iraqi civilian deaths for the same time period, by the Iraq Body Count consortium of academics, who counted deaths reported independently

3,120 Number of U.S.-led coalition soldiers who died in the Iraq War from March 2003 through November 25, 2006—the point at which America's involvement in the war became longer than its involvement in World War II

2,873 Number of those casualties who were from the U.S. Britain incurred 126 deaths, and all other nations, 121

Most at Risk of Premature Death from War

WORLDWIDE DEATH RATES, 2002
(per 100,000 population)

AGE	MALE	FEMALE
0–4	0.1	0.1
5–14	0.3	0.4
15–29	8.4	0.4
30–44	8.5	0.7
45–59	4.8	1.1
60–69	5.2	1.2
70+	3.6	1.2

Main Cause

Politics

Prevention

- BE COMPASSIONATE
- GET EDUCATED
- BE HAPPY

#1 Cause of death in the world
2002 (age 70+)

#1 Cause of death in the USA
2001 (age 75+)

Age

The Inevitable

QUESTION: How many U.S. states have more than 15% of their population over age 65?

ANSWER: 3

In 2003 these were Florida, 17%, Pennsylvania, 15.4%, and West Virginia, 15.3%.

Q How many times worse are you as a driver when you're old versus young? **A: Almost 1½ times**

Death rates for the 25–34-year-age group in the U.S. are 17.8 per 100,000 versus 25.7 for the 75–84 group.

Q Are you more likely to die old from TB or murder? **A: Murder**

355 people over age 75 died in the U.S. from tuberculosis versus 391 who were murdered, in 2001.

Q Are you more likely to commit suicide when you're young or old? **A: Old**

In the U.S., rates of death from suicide are highest for ages 75+.

Q How many countries in the world have longer life expectancies than the U.S.? **A: 17**

In 2003, in addition to the top 10 listed in this chapter's section "The Long and Short of It,"
the U.S. follows Austria (78.9), Netherlands (78.6), Germany (78.4), Belgium (78.4), the UK (78.2), Finland (78.2), and Jordan (78.1).

Q What is more likely your final resting place, a nursing home or the hospital? **A: Nursing home**

Of those Americans 85 or older in 2002, 289,646 died in nursing homes versus 219,317 in the hospital and 112,878 at home.

Q How many countries in the world have more than 15% of their population over age 65? **A: 15**

In 2003, Italy had 18.8% over age 65, followed by Japan, Greece, Germany, Spain, Sweden, Belgium, Bulgaria, Portugal, France, the UK, Austria, Finland, Switzerland, and Ukraine.

Q What's scarier when you're older, surgeons or stairs?

A: Stairs

907 folks over 75 in the U.S. died on stairs versus 46 who died from a surgical mishap.

Q How many fewer men than women are there at age 85+?

A: 58%

Five percent more males than females are born in the U.S., but males are 58% fewer by the age of 85.

Old Age World Death Rates
by WHO Region (per 100,000 population)

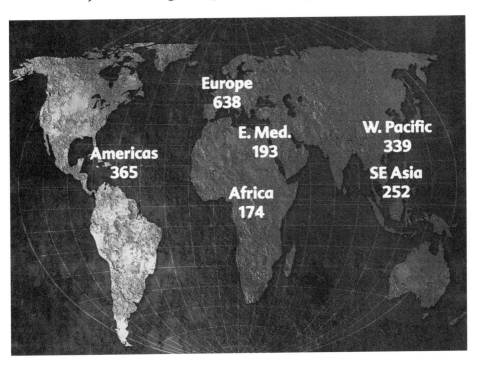

Europe
638

E. Med.
193

W. Pacific
339

Americas
365

SE Asia
252

Africa
174

OLD AGE DEATHS, 2002—AGE 70+

Americas (incl USA):
3,115,114

USA (age 75+): **1,357,465***

Europe: **5,598,380**

E. Mediterranean: **970,525**

Africa: **1,171,534**

W. Pacific: **5,825,068**

Southeast Asia: **4,012,416**

* USA totals are for 2001.

Old Age Deaths Worldwide, 2002

Cause	Deaths
Broken heart	10,267,540
Bad breath	3,441,653
Cancer	3,136,730
Bad plumbing	1,096,099
Bugs	774,757
Hormones	598,115
Bad wiring	596,830
Accidents	490,036
Suicide	100,469
Bad framing	98,126
Starvation	87,090
Murder	24,924
Drugs	10,916
War	6,148
Childhood	5,134
Law	1,110
Giving life	7
Total	**20,735,684**

SOME SAY that old age doesn't kill anyone: older people die of specific causes such as pneumonia, heart attack, stroke, or emphysema. But that's like saying nobody ever dies from a car accident: They're killed instead by organ or brain damage, trauma, or blood loss. Technically true—but none of those things would've occurred without the car accident. Even if we take good care of ourselves and are lucky, we'll still end up smothered by the accumulated weight of our years. Even the most healthy people don't seem to make it past some personal built-in threshold age, whether 80 or 100 or, in the oldest documented case, 122. So while we'll give a nod to the nominal causes of death throughout this chapter, we're also talking about things breaking down because of the natural limits of our lives.

GOIN' HOME

Quick & Dead Summary for the U.S.

1,353,379 Number of U.S. deaths among people 75 years and older

47 Percentage dying from heart-related causes

Top 5 Causes of Death

632,257 Number of broken-heart deaths, most from heart attacks, 53% age 85+

251,493 Number of cancer deaths, 32% age 85+

155,605 Number of bad-breath deaths, most from pneumonia and chronic obstructive pulmonary disease (COPD), 47% age 85+

110,815 Number of bad-wiring deaths, most from Alzheimer's and dementia, 59% age 85+

79,937 Number of bad-plumbing deaths, approximately 50% from kidney and urinary tract disorders, 48% age 85+

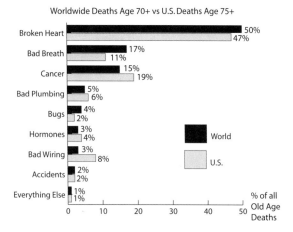

Worldwide Deaths Age 70+ vs U.S. Deaths Age 75+

Old Folks at Home

605 million Estimated number of world population 60 years and older in 2000

54 Percentage of people over 60 who live in Asia. The second highest group (24%) live in Europe

86 Percentage of U.S. women over 65 who reported taking a prescription drug within the previous month in 2000

78 Percentage of U.S. women over 65 who reported the same thing a decade earlier. Males over 65 taking prescription drugs increased from 67% to 81% during the same period

2 billion Projected number of people over 60 who will be alive in 2050. This would be the first time in history in which the number of people over 60 outnumbers the number of children under 14

12 Percentage increase in Americans over 65 between the censuses of 1990 and 2000. However, for the first time in census history, this growth rate rate was actually lower than that of the rest of the population (23.2%)

38 Percentage increase in Americans over 85 during the 1990s, making it the fastest-growing segment of the population

1 in 7 Proportion of the U.S. population at least 65 years old in 2000

1 in 15 At least 75

1 in 58 At least 85

1 in 737 At least 95

The Bible claims that Moses died at age 120 after climbing a mountain to talk with God.

433

I rving Berlin and Grandma Moses both lived longer than comedian George Burns—one year, to be exact—but Burns ("I'd love to date women my own age—but there are no women my own age") is probably the most famous of famous old people. Along with his trademark cigar, he made his old age part of his comedy routine for years, even booking himself to play the London Palladium on his 100th birthday. Unfortunately, an injury sidelined him a couple of years before, so he couldn't get around well enough to perform. Burns died 48 days after his 100th birthday, in 1996.

Cancer Rising

251,493 Number of American cancer deaths in patients 75 and older

TOP 10 OLD AGE (AGE 75+) CANCER DEATHS IN THE U.S.

RANK	CAUSE OF DEATH	# OF DEATHS
1	Trachea, bronchus, and lung	60,031
2	Colon, rectum, and anus	28,786
3	Prostate	21,825
4	Breast	15,574
5	Pancreas	13,732
6	Non-Hodgkin's lymphoma	10,875
7	Leukemia	10,281
8	Bladder	7,524
9	Ovary	5,913
10	Kidney and renal pelvis	4,730

OTHER CAUSES OF OLD-AGE (AGE 75+) DEATHS IN THE U.S.*

RANK	CAUSE OF DEATH	# OF DEATHS
6	Hormones (68% diabetes)	53,828
7	Accidents	26,439
8	Bugs (mainly blood poisoning)	24,260
9	Bad framing	10,826
10	Starvation	3,226
11	Suicide	2,961
12	Childhood birth defects	784
13	Murder	422

* For Top 5 causes please see page 432.

Accidental Departure

26,439 Number of U.S. accidental deaths to ages 75 and older

9,790 Number of those deaths from falls

4,535 Number from motor vehicle accidents

15–24 Age of the only group having more fatal motor vehicle accidents (rate of 28.2 per 100,000 population versus

25.7 age 75–84 and 28.0 age 85+)

2,516 Number of deaths from accidentally inhaling food, drink, or vomit

2 to 1 Odds of an older American dying from complications of medical care (1,428) compared to smoke and fire (677)

Skin and Bones

1,662 Of the 10,826 U.S. bad-framing deaths in ages 75+, the number from arthritis

1,591 From osteoporosis

1,304 From bedsores

Human Tragedy

77 Percent increase in suicide rates among the elderly (17.5 per 100,000 age 75+) versus 15–24-year-olds (9.9 per 100,000 teens/young adults)

U.S. SUICIDE RATES BY AGE, 2002 (per 100,00 popilation)	
AGE RANGE	DEATH RATES
Under 1	0
1–4	0
5–14	1
15–24	10
25–34	13
35–44	15
45–54	16
55–64	14
65–74	14
75–84	18
85+	18

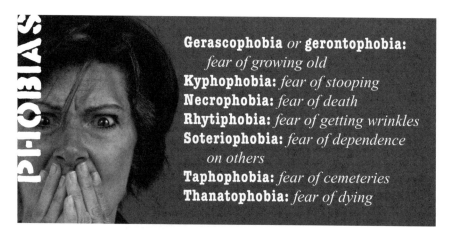

PHOBIAS

Gerascophobia *or* **gerontophobia:** *fear of growing old*
Kyphophobia: *fear of stooping*
Necrophobia: *fear of death*
Rhytiphobia: *fear of getting wrinkles*
Soteriophobia: *fear of dependence on others*
Taphophobia: *fear of cemeteries*
Thanatophobia: *fear of dying*

TOP 5 U.S. IN-HOSPITAL DEATHS, AGES 85+, 2002

RANK	CAUSE OF DEATH	NUMBER OF DEATHS
1	Pneumonia	23,654
2	Heart attack	17,122
3	Blood infection	17,103
4	Congestive heart failure	15,695
5	Stroke	14,926

Go In, Never Come Out

58 Percentage of Americans over 75 who died in a hospital or medical center

28 Percentage who died in a nursing home

10 Percentage who died at home

Keeping Up the Family Spirits

Dying at home is important to the hill people of the Golden Triangle area of Thailand, Burma, and Laos. They believe that if a body dies away from familiar places, its spirit will wander forever; its absence from the company of other family spirits will weaken the family and cause sicknesses to its survivors.

States of Life and Death

1 Rank of North Dakota among states for old-age deaths

70 Percentage of North Dakota's 9,817 deaths occurring to people over 75

8 Number of states among the 10 ten over-75 death rates located in the Mid-west: besides North Dakota (#1), they are Nebraska (#2), Iowa (#3), South Dakota (#4), Minnesota (#5), Kansas (#6), Wisconsin (#8), and Ohio (#10)

2 Number of non-Midwestern states in the top 10: Pennsylvania (#7) and Louisiana (#9)

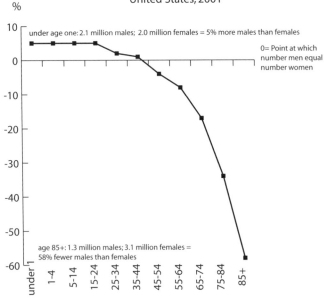

Change In Percentage of Males to Females by Age
United States, 2001

%

under age one: 2.1 million males; 2.0 million females = 5% more males than females

0= Point at which number men equal number women

age 85+: 1.3 million males; 3.1 million females = 58% fewer males than females

The Long and Short of It

1 Rank of Japan in worldwide life expectancy in 2003: 80.9 years. It's followed closely by Sweden and Switzerland (80.3), Australia (80.1), Canada (79.8), Italy (79.4), France (79.3), Spain and Israel (79.2), and Greece (78.9)

77.4 Average life expectancy in years for a baby born in the United States in 2003

74.6 Average life expectancy for a baby boy

80.4 Average life expectancy for a baby girl

67.6 Weighted average worldwide life expectancy in 2003

35.2 years Average 2003 life expectancy in Zambia, the lowest in the world. The rest of the bottom ten include Malawi (37.5), Mozambique (38.2), Zimbabwe (39.0), Rwanda (39.2), Ethiopia (41.2), Afghanistan (42.0), Sierra Leone and Côte d'Ivoire (42.7), and Burundi (43.4)

According to the Guinness Book of World Records, French-born Jeanne-Louise Calment was the oldest person ever whose age has been authenticated. Born in 1875, she lived 122 years and 164 days. Calment attributed her old age to copious amounts of chocolate, olive oil, and port. However, her active lifestyle also deserves some credit: She learned to fence at 85, still rode her bicycle at 110, and played herself in the movie *Vincent and Me* at the age of 114, making her the oldest film actress in history.

ADDITIONAL SOURCES

MAKING SENSE OF STATISTICS AND MEDICAL TERMINOLOGY
A. The International Statistical Classification of Diseases and Related Health Problems 10th Revision (ICD-10) is a coding system by which the World Health Organization (WHO) and the Center For Disease Control (CDC) track death statistics. The codes are here: www.who.int/classifications/apps/icd/icd10online
B. To determine the ICD-10 code for deaths recorded on WHO Global Burden of Disease reports (GBD) see Annex Table 3 attached to the "Global Burden of Disease in 2002: data sources, methods and results." Discussion Paper No. 54: www.who.int/healthinfo/paper54.pdf
C. To understand medical terminology, see the U.S. National Library of Medicine and The National Institutes of Health Medical Dictionary: www.nlm.nih.gov/medlineplus/mplusdictionary.html

GENERAL STATISTICS
(Referenced for all or most Chapters)
1. World Health Organization (WHO): www.who.int
   a. Revised Global Burden of Disease (GBD) 2002 Estimates: www.who.int/healthinfo/bodgbd2002revised/en/index.html
2. CIA: The World Factbook:www.cia.gov/library/publications/the-world-factbook/index.html
3. U.S. Center for Disease Control and Prevention (CDC): www.cdc.gov
   a. Mortality Data from the National Vital Statistics www.cdc.gov/nchs/deaths.htm
   b. Mortality Tables:www.cdc.gov/nchs/datawh/statab/unpubd/mortabs.htm
   c. *Health, United States* Annual Report: www.cdc.gov/nchs/hus.htm
4. U.S. Census Bureau's Statistical Abstract for the National Data Book publication: www.census.gov/compedia/statab
5. U.S. Department of Labor: Bureau of Labor Statistics (BLS): www.bls.gov
6. U.S. National Library of Medicine: www.nlm.nih.gov

7. U.S. Department of Health & Human Services:www.hhs.gov
   a. Bureau of Health Professionals: bhpr.hrsa.gov

CANCER

1. International Agency for Research on Cancer: www.iarc.fr
2. National Cancer Institute: www.cancer.gov
3. Cornell University: Program on Breast Cancer and Environmental Risk Factors: envirocancer.cornell.edu
4. Oxford Journal: Carcinogenesis: carcin.oxfordjournals.org
5. Epidemiology Scientific Journal:www.epidem.com
6. Society for Women's Health Research: www.womenshealthresearch.org

BROKEN HEART

1. American Heart Association: www.americanheart.org
2. American Heart Association Journals: www.ahajournals.org
3. Cardiology Channel: Heart Attack article: www.cardiologychannel.com/heartattack
4. The Organ Procurement and Transplantation Network: www.optn.org
5. Deep Vein Thrombosis: www.dvt.net
6. Health24.com Heart Attack During Sex: www.cardiologychannel.com/heartattack
7. Sherwin B. Nuland book *How We Die*: www.randomhouse.com/vintage/catalog/display.pperl?isbn=978067942449
8. Dr. Judith Mackay and Dr. George A. Mensah book *The Atlas of Heart Disease and Stroke*: www.who.int/cardiovascular_diseases/resources/atlas/en/

ACCIDENTS

1. WHO: World Report on Road Traffic Injury Prevention: www.who.int/violence_injury_prevention/publications/road_traffic/world_report/en/index.html
2. National Highway Traffic Safety Administration (NHTSA): www.nhtsa.gov
   a. NHTSA Traffic Safety Facts Annual Reports: www-rd.nhtsa.dot.gov/CMSWeb/listpublications.aspx?Id=E&ShowBy=DocType
3. National Safety Council (NSC) Resources:www.nsc.org (Recommended Statistics book "Injury Facts" only available in print)
4. U.S. Consumer Product Safety Commission: cpsc.gov

5. U.S. Bureau of Labor Statistics: Census of Fatal Occupational Injuries: www.bls.gov/iif/oshcfoi1.htm
6. U.S. Environmental Protection Agency (EPA): www.epa.gov
7. U.S. Food & Drug Administration: www.fda.gov
8. AVweb—Independent Aviation News Resource Links: www.avweb.com/aviationlinks
9. National Geographic News: news.nationalgeographic.com/news/index.html

ACCIDENTS—FLORA AND FAUNA

1. National Oceanic and Atmospheric Administration (NOAA): www.noaa.gov
2. Florida Fish and Wildlife Fish and Conservation Commission: Fish and Wildlife Research Institute: www.floridamarine.org
3. Alaska Science Center: Biological Science: alaska.usgs.gov/science/biology/index.php
4. American Humane Society: www.americanhumane.org/site/PageServer
5. The Humane Society of the United States: www.hsus.org
6. Dog Bite Law (non commercial, non governmental website): www.dogbitelaw.com
7. California Academy of Sciences: Research: research.calacademy.org/research
8. National Center for Biotechnology Information: www.ncbi.nlm.nih.gov
9. Global Invasive Species Database: www.issg.org/database/welcome
10. Extreme Science: www.extremescience.com
11. Australian Museum Fish site: www.amonline.net.au/fishes
12. Environment Canada: www.ec.gc.ca
13. Florida Museum of Natural History: www.flmnh.ufl.edu
14. The Medical Journal of Australia: www.mja.com.au
15. Infectious Disease Surveillance Center: idsc.nih.go.jp
16. Texas A&M University: Discover Entomology: insects.tamu.edu
17. Headlice.org: www.headlice.org
18. Entomology Dept. at University California, Riverside: spiders.ucr.edu
19. American Association of Poison Control Centers: www.aapcc.org
20. UC Berkeley: Essig Museum of Entomology: research.chance.berkeley.edu/page.cfm?id=78
21. Mongabay.com: www.mongabay.com

22. African Conservancy: www.africanconservancy.org
23. African Wildlife Foundation (AWF): www.awf.org
24. Born Free: www.bornfree.org.uk
25. Elephant Care International: www.elephantcare.org
26. All Africa.com: www.allafrica.com
27. Travel & Leisure: Golf: www.travelandleisure.com/tlgolf
28. Kruger National Park: www.krugerpark.co.za
29. Safari Bwana: www.safaribwana.com
30. The Pulitzer Prizes website (see 2001 article international-reporting by Paul Salopek on Africa): www.pulitzer.org
31. Marine-Medic.com: www.marine-medic.com.au

ACCIDENTS—NATURE

1. U.S. Committee on Science & Technology: science.house.gov
2. U.S. Geological Survey: www.usgs.gov
3. Federal Emergency Management Agency: www.fema.gov
4. NASA: www.nasa.gov
5. U.S. Earth System Research Laboratory: Global Monitoring Division: www.esrl.noaa.gov/gmd
6. Department for Environment and Heritage Government of South Australia: www.environment.sa.gov.au
7. Australian Academy of Science:www.science.org.au
8. International Federation of Red Cross and Red Crescent Societies: www.ifrc.org
9. U.S. National Climactic Data Center (NCDC): www.ncdc.noaa.gov/oa/ncdc.html
10. U.S. National Weather Service: Storm Prediction Center: www.spc.noaa.gov
11. Centre for Research on Epidemiology of Disasters (Belgium): www.cred.be
12. Atlantic Oceanographic and Meteorological Laboratory: www.aoml.noaa.gov
13. Worldwatch Institute: www.worldwatch.org

ACCIDENTS—SPORTS

1. Lucille Packard Children's Hospital at Stanford (search on "sports"): www.lpch.org

2. National Center for Catastrophic Sport Injury Research: www.unc.edu/depts/nccsi

3. U.S. Dept. of Health and Human Services (search on "physical activity"): www.os.dhhs.gov

4. Sportscience: www.sportsci.org

5. Kidsource Online (search on "safety"): www.kidsource.com

6. NHRA Championship Drag Racing: www.nhra.com

7. National Collegiate College Athletic Association: www.ncaa.org

8. Education Development Center, Inc. (search on "athletes"): main.edc.org

9. Children's Hospital Boston (search on "sudden death"): www.childrens hospital.org

10. Canada Safety Council: www.safety-council.org

11. USA Boxing: www.usaboxing.org

12. World Boxing Council (search on "fight statistics"): www.wbcboxing.com

13. Journal of Combative Sport: ejmas.com/jcs/jcsframe.htm

14. CDC Web-based Injury Statistics Query and Reporting System (WISQARS): www.cdc.gov/ncipc/wisqars

15. Corsinet (search on "last death"): www.corsinet.com

16. In Defense of Animals: www.idausa.org

17. U.S. Dept. of Labor: Fatal Occupational Injuries to Athletes 1992–2002: www.bls.gov/opub/cwc/sh20040719ar01p1.htm

BAD BREATH

1. U.S. Environmental Protection Agency: Office of Air and Radiation: www.epa.gov/air

2. American Lung Association: www.lungusa.org

3. National Asthma Council Australia: www.nationalasthma.org.au

4. National Institute of Allergy and Infectious Disease: www3.niaid.nih.gov

BAD PLUMBING

1. New Mexico American Indian Health Status Report 2005: www.health.state.nm.us/pdf/health_status_report_final.pdf

2. Medicinenet.com (kidney stones): www.medicinenet.com/images/illustrations/kidney_stone.jpg

3. Allrefer Health.com: health.allrefer.com

4. Answers.com: www.answers.com
5. University of Minnesota Children's Hospital, Fairview (search "lymph nodes and vessels"): www.uofmchildrenshospital.org
6. Transweb.org: www.transweb.org
7. World Health Organization Regional Office for Europe: www.euro.who.int

HORMONES

1. World Health Organization (WHO): Obesity and overweight: www.who .int/dietphysicalactivity/publications/facts/obesity/en
2. CDC: National Diabetes Fact Sheet: www.cdc.gov/diabetes/pubs/factsheet .htm
3. U.S. Dept. of Health & Human Services: Women's Health.gov (search "Graves' Disease"): www.4woman.gov
4. Medlineplus article on Diabetes: www.nlm.nih.gov/medlineplus/ency/ article/001214.htm
5. National Endocrine and Metabolic Diseases Information Service: www.endocrine.niddk.nih.gov/pubs/acro/acro.htm
6. Wrong Diagnosis.com article on Hypopituitarism: www.wrongdiagnosis .com/h/hypopituitarism/intro.htm
7. Nature Neuroscience (search on "sleep disorders"): www.nature.com/neuro/ index.html
8. Little People of America Medical Resource Center: medical.lpaonline.org
9. The Pituitary Foundation: www.pituitary.org.uk

BUGS

1. National Institute of Allergy and Infectious Diseases: www3.niaid.nih .gov
2. The Body (The Complete HIV/AIDS resource): www.thebody.com
3. CDC: National Center for Health Statistics: *Health, United States*: www.cdc.gov/nchs/hus.htm
4. U.S. National Library of Medicine: www.nlm.nih.gov
5. World Health Organization: Regional Office for South-East Asia: www.searo.who.int
6. "First 500,000 AIDS cases—United States, 1995"; via TheBody.com: www.thebody.com/content/art17141.html

7. Institute of Medicine of the National Academies: www.iom.edu
8. CDC: National Nosocomial Infections Surveillance System (NNIS): www.cdc.gov/ncidod/dhqp/nnis_pubs.html
9. PBS: *Now*: Smallpox overview: www.pbs.org/now/science/smallpox.html
10. Cleveland Clinic: Hepatitis A: clevelandclinicmeded.com/medicalpubs/diseasemanagement/gastro/hepatitis_a/hepatitis_a.htm
11. Stanford University: "Influenza Pandemic of 1918": www.stanford.edu/group/virus/uda
12. New Yorker Article "What Money Can Buy" by Michael Specter: www.michaelspecter.com/ny/2005/2005_10_24_gates.html
13. Medi-Smart: Nursing Education and Career Resources (search "MRSA"): www.medi-smart.com

SUICIDE

1. World Health Organization (WHO): Violence and Injury Prevention: www.who.int/violence_injury_prevention/en
2. CDC: National Center for Health Statistics—FASTATS: www.cdc.gov/nchs/fastats/suicide.htm
3. CDC: (search on "suicide"): www.cdc.gov/search.do?queryText=suicide&action=search
4. WHO: Evolution 1950–2000 of Global Suicide Rates: www.who.int/mental_health/prevention/suicide/evolution/en
5. CDC: Youth Risk Behavior Surveillance System: www.cdc.gov/HealthyYouth/yrbs
6. University Oulu: "Seasonal Variation of Suicide and Homicides in Finland": excerpt of Chapter 2: herkules.oulu.fi/isbn9514256042/html/x335.html
7. National Institute of Mental Health (search on "suicide"): www.nimh.nih.gov/health/topics/index.shtml
8. Bureau of Labor Statistics: Census of Fatal Occupational Injuries: www.bls.gov/iif/oshcfoi1.htm
9. Federation of American Scientists CRS Report for Congress: "American War Military Operations Casualties": (see Self Inflicted Military Deaths): www.fas.org/sgp/crs/natsec/RL32492.pdf
10. Health & Literacy Special Collection: "The History, Economics & Hazards of Tobacco": healthliteracy.worlded.org/docs/tobacco/Unit4/1whats_in.html

11. USC News "Suicide by Cop" article by Paul Dingsdale:
www.usc.edu/uscnews/stories/4081.html

BAD WIRING

1. Alzheimer's Association: www.alz.org
2. Minnesota Epilepsy Group: www.mnepilepsy.org
3. Agency for Toxic Substances and Disease Registry: Multiple Sclerosis fact sheet: www.atsdr.cdc.gov/DHS/MS_Fact_Sheet.html
4. National Institute of Mental Health: www.nimh.nih.gov
5. International Community for Alien Research: www.icar1.com
6. U.S. Department of Veterans Affairs (search on "depression"): www.va.gov
7. Centre for Asia-Pacific Initiatives Anorexia in Japan anorexia article: www.capi.uvic.ca/pubs/oc_papers/a-ruelle.pdf

BAD BIRTH

1. United Nations: Department of Economic and Social Affairs: Population Division: www.un.org/esa/population
2. CDC: National Center for Health Statistics: "Supplemental Analysis of Recent Trends in Infant Mortality": www.cdc.gov/nchs/products/pubs/pubd/hestats/infantmort/infantmort.htm
3. CDC: "Achievements in Public Health, 1900–1999": www.cdc.gov/mmwr/preview/mmwrhtml/mm4838a2.htm
4. March of Dimes: www.marchofdimes.com
5. CDC: MMWR article "Abortion Surveillance—United States: www.cdc.gov/mmwr/preview/mmwrhtml/ss5309a1.htm
6. CDC: MMWR article "Smoking During Pregnancy—United States, 1990–2002": www.cdc.gov/mmwr/preview/mmwrhtml/mm5339a1.htm
7. CDC: Smoking and Tobacco use (search on "reproductive effects"): www.cdc.gov/tobacco
8. Down Syndrome: Health Issues "Trisomy 21: The Story of Down Syndrome" by Len Leshin: www.ds-health.com/trisomy.htm

MURDER

1. Bureau of Labor Statistics: Census of Fatal Occupational Injuries: www.bls.gov/iif/oshcfoi1.htm

2. Bureau of Justice Statistics (search on "homicide trends"): ojp.usdoj.gov/bjs
3. FBI: Uniform Crime Reports: www.fbi.gov/ucr/ucr.htm
4. United Nations: Office on Drugs and Crime: www.unodc.org
5. The Journal of the American Medical Association (JAMA): "Enhanced Surveillance for Pregnancy-Associated Mortality—Maryland, 1993–1998": jama.ama-assn.org/cgi/content/abstract/285/11/1455
6. International Journal of Epidemiology Firearm-related deaths article: ije .oxfordjournals.org/cgi/content/abstract/27/2/214
7. American Journal of Public Health (search on "murder" or "homicide"): www.ajph.org
8. Small arms survey: www.smallarmssurvey.org
9. The Journal of the American Medical Association (JAMA) (search on "pregnancy-Associated Mortality"): jama.ama-assn.org
10. CDC: MMWR: "Occupational Injury Death of Postal Workers—United States, 1980–1989": www.cdc.gov/mmwr/preview/mmwrhtml/00032345 .htm

DRUGS

1. United Nations: Office on Drugs and Crime: "The Seventh United Nations Survey of Crime Trends and Options of Criminal Justice Systems, Covering the Period 1998–2000": www.unodc.org/pdf/crime/seventh_survey/7sc .pdf
2. Bureau of Justice Statistics Drugs and Crime Facts: www.ojp.usdoj.gov/bjs/ dcf/contents.htm
3. CIA World Factbook (search on "illicit drugs"): www.cia.gov/library/ publications/the-world-factbook/fields/2086.html
4. Merck Manual: Drug Use During Pregnancy: www.merck.com/mmhe/sec22/ ch259/ch259a.html
5. National Center on Substance Abuse and Child Welfare: www.ncsacw .samhsa.gov
6. Interpol: Heroin: www.interpol.int/Public/Drugs/heroin/default.asp
7. Erowid website about psychoactive plants and chemicals: www.erowid .org/chemicals/heroin/heroin_dose1.shtml
8. UCSF: News Office: 1999 article on heroin: pub.ucsf.edu/newsservices/ releases/2004010774

9. Caffeine Research Today: caffeine.researchtoday.net/about-caffeine.htm
10. Opiods: Opium History Up to 1858 A.D. by Alfred W. McCoy: opioids
    .com/opium/history/index.html
11. Drug Policy Alliance: "Fatal Heroin Overdose: A Review": www.drugpolicy
    .org/library/darke2.cfm
12. National Institute on Drug Abuse: www.nida.nih.gov
13. World Health Organization WHOSIS (search on "Alcohol"):
    www.who.int/whosis/en
14. Executive Office of the President: Office of National Drug Control Policy:
    Drug Use Trends (October 2002): Drug Policy Information Clearing House:
    www.whitehousedrugpolicy.gov/publications/factsht/druguse
15. Mayo Clinic: "Understanding Miscarriage" (see "caffeine," "alcohol"):
    www.mayoclinic.com/health/miscarriage/PR00097
16. American Journal of Epidemiology: "Coffee and Fetal Death": aje
    .oxfordjournals.org/cgi/content/abstract/162/10/983

BAD FRAMING

1. CDC: Morbidity and Mortality Report: www.cdc.gov/mmwr
2. Scleroderma Foundation: www.scleroderma.org
3. The New Yorker: Annals of Medicine: "Bloodsuckers" article by John Cola-
   pinto: www.newyorker.com/archive/2005/07/25/050725fa_fact_colapinto
4. Nursing Home Abuse Resource: www.nursing-home-abuse-resource.com
5. Talk Surgery, Inc.: Plastic Surgery Information Service, Safety Zone:
   www.talksurgery.com/consumer/safety
6. Cedars-Sinai: Rheumatology: www.cedars-sinai.edu/6048.html

STARVATION

1. Unicef: www.unicef.org
2. World Health Organization (WHO) Regional Office for South-East Asia
   (search on "nutrition"): www.searo.who.int
3. World Health Organization WHOSIS (search on "underweight" and
   "overweight"): www.who.int/whosis/database/core/core_select.cfm
4. World Food Programme: www.wfp.org/english
5. Bill and Melinda Gates Foundation (search on "starvation"):
   www.gatesfoundation.org/Search/default.htm

6. Historical Atlas of the 20th Century by Matthew White (see starvation resulting from war stats): users.erols.com/mwhite28/20century.htm
7. Jewish Virtual Library (search on WW II starvation): www.jewishvirtuallibrary.org
8. Harvard School of Public Health: www.hsph.harvard.edu

CHILDBEARING

1. WHO: Mother-Baby Package: Implementing Safe Motherhood In Countries: www.who.int/reproductive-health/publications/MSM_94_11/contents .html
2. CDC: Reproductive Health: www.cdc.gov/reproductivehealth
3. CDC: MMWR article "Achievements in Public Health, 1900–1999": www.cdc.gov/mmwr/preview/mmwrhtml/mm4838a2.htm
4. The University of Iowa Health Dept. of Obstetrics and Gynecology: http:// obgyn.uihc.uiowa.edu
5. bnet article "The Public Health Impact of Legal Abortion: 30 Years Later-Comment" by Willard Cates, Jr. David A. Grimes and Kenneth F. Schulz: findarticles.com/p/articles/mi_m0NNR/is_1_35/ai_97873955/pg_1
6. emedicine article on Pregnancy, Postpartum Hemorrhage: www.emedicine .com/emerg/topic481.htm
7. National Library of Medicine Pub Med (search on "unsafe abortion"): www.ncbi.nlm.nih.gov/sites/entrez
8. American Journal of Public Health (search on "underreporting of maternal deaths"): www.ajph.org
9. CDC "Family Planning Methods and Practice: Africa" re. Adolescent Women and Reproductive Health (Chapter 4 starting on page 47): www.cdc.gov/reproductivehealth/Products&Pubs/Africa/Africa_bk.pdf
10. Eastern Mediterranean Health Journal article "Early teenage marriage and subsequent pregnancy outcome" by S. Shawky and W. Milaat: www.emro.who.int/publications/emhj/0601/06.htm

LAW

1. United Nations: Office on Drugs and Crime: www.unodc.org
2. United Nations: Office on Drugs and Crime: "The Seventh United Nations Survey on Crime Trends and the Operations of Criminal Justice Systems

(1998–2000)": www.unodc.org/unodc/en/data-and-analysis/Seventh -United-Nations-Survey-on-Crime-Trends-and-the-Operations-of -Criminal-Justice-Systems.html

3. Bureau of Justice Statistics (search on "capital punishment"): ojp.usdoj.gov/bjs

4. Bureau of Justice Statistics: Sourcebook of Criminal Justice Statistics: www.albany.edu/sourcebook

5. Death Penalty Information Center: www.deathpenaltyinfo.org

6. The National Center for Education Statistics (NCES): nces.ed.gov

7. National Institute for Literacy article "Correctional Education Facts": www.nifl.gov/nifl/facts/correctional.html

8. Amnesty International (search on "death penalty"): www.amnesty.org

9. Article on History of British Judicial hanging: www.richard.clark32 .btinternet.co.uk/hanging1.html

10. Inter-University Consortium for Political and Social Research (search on "executions the Espy File"): www.icpsr.umich.edu

11. American Psychiatric Foundation article: "Averting Prison Suicides Requires Special Strategies": pn.psychiatryonline.org/cgi/content/full/39/24/15

12. The Christian Science Monitor (search on "death row"): www.csmonitor.com

13. Cabinet Magazine Online: "Animals on Trial": www.cabinetmagazine .org/issues/4/animalsontrial.php

14. American Civil Liberties Union (ACLU): Capital Punishment Project: www.aclu.org/capital/index.html

WAR

1. Matthew White's personal "Source List and Detailed Death Tolls for the Man-made Megadeaths of the Twentieth Century": users.erols.com/ mwhite28/warstats.htm

2. U.S. Department of Defense: www.defenselink.mil

3. International Campaign to Ban Landmines: www.icbl.org

4. American Historical Society: www.historians.org

5. The U.S. Army: www.army.mil

6. HQMC—United States Marine Corps Headquarters: hqinet001.hqmc.usmc.mil

7. U.S. Air Force: www.af.mil

8. Naval Historical Society: www.history.navy.mil

9. Library Spot Network: America's Wars and Casualties: www.libraryspot.com/lists/listwars.htm
10. World History at KMLA: www.zum.de/whkmla/about.html
11. Piero Scaruffi's personal website: www.scaruffi.com/politics/dictat.html
12. United Human Rights Council: www.unitedhumanrights.org
13. Amnesty International: www.amnesty.org
14. R.J. Rummel's personal website: www.hawaii.edu/powerkills
15. Sven Lindqvist's personal website, author of *A History Of Bombing*: www.svenlindqvist.net
16. University of Michigan Documents Center Statistical Resources on the Web Military and Defense: www.lib.umich.edu/govdocs/stmil.html
17. Australian Government: Geoscience Australia: www.ga.gov.au/oracle/nukexp_form.jsp
18. U.S. Dept. of State Office of the Coordinator for Coordination of Counterterrorism: www.state.gov/s/ct
19. U.S. Dept. of Health & Human Services: www.healthfinder.gov
20. U.S. Department of Veteran Affairs: www1.va.gov/opa/fact/amwars.asp
21. Vietnam Veterans of America: Fact sheet: America's Wars: www.vva.org
22. Come Clean WMD Awareness Program: www.comeclean.org.uk
23. New Mexico State University: Homeland Security: spectre.nmsu.edu/dept/academic.html?i=512&s=sub
24. World Socialist website (see article on "depleted uranium weapons in Balkan War"): www.wsws.org
25. Stockholm International Peace Research Institute: www.sipri.org

OLD AGE

1. Health Care Cost and Utilization Project (HCUP): HCUP Fact Book No. 6: Hospitalization in the United States, 2002: www.ahrq.gov/data/hcup/factbk6/factbk6b.htm
2. The U.S. Administration on Aging: www.aoa.gov
3. U.S. Census Bureau article "The 65 Years and Over Population: 2000": www.census.gov/prod/2001pubs/c2kbr01–10.pdf
4. U.S. Government Accountability Office (U.S. GAO) (search on "nursing home"): www.gao.gov

INDEX